GIVING NOTICE

GIVING NOTICE

Why the Best and the Brightest Leave the Workplace and How You Can Help Them Stay

Freada Kapor Klein

Level Playing Field Institute

Martha Mendoza

Kimberly Allers

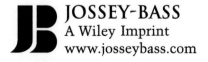

JOSSEY-BASS
A Wiley Imprint
www.josseybass.com

Published by Jossey-Bass
A Wiley Imprint
989 Market Street, San Francisco, CA 94103-1741—www.josseybass.com

Jossey-Bass books and products are available through most bookstores. To contact Jossey-Bass directly call our Customer Care Department within the U.S. at 800-956-7739, outside the U.S. at 317-572-3986, or fax 317-572-4002.

Jossey-Bass also publishes its books in a variety of electronic formats. Some content that appears in print may not be available in electronic books.

Library of Congress Cataloging-in-Publication Data

Klein, Freada Kapor, 1952-
    Giving notice : why the best and the brightest leave the workplace and how you can help them stay / Freada Kapor Klein, Kimberly Allers, Martha Mendoza. — 1st ed.
      p. cm.
    Includes bibliographical references and index.
    ISBN 978-0-7879-9809-7 (cloth)
    1. Diversity in the workplace—United States. 2. Minority professional employees—United States. 3. Personnel management—United States. 4. Corporate culture—United States. 5. Multiculturalism—United States. I. Allers, Kimberly Seals. II. Mendoza, Martha. III. Title.
    HF5549.5.M5K59 2007
    658.3'14—dc22   2007020670

Printed in the United States of America
FIRST EDITION
HB Printing   10 9 8 7 6 5 4 3 2 1

CONTENTS

To the Level Playing Field Institute's IDEAL and SMASH Scholars, whose accomplishments and enthusiasm illustrate how much can be achieved if hidden bias and hidden barriers aren't in the way.

INTRODUCTION

When CEOs are asked what keeps them up at night, two key concerns usually rise to the top of their short list: finding and keeping top talent and figuring out how to compete in a global marketplace. But rarely do CEOs realize that these issues are related. When a senior manager can't crack the code of expanding to new markets, does it have anything to do with not recognizing talent when it shows up in a different package? When business leaders learn how to listen across boundaries—geographic and personal characteristics—new markets of customers/clients *and* talent are unlocked.

Do senior managers truly know why they're losing top talent, and do they know where their former employees are going? Do male and female professionals and managers leave their jobs for the same reasons? And people of color and Caucasians, or gays, lesbians, and heterosexuals? Are top employees being pulled out by bigger paychecks and bigger opportunities, or are they being pushed out by an unwelcoming and exclusionary work environment?

In *Giving Notice* you'll hear the *real* reasons talented managers and professionals from a cross section of industries left their employers—not the safe, half-truths they told during their exit interviews. Each and every barrier that is discussed—whether hidden or blatant, whether a glass ceiling or a brick wall—was faced by someone we interviewed at a top-tier corporation or professional services firm. Their stories are woven together with data from an innovative national survey to tell us what this exodus is costing corporate America.

THE $64-BILLION-A-YEAR PROBLEM

Sixty-four billion dollars a year: That's the conservative estimate of what voluntary turnover due solely to unfair treatment costs U.S. employers every year. *Giving Notice* points the way to reclaiming those lost dollars and lost talent. The book introduces three fictional characters—Eric Johnson, Kristen Van Der Camp, and Miguel Rodriguez—as they negotiate life in a high-end corporate workplace. Their formative experiences in their upbringings and throughout their educations (from elementary school through MBA) are also periodically referenced. These individuals are fictional characters, *composites*, based on stories I have heard and data I have collected during my three decades of work as a consultant, trainer, and researcher for a range of organizations—from top-tier international law firms, to Wall Street investment banks, to high-flying Silicon Valley startups. When people of color, lesbians or gays, or white women told us why they left their jobs at Microsoft, Home Depot, Goldman Sachs, or Skadden Arps (to name only a few), their experiences had an opportunity to become the experiences of Eric, Kristen, and Miguel in *Giving Notice*.

Being Put to the Test

When I became the first head of employee relations at Lotus Development Corporation, my charter was to make the company the most progressive employer in the United States. Shortly after my arrival, the three whiz-kid engineers who were working on 1-2-3 (the spreadsheet dubbed "the killer app" that made the IBM personal computer ubiquitous in business) came to see me. They told me that they were aware of problems in engineering, and they understood that it was my job to help fix things. However, if I didn't know anything about software development, how could I really help them? The obvious logic was compelling. They generated a reading list of materials that could be obtained down the street from the MIT bookstore, and I was to call them when I had completed my "homework" so they could quiz me. If I passed, I would be entitled to help them. As it turned out, this reading list and their grilling rivaled anything I did to earn my Ph.D., but it was well worth the trouble. Having passed, I earned the right to help them. Every person working on human capital strategies should know enough about the fundamentals of his or her business to be a genuine contributing business partner.

From my early days at Lotus and through decades of consulting, training, and conducting research, I have professed the critical importance of rigorous methodology; the creation of fair, confidential, and effective complaint channels; and the development of people strategies that are truly integrated with business strategy. All of these issues are covered in *Giving Notice.*

THE LEVEL PLAYING FIELD INSTITUTE

In 2001, I founded the Level Playing Field Institute (www.lpfi.org). This non-profit's mission is to provide innovative approaches to revealing and removing barriers along the path from the classroom to the boardroom. Several issues prompted my founding the institute: among them, I was genuinely perplexed as to why diversity efforts in corporate America had consumed so much time and money and were having such an anemic return on investment. Someone needed to address this.

Although the Institute's workplace research and programs are most directly relevant to this book, our scholarship and leadership programs also play a key role in our work and mission. More than 150 San Francisco Bay Area high school and college students participate in our education programs. They are all underrepresented students of color: most are the first in their families to be college bound, and many hail from some of the most dramatically under-resourced schools imaginable. They provide us with constant inspiration and motivation. They have survived poverty, violence, and low expectations. Now that they are achieving and excelling academically, I hope to see a myriad of employers recognize their gifts, welcome them, and let them contribute.

WHAT'S INSIDE *GIVING NOTICE*

As you will see, the content of *Giving Notice* speaks to a broad audience: CEOs and other senior management, job seekers, career coaches, recruiters and hiring managers, HR professionals, diversity officers, consultants and trainers, business school professors and students, and high school and college career counselors. This book is for all the "gatekeepers" and all those aspiring professionals and managers who are committed to fair and inclusive workplaces.

The early chapters of *Giving Notice,* after introducing several key concepts, illustrate the direct and profound effect the daily landscape of false/misguided assumptions and stereotyping has upon turnover. They reveal the deadly gap between what is stated and what is actually practiced in corporate America. In Chapter Four, upon demonstrating the individual and human cost of subtle bias, findings from a national survey of professionals and managers are used to calculate the staggering dollar cost of allowing unfairness to prevail in the workplace. Chapter Five begins with an understanding of how even the most well-intentioned person can harbor unconscious bias and perpetuate stereotypes. Chapter Six introduces mechanisms to dismantle hidden biases and hidden barriers. Chapter Seven presents the due diligence that any savvy job seeker can conduct to find a fair and welcoming work environment. Chapter Eight discusses the similarities in experiences of bias and unfairness faced by professionals and managers throughout the increasingly global marketplace, and it reveals how an organization can establish a consistent corporate culture worldwide and still maintain respect for cultural differences. Chapter Nine examines how educational backgrounds/opportunities lay the groundwork for success or failure in the corporate work environment. Lastly, Chapter Ten offers a better way to create a successful, nimble company that is also a welcoming place to work for people from a wide range of backgrounds.

Giving Notice is about reframing the conversation. It's time to rethink what it means to build welcoming, respectful, and productive workplaces. When I look at top-tier, U.S.-based, global businesses, I struggle to think of any that I would wholeheartedly endorse to the high school and college students who participate in the Level Playing Field Institute's education-related programs. After dodging bullets, figuratively and sometimes literally, for the first two decades of their lives, don't they deserve a fair chance? Doesn't everyone? At an annual cost of $64 billion, eliminating workplace unfairness is as much about "doing the right thing" as it is about protecting the U.S. economy.

GIVING NOTICE

Chapter One

The Meritocracy Myth:
Is the Playing Field Level?

I arrived in the lobby of the New York headquarters at 2:47 P.M. It was Thursday. The highly respected general counsel of the corporation came down to greet me. The sound of his Berluti shoes against the marble floors heralded his arrival long before we shook hands. He quickly escorted me past security and up to the 34th floor, where I would meet three of the CEO's most trusted advisers. Going from office to office and from pinstripe suit to pinstripe suit, I began to sense the unspoken dynamics of this company. After decades of advising international law firms, major financial services institutions, and other multinational conglomerates on organizational development and diversity issues, I've developed keenly astute antennae for detecting the kind of subtle issues that aren't addressed by typical diversity protocols. The uniformity of these offices and the senior managers in them were disturbing. Each one felt exactly the same as the next: impressionist style artwork on the walls, deep mahogany furniture arranged in identical fashion, and one family photo placed at the upper-right corner of the desk. By the time I was introduced to the last executive, I was convinced that this company had a complex, systemic problem, but it was not the problem the firm had called me to address.

These are the types of companies that highly paid diversity consultants visit every day. Usually, management calls in the consultants because an "incident" has occurred. The consultants are often afterthoughts, contacted only when a potentially litigious problem surfaces. And the solutions offered by the majority of diversity gurus are mostly superficial, cookie-cutter programs that don't address the root issue: unearthing and removing hidden bias in organizational structures. They can offer boxed solutions for the blatantly obvious, but nobody is checking for the subtle signs of hidden agendas. This is the disturbing void in current diversity methodologies.

A CONTRADICTORY PICTURE

Even as corporate America applauds its diversity efforts, hails the triumph of a true meritocracy in the workplace, and parades its principles of fairness, decades of research documenting thousands of workplace experiences of people of color, women, and gays and lesbians paint a nettlesome, contradictory picture. The quantitative and qualitative findings lead to one sobering conclusion: the twenty-five-year diversity crusade by corporate America has been a costly failure leading to stunted careers, wasted money, and disillusioned observers.

This unfortunate reality exists despite the estimated $8 billion spent annually on diversity efforts—including advice on recruitment, diversity training, career development, and community outreach—according to Thomas Kochan of MIT's Sloan School of Management (Hansen 2003). Further, a recent study by researchers at the University of California, Harvard University, and the University of Minnesota concludes that diversity training may, in fact, increase managerial bias (Kalev et al. 2006). Often the end result is even more damaging and leaves employees dissatisfied. A two-year study released in 2004 by the National Urban League found that only 32 percent of 5,500 American workers surveyed believed that their employers had an effective diversity initiative (Peoples 2004). Why? Because corporate America and much of the diversity consultant industry has operated, and continues to operate, under some fundamentally flawed assumptions about what works and what doesn't.

Consider these faulty assumptions:

- The most qualified person for a job can be clearly determined.
- Businesses hire the most qualified people.
- Most managers aren't biased.
- Objective performance criteria can be easily established for any job.

- Once a person is hired, everyone has an equal opportunity to succeed, limited only by individual abilities.
- If a person works hard enough, he or she will be recognized and rewarded.

Each of these assumptions undoubtedly harbors an element of truth, and we more readily recognize experiences that confirm these assumptions rather than those that raise questions as to their validity. Yet each contains a substantial helping of subjectivity. (More information about how the brain works and the "brain–hidden bias connection" is presented in Chapter Five.)

For example, at many companies, employees are evaluated by their ability to bring in new customers or clients. Sounds objective, right? But what about those customers or clients whose experiences and comfort zones may put women, gays and lesbians, and people of color at an unfair disadvantage? Consider these scenarios:

- An older male client might not be comfortable dining out alone with a young female salesperson. He may worry about appearances at least and temptation at most.
- If a client has never worked with or befriended a person of color, would the client feel comfortable placing a major order or signing a hefty services contract with a person of color?
- Suppose a prospective customer is expected to socialize with a gay vendor but can't imagine bringing her spouse to dinner with the vendor and his partner.
- A Caucasian child of privilege walks into the new job with a Rolodex full of wealthy and well-positioned family friends. Is it fair to compare this worker's business development or sales results with others who do not have privileged access?

Despite such challenges, "Bringing in business is an objective measure of performance" is a frequent refrain of companies' senior managers responsible for hiring, promoting, and firing.

Consider another example. Most companies espouse an "Our client comes first" position. But what does a manager do when a client makes a thinly veiled racist comment? In one of the incidents recorded during research by the Level Playing Field Institute, a senior manager faced this circumstance: During a conference call, a client said, "This is a really big deal. I don't want any affirmative action hires on this one." In such a case, does the client still come first? If the manager already intended to put a highly competent African American saleswoman on the deal, would he change the assignment to suit the client? Would that be fair? At first glance, the "client first" policy sounds wholly reasonable and within the bounds of acceptable practice, but as it plays out in the context of racism and bias, it becomes problematic.

With so many nuances tied to conventional ideas of what is a fair workplace for all, it becomes even more clear that the belief that diversity efforts should be heavily focused on recruitment—getting talented people from various racial, ethnic, and cultural backgrounds in the door and everything that follows will occur organically—is overly simplistic and misguided. It's a pedestrian approach, devoid of any understanding of the intangible issues that dominate workplace environments, such as an unwelcoming culture, self-serving delusions about meritocracy, and the subtleties of bias.

When a senior human resource executive prefaces every mention of an applicant of color by calling her a "qualified" applicant, the unstated assumption is that most female applicants of color are unqualified, so this particular issue must be categorized differently. That's subtle bias at play. When a CEO whose company's products have a direct connection to consumers of color doesn't see the business case for diversity, it signals a willful ignorance that will surely permeate that company's culture and adversely affect employees.

Based on my decades of experience conducting workplace surveys, designing and delivering training, and consulting to employers who are concerned about issues of bias, discrimination, and/or harassment, a framework has emerged to describe the large "buckets" of issues I've encountered. The framework was further refined by thousands of conversations with managers and professionals who had voluntarily left their employers due to the cumulative effects of experiencing subtle, hidden bias. This hidden bias, exhibited (in many cases) by well-intentioned individuals, evolved into hidden barriers in companies. Often barriers were the seemingly neutral or objective systems used for hiring, assigning, evaluating, promoting, and firing employees.

Development of Hidden Barriers

For people of color, gays and lesbians, and women of all backgrounds, hidden biases can become hidden barriers in three major areas:

- **Commitment of the Leadership** If senior managers' experiences are vastly different from those of their employees, can management really empathize? Do they really understand the experiences and perceptions of those who are different? Do their day-to-day business decisions actually reflect the laudatory diversity goals of their companies?
- **Mentoring, Career Development, and Feedback** Who gets shown the ropes? For whom is a misstep a predictable point on the learning curve, versus a confirmation of incompetence? Who is given direct, specific performance feedback in a timely fashion so that they know what to continue doing and what to change?
- **Unwelcoming Environment** These instances take the forms of omission and commission. Who is never considered for the "stretch assignment" or the after-work drink? Who gets peppered with well-meaning, but nonetheless offensive, comments, questions, or jokes?

People of color and gays and lesbians are further confronted with another category:

- **Stereotypes** Can they ever simply be seen as typical individuals with quirks and strengths, or are they always representatives of their "groups"? Being African American, Latino, or gay is often a key part of one's identity and experiences in the world, but this doesn't predict all of a person's interests, traits, and abilities.

Women of all backgrounds face an additional hurdle:

- **Balancing Career and Family** Can a woman who has stepped off the fast track ever get back on?

Every employer can benefit from auditing company practices and culture from this framework. How much do the experiences and perceptions of employees diverge by race/ethnicity, gender, or sexual orientation (or a number of other factors)? In an era of fierce global competition, if businesses need teamwork more than ever, how can a well-functioning team be built to include those who traverse the same hallways but whose experiences are dramatically different?

Those who "voluntarily" leave their jobs constitute unwanted turnover for everyone: the employer who has invested in training, the employee who invested his or her education and hopes, and the society that needs efficient, well-run enterprises. Still, one breed of CEO tries to explain away anemic retention rates by saying that certain employees aren't "team players" and "don't fit in." These may sound like perfectly logical explanations, but they are subjective, destructive terms that indicate idiosyncratic, cultural norms that often exclude people of color, women, and gays and lesbians.

A remarkable pattern of rewriting history occurs after employees walk out the door. The previous star performer is too often recast by management as a marginal employee, not tough enough to survive the brutal pressures of global business. This is just one example of many types of hidden barriers and psychological hazards that hardworking employees face every day. These barriers, though not the blatantly discriminatory practices that can be fought in the courts, remain the largest impediment to success for many workers across the nation.

Incivility + Unfairness = Turnover

American workplaces are increasingly characterized by a lack of civility and a lack of fairness. The gap between what is stated and what is practiced, or between aspirations and actualities, is widening. Cynicism and a broken compact between employer and employee are filling an ever-expanding space. What is the relationship among growing incivility, unfairness, and unwanted turnover?

This is what the Level Playing Field Institute, in cooperation with Knowledge Networks, recently set out to determine. We began with a nationally representative sample of 19,000 people; this, in turn, yielded 1,700 professionals and managers who met our criteria of salaried individuals who voluntarily chose to leave their jobs between 2001 and 2006. We sought to answer three questions:

1. What is the effect of unfairness on an employee's decision to leave his or her employer?
2. What is the financial cost to employers due to voluntary turnover based on unfairness?
3. What, if anything, could employers have done to retain employees who left a job due to unfairness?

As it turns out, managers and professionals from all walks of life and across all sectors are subjected to a barrage of uncivil treatment. Not only does inappropriate conduct raise questions in the minds of employees about their company's commitment to fairness, but it also affects morale, productivity, and corporate reputation. All of these outcomes have a measurable negative consequence on the bottom line.

THE PRICE TAG

What's the impact of working while being mistreated? In one year, 5.5 percent of the managers and professionals in our survey voluntarily left their jobs, citing *unfairness* as the *only* reason for their departure. (A list of the unfair/negative behaviors that they experienced "during the past year" at their former employer is shown in Table 1.1.) A full 43.5 percent of survey respondents cited their negative experiences as having "a great deal" of influence on their decision to leave a position. And what is the annual cost to U.S. businesses for the voluntary turnover of managers and professionals due solely to unfairness? An eye-popping $64 billion.

Let's put the $64 billion in context: here are other expenditures totaling the same sum:

- U.S. government's Information Technology budget for 2007[1]
- 2006 combined revenues of Google, Goldman Sachs, Starbucks, and Amazon.com[2]
- Amount allocated by the United Nations in oil revenues during the lifetime of the "Oil-for-Food Program" in Iraq[3]
- India's estimated outsourcing industry's value by 2012[4]

TABLE 1.1. BEHAVIORS EXPERIENCED IN PAST YEAR AT PREVIOUS EMPLOYER

Rudeness	50.4 percent
Having co-workers at a similar or higher level who are less educated or less experienced than you	46.1
Others taking credit for your work	39.0
Being given assignments that are usually considered below your job level	38.9
Feeling excluded from the team	35.7
Being stereotyped	23.5
Being bullied	22.9
Being excluded from key social groups	22.8
Being unable to acquire benefits	20.2
Offensive jokes	19.3
Being publicly humiliated	18.8
Being passed over for a promotion due to your personal characteristics	15.7
Being asked about your religious practices	13.7
Having your identity mistaken for someone else	9.2
Unwanted sexual attention, such as pressure for dates, teasing, jokes, remarks, or questions	8.7
Unwelcome questions about your skin, hair, or ethnic attire	7.2
Being subjected to offensive materials, such as photos, Internet sites, or e-mails	7.2
Being asked to attend more recruiting or community- related events than others because of your race, gender, religion, or sexual orientation	5.1
Being compared to a terrorist in a joking or serious manner	2.0

- Cost of pollution to China in 2004[5]
- Amount the entire European Union donated in development aid in 2006, representing 0.42 percent of gross domestic product (GDP)[6]
- Roughly equivalent to the 2005 GDP of Bangladesh (55th largest GDP of the 184 tracked by the World Bank)[7]

The experiences of inappropriate conduct and unfairness that lead to voluntary turnover of professionals and managers are not evenly distributed across all groups. For example, racial minorities experience being stereotyped about twice as often as their Caucasian male counterparts. Gays and lesbians experience rudeness substantially more often than Caucasian heterosexual men. People of color receive requests to attend recruiting/community events nearly five times more often than their white male colleagues. (While this may seem reasonable, if it doesn't "count" toward developmental assignments, bonuses, promotions, or other recognition, their participation is being valued for one and only one dimension.) White women are subjected to materials they find offensive, such as pornographic photos, Internet sites, or e-mails.

Surprisingly, however, practitioners and academics have never fully "connected the dots" among the range of complex dynamics at play in these situations. These dynamics include race and gender stereotyping, exclusion, in-group favoritism, inability to fit in, and the cumulative impact of micro-insults—the daily slights, snubs, bad jokes, and omissions that pose an extreme challenge to corporations everywhere. Nor is anyone exploring the complexities of our beliefs about what is fair or looking at a comprehensive approach as a tenable solution. Companies are too focused on checklists and platitudes, add-on programs, and "Best of . . ." rankings. Ironically, many companies are driving out some of their best talent due to the lack of a rigorous understanding of subtle bias and the hidden barriers that cause underrepresented groups to feel excluded or devalued. This has far-reaching business and economic ramifications.

It is important to note that many of those driven out migrate to non-profits or public service. Many privileged women, especially Caucasian women, stay home with their children after earning advanced degrees and logging a decade or more in top-tier corporations and professional services firms. They bring many skills to their unpaid work as board members of private schools and non-profits.

Similarly, many people of color and gays and lesbians find themselves wanting to do work they believe is more authentic or rewarding. A very gifted programmer, who happens to be gay, is now teaching math in New York public schools. An African American man who completed a Ph.D. in molecular and cell biology and earned a prestigious postdoctoral fellowship at a biotech firm now finds himself wanting to do outreach with inner-city kids to help them stay in school. The real contribution each of these people makes to society should not be overlooked; however, if their previous employers had been more welcoming and more flexible, perhaps they could be contributing in multiple arenas.

DIVERSITY POSTER CHILD— OR PROBLEM CHILD?

A few years ago, a major consumer products giant made a multi-million–dollar investment into expanding its businesses in Asia and spared no expense in attracting a highly sought-after talent pool. The group was run by a hard-driving manager from Texas, who had taken startup divisions and turned them into full throttle, profit-generating machines during his twenty-year tenure with the firm. The manager also had an equally long reputation for telling racial, gender-based, and ethnic jokes that often offended his staff but were generally considered harmless by his superiors.

Focused purely on the manager's proven business acumen, the CEO and his strategic advisers never considered the ramifications and reputational risks of selecting this man to head a division with mostly Asian American employees. But in a few months, a groundswell of complaints reached human resources. He frequently made jokes about Asian food, routinely confused employees with his Texas colloquialisms, and made no concerted effort to pronounce each associate's name correctly. On one occasion, employees finally reached their boiling point: When the manager mispronounced a name, yet again, and was gently corrected, he joked, "Well, your names are all inter-Chang-able." A few hours later, all the Asian American employees in the division resigned—

nearly a dozen people. "If they can't bother to learn my name and to be respectful, why should I stay here sixty-five hours per week making them wealthy?" one argued.

The team's mass resignation cost the company real dollars, both in the short and long terms. The company suffered from lost productivity as the employees felt increasingly demoralized. It suffered reputational damage as the employees told friends from school, in the industry, and clients about their treatment. Servicing existing clients with such a huge shortage of talent caused problems that undoubtedly resulted in lost repeat business. In the aftermath, high costs were incurred with replacing and retraining employees.

A look at this manager's graduate school transcripts or GMAT scores wouldn't reveal his true asset and liability profile. No realistic assessment was made of his cultural competence, implicit bias, or people management skills. Situations like this prove that business needs a fresh approach and a more targeted assessment that would reveal a prospective manager's real net value to a company.

Even more telling, news of the incident that traveled throughout the industry was met with surprise—no one suspected that such a hostile environment existed at this company. After all, last year the CEO and his direct reports approved a final budget of $1.8 million for implementing worldwide diversity efforts. The human resource managers were quick to recite statistics on company-wide Asian representation (which were intentionally misleading, since they included those who actually resided in their respective Asian countries of origin rather than only those who were Asian American). The chief diversity officer could easily deliver a dossier of every diversity training, roundtable, and networking event the company had hosted that included Asian American representation. Managers mentioned the countless career fairs, the formal mentoring program, varied diversity committees and employee resource groups, and the widely distributed, eight-page, superglossy diversity brochures that touted more than forty thousand hours spent on training in the previous year.

It would seem to some that this company was a diversity poster child. It had clear goals and a working strategy. Yet, as in the diversity movement as a whole, something had gone terribly awry. For one, the diversity program was just garnish—something the company added on for cosmetic purposes. It wasn't an ideal that the company had instilled in its corporate culture, starting from the CEO on down. And just like the group of talented Asian Americans that quit en masse, thousands of people of color, women, and gays and lesbians paint a stark and contradictory picture to the much improved landscape some diversity pundits would like to purport.

THE DRIPPING PIPE

In the end, this situation is not about the diversity movement or the deep-pocketed companies that have supported the multi-billion–dollar industry of diversity recruiting, consulting, and training. In the end, the real losers are the talented employees from varied backgrounds who bring their hopes, dreams, and aspirations to the workplace every day in an attempt to reach their full potential. Others show up with the expectations of their parents, extended families, communities, and peer groups weighing heavily on their shoulders in their quest to "make it." But when they arrive at work, they must often leave a part of themselves at the door. They know that they cannot be fully appreciated and valued. They know that the wholeness of their lives and all that their experiences can contribute are not welcome.

Instead, the reality of work for many is a constantly dripping pipe of daily indignities that cumulatively lead to feelings of isolation and distrust—and ultimately to extraordinarily high rates of voluntary turnover that is unwanted, and often unexpected, by the employer and employees alike.

Drip. A company evaluates employees on their ability to work effectively and win the confidence of major existing and prospective customers and clients, but it doesn't consider whether those individuals are capable of exercising objective business judgment any more so than the company's own managers. The customer's management team that likes to take business partners hunting for the weekend or go to strip clubs to celebrate major milestones isn't likely to view a person of color, a woman, or a gay or lesbian co-worker as the same kind of close, trusted business colleague as someone with the same background who shares their tastes in extracurricular activities.

Drip. A sole Latino senior manager at a Fortune 500 company gets frustrated by doing three jobs and being paid for only one. He must do his work impeccably; he must sit on every company diversity task force, participate in every roundtable or conference, and attend every community or recruiting dinner; and he must keep an open-door policy as mentor to every new "minority" hire. And then consider the ever-present sins of omission: "We didn't invite Enrique from accounting for a round of golf because we assumed he doesn't play." Eventually, that kind of exclusion becomes exhausting, but it's a reality that many employees of color must face.

MEET ERIC, KRISTEN, AND MIGUEL

Eric Johnson is a Princeton graduate and Stanford MBA who grew up in a working-class African American neighborhood outside Detroit, where everyone, including his parents, worked for the automobile industry. (In Eric's case, his parents worked for companies producing parts for the automakers, so they lacked the better pay and benefits accorded to union members.) Eric thinks in shifts and in calculated time blocks for his personal and professional goals. More strikingly, in Eric's life, his family fortunes and misfortunes, happy and unhappy moments, were dictated by big business. When things were going well for the auto industry, things were good at home. His parents got along well and provided the family with gifts, vacations, and new clothes. But when things were bad at work, Eric experienced the stress and anxiety of economic downturn at the dinner table. It permeated the air in his home. So it seems odd that Eric is so vehemently drawn to big business and its dynamics. But he is resolved to overpower big business—to understand it, tame it, and subjugate it. This determination has fueled his career ambitions.

Kristen Van Der Camp is a resolute white woman who grew up on a farm in Nebraska and focused on her books after being teased in school for wearing thrift-store clothes. The agricultural economy of rural America was just as fickle and unpredictable as the forces that had influenced Eric's upbringing. Droughts and hailstorms could destroy a farm family's source of income without warning. For Kristen, a job in the business world was the key to escaping a life of constant financial uncertainty.

Miguel Rodriguez was raised by his mother in New York City. Miguel's father had come to America seeking refuge from the political turmoil of Cuba, but he died when Miguel was five years old after he received poor medical care for what began as an easily treatable condition. As a boy, Miguel often accompanied his mom on weeknights to her late night shifts cleaning offices. There, he saw the computers and users' manuals for Lotus 1-2-3 as the first sign of professionalism and success. Twenty years later, he had the opportunity to meet the founder of Lotus, who funds scholarship programs for underrepresented students of color. Miguel's wife is employed as a teacher in one of the programs.

In this book, you'll follow Eric, Kristen, and Miguel on their respective journeys as they encounter and address hidden barriers and other subtle effects of bias in their workplaces and personal lives. They are composite characters based on three decades of consulting work and material gathered from surveys, interviews, and focus groups with hundreds of thousands of employees from around the globe.

The stories from which Eric, Kristen, and Miguel's experiences are culled were part of what motivated me to found the Level Playing Field Institute—a San Francisco–based non-profit that promotes innovative approaches to fairness in higher education and workplaces by removing barriers to full participation.

When persons of color, lesbians or gays, or women share with Level Playing Field Institute researchers reasons for their leaving jobs at Bank of America, General Foods, Cisco, Deloitte Touche, or any one of dozens of other companies, their experiences and perspectives are reflected in the career journeys of Eric, Kristen, and Miguel. In this book, they are presented as whole individuals— you'll have insights into their family backgrounds and other circumstances that impacted their life choices, education, academic affiliations, work experiences, and the colleagues and mentors who influenced them. You'll begin to understand that only by considering the whole individual can we create a new value system that effectively roots out the hidden biases that beget hidden barriers in the workplace.

You will see both differences and similarities in their stories. For examples, Eric's determination to subjugate business is much like Kristen's ardor to get off the farm, which she did—landing in the belly of Boston due to an academic scholarship to Harvard, where she received her BA and MBA. She was among the top of her class and received multiple awards and job offers, but she still had a hint of a farm girl's earnest need to succeed simply by working hard, along with some traditional ideas about the importance of family. These tenets are sorely tested in her career, where organizational culture and informal policies often determine success as she toils for a company that offers no flex-time, long hours that snuff out any social or family life, and no childcare facilities.

Miguel's cultural background also taught him to succeed on his own terms. As a boy, he lived in a small, cramped apartment shared with extended family members. By accompanying his mother at night to empty the wastebaskets and clean the toilets of those who, by accident of birth, were in charge, he was taught the value of working hard, the importance of community and caring for extended family members, and the quiet strength of humility. Miguel had a will to succeed and showed signs of academic excellence early in his school career, but his mother warned him not to brag or think too highly of himself and his accomplishments. She would say, "*!Ay, qué espectáculo!*" Although he is not fluent in Spanish, he has picked up such idioms from their constant refrain. How will Miguel and these cultural beliefs fare in a work environment that favors self-promotion as he competes with colleagues who actively practice impression management techniques?

CONCLUSION

Clearly, whether on an individual, company, or societal level, a fresh approach to diversity is required—not a one-size-fits-all way of thinking that starts with a legal framework (you're either a protected class and can sue us or not) but a deeper and richer approach, based on rigorous research that distinguishes between the different levels and types of hidden barriers. This approach must provide a deep understanding of bias and how it pervades business and hiring decisions. It must allow for a broader evaluation of what actually makes a candidate qualified. This new approach to creating fair workplaces is laced with an acute understanding of the business imperative to stem the loss of talented women, people of color, and gays and lesbians from America's top companies. Without these talented employees, American businesses will face defeat in the increasingly competitive global landscape.

CHAPTER TWO

SLIGHTS UNSEEN

For the past three years, co-workers Eric Johnson, Miguel Rodriguez, and Kristen Van Der Camp have been meeting at a small table in the back of a labyrinthine Italian café, about three blocks outside the typical lunch radius of their other co-workers, for what they call "the quarterly report," code word: 10-Q.

Three years ago, a random draw brought them together for a team-building activity during orientation. Since that time, they have evolved into a group of strange bedfellows—an African American gay male, a Latino, and a white woman—who meet every three months to commiserate, compare experiences, and spur each other forward. It seems like only yesterday they were donning name tags, sizing up the competition, and teetering on that fine line between apprehension and panic as they began the orientation for the associate training program.

Back then, they were fresh-baked MBAs from three of America's most prestigious schools, feeling optimistic and full of promise. Today, their perspectives have shifted. On most days, they are not treated much differently from their cohorts. And over the course of time, the number of incidents tagged to race and gender bias has not been huge, but it has been disturbing. In fact, several occurrences have left them perplexed as to whether race, gender, or sexual orientation has influenced their experiences.

Over the years since his hire, Eric put in long hours trying to prove he was "on board," toiling away on pitch books, crunching numbers, even doing the grunt work that no one else wanted to do. All the while, he had coded phone conversations with his boyfriend, faked locker room talk with his managers, and created new "date" stories every Monday to share with his boss. His strategy seemed simple: after proving himself and earning the respect of his peers and managers, he would come out of the closet. "Once I've got some positive performance reviews under my belt," he told himself, "I'll be able to come out safely. They will know I'm contributing more than most people in the department, and that's what should matter."

One big problem to Eric's strategy, however, was a close-minded, bigoted manager in his department. Although he wasn't Eric's direct boss, this man would be involved in his upcoming evaluation. Lately, the manager had become increasingly vocal in his denunciations of others' "lifestyle choices." Women with live-in boyfriends were chastised. Homophobic remarks and humor were common. Meanwhile, all the obvious signs of a troubled department—high turnover of women, Jews, Muslims, and people of color; rejection of nonconservative candidates, even though they were seen as top contenders by others—went unnoticed by human resources. This continued for months. Eric noticed that others in the department were faking equally offensive views to curry favor. He had even overheard a Jewish co-worker agreeing with the manager about some anti-Semitic comments made on a talk radio show that was playing in the employee lounge.

One day at the café, Eric desperately needed to share his conundrum with Miguel, but Miguel was distracted by his own challenges. "Last week they told me I was going to be on some rotation. I have to spend six months working with the Spanish-language media clients, and then with the consumer products companies that are making the Latino push. And I don't even speak Spanish. But no one has ever asked me!" he blurted out before the bread even arrived.

"You're kidding me," said Eric.

"I wish I were. It's insulting."

Miguel couldn't understand why he was being pigeonholed into niche marketing campaigns, when all of his experience showed his strong quantitative background and business development skills. Suddenly, he was overwhelmed by a feeling that something wasn't right—the same sensation he'd had after completing his initial interview and later at orientation.

Kristen had worries of her own. "I was making a point about the business strategy if the merger goes through, and the CFO is staring at my chest," Kristen said. "Then when Hudson Carrington picked up on my theme a few minutes later, everyone was overwhelmed with his brilliance."

"Other times we're in client meetings, and I'm being asked to get coffee, order lunch, or make photocopies. Obviously I can't contribute to the presentation when I'm off running errands," she continued. "But when I raised my concerns to one of the stars in our department (who happens to be a white male and a third-generation Andover-Yale-Harvard Business School grad), he told me impatiently that it had nothing to do with gender, since he had just been asked the other day to retrieve a client's suit jacket from the conference room after a meeting. But I know that's not true."

THE FIRST HINT OF TROUBLE

During their first months at the company, Eric, Miguel, and Kristen came to realize that those in power honestly believed that they themselves had reached the top through ambition and smarts alone. These people were equally convinced of their own adroitness in recognizing potential in others. But the trio knew that the managers were grossly mistaken. In reality, like many senior managers gracing the upper echelons of corporate America today, they perceive talent only if it comes in familiar packaging—that is, looking and acting exactly as they do.

The first hint that women, gays and lesbians, and people of color were often not reflected in this firm's corporate thinking came during some arduous orientation weeks. The economically privileged employees handily outpowered those who were disadvantaged, and connections proved more meaningful than bootstrapping. Resumes reflected prestigious boarding schools (often legacy admits), Ivy League educations (often early decision, where the odds are more favorable and only those not in need of financial aid can take the risk), and summer internships at top-flight institutions (often obtained through the elaborate network of parents trading favors with colleagues, neighbors, and clients). Those for whom the environment was familiar, without the crushing burden of six-figure student loans, who knew how to dress and where to see and be seen, had a psychic comfort that can never be measured but confers great advantage.

The ten-person team on which Kristen, Eric, and Miguel found themselves consisted of seven white males who had *Entitlement* emblazoned on their lapels. One bragged about his uncle, who was on the board of their employer's largest client. Another was the son of a managing director—not in this division, mind you. And one had grown up playing golf with the CEO's son.

Each had a confidence and assuredness that Eric envied. After all, his own confidence was just a facade to mask his true fear that he was always one mistake away from a pink slip. During the interview process weeks earlier, Eric had considered mentioning that he was gay, but every male recruiter made constant sports allusions and references to dating women, and Eric desperately wanted to establish rapport. He decided it was better to remain closeted and to pretend. During the orientation, the HR department spent hours bragging about the company's comprehensive benefits. Eric listened intently for any mention of domestic partner benefits. None were mentioned. Instead, a VP talked excitedly of a new pet insurance plan. The HR specialist proudly rattled off a long list of pets that could be covered: dogs, cats, snakes, gerbils, even potbellied pigs. It was, at best, demoralizing.

As for Miguel, he had arrived overprepared for the initial interview weeks earlier, ready to discuss the research he had accomplished on some of the challenges the company was facing as it competed with startups. Based on his deep understanding of technology, he would propose an innovative approach to launching an in-house unit for seed-stage investment in startups. Under his proposal, if the companies were successful, they could be aligned as business partners rather than threatening competitors. His proposal showed a lot of potential.

Instead of sharing his carefully honed insights and novel thinking, he found himself answering questions related to his race and ethnicity. How could the firm attract more Latinos? Would he be comfortable speaking to the Latino community on behalf of the company? Would he be interested in sitting on the company's diversity committee? Weeks later, as he scanned the orientation room, he quickly surmised that he was the only Latino in the group, and that uncomfortable sense resurfaced.

During the long days and short breaks of orientation, Miguel was acutely aware of the "perception problem" of talking to other minorities. With so few minorities in the group, it was easily noticed and easily misconstrued. He risked being perceived as someone who was "not a team player" and who "didn't fit in." Worse yet, he feared his co-workers would see this as "plotting to play the race card." So Miguel said nothing, exchanged sympathetic glances with Eric, and limited conversation to the typical pleasantries.

During one lunch break, Miguel was about to take the empty seat next to Eric, for no other reason than that it was the closest available, but he quickly remembered the unwritten rules and moved on. Instead, he sat next to Kristen. Miguel didn't know her well, but to him, Kristen looked like the kind of blonde who had no problems, down to the three-carat, princess-cut diamond engagement ring on her finger. But as he would soon learn, Kristen had felt as overwhelmed and undervalued as Miguel and Eric.

STEREOTYPING

Eric, Miguel, and Kristen are trapped inside a false meritocracy. They are invisible as individuals, woefully unable to break out of the filters through which the firm's managing directors see them. Despite their unique skills and interests, they are still primarily seen as "diversity hires." Some co-workers believe Eric, Miguel, and Kristen got in the corporate door only because of their demographics, so the three are assumed to be underqualified and underprepared for their positions. Their value to the firm is realized only in their superficial differences, not their real differences in perspective and knowledge based on their experiences. However, since no one is facing blatant discrimination—nobody's using derogatory names or paying them inferior salaries—Eric, Miguel, and Kristen's experience of enduring dozens of microinsults is easily written off.

Stereotyping, on any basis, is the single most common form of inappropriate conduct experienced by American employees. A groundbreaking, methodologically rigorous study conducted jointly in 2003 by the Level Playing Field Institute and the University of Connecticut Center for Survey Research & Analysis found that stereotyping occurs more frequently than bullying, racial slurs, or sexist jokes. A full 53 percent of employees of color and 39 percent of white employees report experiencing stereotyping on the job in the year 2002.

The experience of daily discomfort is equally degrading. A Latina worker may wonder, "Did something happen to me (or not happen to me) because of my being Latina or female rather than because of my interests and insights?" The questions swirl, affecting productivity and self-confidence. Everybody loses when we can't see past a person's exterior: the employees, the company, and society.

Miguel, Eric, and Kristen are demoralized and unlikely to give their best effort to their work or to speak highly of their employer. Indeed, people are statistically significantly far less likely to recommend their employers' products and services if they believe they've been treated unfairly at work.

Because of bias, the company is losing what each of these people has to offer. Eric has a keen sense for project demands and managerial technique. Miguel has a sophisticated grasp of how to recognize potentially disruptive technologies and bring them in-house before they become business threats. Kristen understands the nuances of merging business cultures, not just balance sheets. But if these workers don't have a fair shot at being heard, they will eventually leave the company. In fact, while they are likely to leave the company, they are even more likely to leave their work sector altogether—just when America needs all the intellectual power it can harness to maintain its edge in a brutally competitive global landscape. If their bosses can't recognize and overcome their own biases, we all suffer.

The Tipping Point

Eric, Miguel, and Kristen endured a litany of indignities, as young professionals often do. Their cumulative experiences, however, eventually led to a tipping point, when their perceptions of their jobs changed for good.

One weekend, Eric came into the office to put in more time on an important project. Dressed casually in a sweatshirt, jeans, and baseball cap, he was stopped by the security guard. Again. It didn't take long to recall the other occasions when the guards had stopped him on working weekends when he came to the office casually dressed. This time, the guard fired off a barrage of questions about where he was going, what department he worked in, how long he planned to stay, and why he was at the office on a Saturday night. This time, Eric's company photo ID would not suffice, and he was asked to produce a driver's license to "validate" his identity. Then the guard asked him to remove his cap. As he did, Eric couldn't help but notice a white man in a baseball cap and jeans whizzing past the security checkpoint with barely a flash of his ID. At that moment, Eric's enthusiasm for work was gone, his desire to put in the extra time for the team evaporated, and his company loyalty faded. After getting the OK to proceed to the elevator banks, Eric simply turned around and walked out.

Although the guard wasn't someone who controlled Eric's career, or even worked for Eric's firm, Eric's treatment during this ordeal contributed to the cumulative effect. Such barriers are visible only to those who run into them. The mere fact that Eric's white co-workers never even thought about how to dress on the weekend, or never questioned their entitlement to go to their offices whenever they wanted, was an unfair advantage for them. Every instance of his being reminded that "folks like you" don't usually work in "places like this" and every instance of him checking himself at the door detracted from his ability to focus on the firm's business and commit to the firm and its clients.

Miguel and Kristen's experiences were different but equally troubling. Miguel was loathe to recall how many times someone had remarked that his English was "so good," or how many times he was asked to teach a colleague how to salsa dance. Lately the well-intentioned but nonetheless hurtful comments surrounded the immigration debate. Despite being Cuban American, he was asked by near-strangers whether he favored a guest-worker program and even whether he would be sent back to his country if a particular piece of pending legislation passed. One of his team members from his first days in the company asked if he had any family members looking for more apartments to clean. Miguel knew there was no optimal way out of this encounter: asking his colleague in any way to question his own assumptions was too risky. So he merely said he didn't have family in the area.

Kristen carefully camouflaged her ambitions of marriage and family, being cautious never to show any desire to have children. She remembered her interviews and how the managers asked veiled questions such as, "What are your plans for the future?" and "What kind of hours are you looking for?" She knew it was all code; they were trying to determine whether she planned on having children anytime soon, so she strategically crafted her responses. "No, I don't plan on having children," she would say. "My career is my first priority." It was all a lie, and Kristen reluctantly realized that, given the company culture, she had no meaningful or lasting future here.

An even deeper level of awareness evolved after she was assigned a mentor. The perfunctory e-mail introduction was followed by promises of meeting up for coffee or lunch that never materialized. As a woman in a male-dominated work environment, Kristen viewed a mentor as a lifeline she desperately needed. One day, she stopped by his office and asked his secretary if she could leave a note on his desk, but when Kristen approached his desk, she saw graphic pornography displayed on his computer screen. Shocked, she quickly exited without leaving her note. She knew this manager to be a high producer and a client "golden boy," but now she concluded that the rumors of his chauvinistic comments and lewd jokes were more than just company lore.

These are examples of the double standards of too many companies when it comes to enforcing their policies about harassment and discrimination. If a rainmaker continues to generate revenues for the firm, the company easily excuses that person's bad behavior with comments like, "Oh, he didn't really mean it," or "That's just Joe. He loves a good time, and clients love him." Employers have been known to go as far as paying such workers' legal bills and coaching fees, settling complaints with gag orders and severance pay, and then proudly declaring, "That's just the cost of doing business. Do you know how much money he brings in? It's a rounding error to buy someone out and simply let Joe be Joe."

THE FIRST PERFORMANCE REVIEW

By the time the first annual performance review for Kristen, Miguel, and Eric came around, they were experiencing a full menu of emotions and concerns with an awakening that their career paths may not take the course they originally hoped. Like most new employees, they met their reviews with some fear and anxiety, but they also felt an unexpected glimmer of hope, an expectant feeling that maybe this was their chance to be evaluated on paper only, with an unbiased look at their accomplishments, raw numbers, productivity gains, and new clients won.

Much was riding on the performance reviews on both sides of the table. The company invested heavily in its performance management system, developing templates and special software for peer reviews, upward reviews of managers by employees, grids explaining core competencies, and examples of achieving them at levels of exceptional versus satisfactory versus substandard performance. The trouble was that the company's elaborate system merely feigned objectivity; after all, when you assign numbers to subjective criteria and add them up, they're still subjective. Telling a young associate that his or her presentation style with clients doesn't match the company's norm merely tells the employee that he or she doesn't fit the company mold. That's exactly the kind of feedback that ignores the question of whether or not different presentation styles might, indeed, be equally as effective with different clients. To be clear, quantifying bias doesn't make it objective.

When Miguel entered his manager's office, he was confident and looking forward to discussing his recent achievements. In his "spare" time, when he wasn't working with clients on Latino business development, he had overseen a difficult internal restructuring of the media buying department that enabled the firm to better to utilize Web advertisements, halve the niche marketing budget, and reach a more valuable audience. Thirty minutes after his review discussion, he was back at his desk wondering what had just happened. The experience felt more like speed-dating in New York City than a meaningful conversation about his goals and objectives. The conversation went something like this:

"Miguel, you're a smart guy. You've done an outstanding job with the marketing and media department reorganization. But there's some concern about your commitment to the team. We're disappointed that you haven't been able to recruit more Latino clients to the firm." As further evidence that Miguel hadn't been committed to the team, his manager mentioned that Miguel had missed the annual staff retreat. When Miguel explained that he chose to stay at the office and complete his report instead of attending, his manager responded by asking, "Were you trying to make the rest of us look lazy?"

"No," Miguel retorted. He chose to back off rather than explain how he had been less than enthused about the retreat after a firm executive mistook him for the table busser at the previous year's retreat and asked him to refill his water glass.

Miguel had hoped to use the review as an opportunity to ask for a new assignment that was more suited to his business development and technology management background. Instead, he walked out of the meeting feeling defeated.

Kristen's review was also a disappointment. Kristen thought she was learning the ropes and establishing connections with some of the key players at major clients. A newly anointed female CFO at one client firm was outspoken in the business press about how women needed to support each other. Kristen had been added to this client's team solely because of her gender; for once, it had worked in her favor. But recently, her manager had been complaining about how much money the firm wastes training women who follow their husbands' careers or who leave to have babies and never come back. Kristen knew she had to figure out a way to leave this manager's business unit. She knew that she would become invisible to him as soon as she asked for time off for her wedding.

Eric's review was also disturbing. It began like this: "Eric, the senior management team is delighted you're on board. Everyone has recognized that you're a real team player. Given some of our clients' real diversity push lately, you can open many doors for us. After the last pitch meeting you attended, the general counsel of [the prospective client] even said you were the smartest black man he had ever met. Praise like that is worth a mint to us."

Instead of receiving a meaningful review with the type of honest feedback that enriches and enhances a career, the responses Eric heard were superficial, the advice was personal and not work related, and he received no action plans for future goals and targets. As is typical in the review process for people of color, gays and lesbians, and women, fear of crossing any legal boundaries suffocated honest dialogue and effective feedback.

Soon after Eric started, he let a client slip through the cracks—a typical learning curve issue that could have been addressed by constructive correction. But his manager did not want to appear racist by giving him anything but a bland review. By not telling Eric about the client's concerns, his manager prevented Eric from learning from his mistakes and changing his practices. Instead, Eric was left clueless and more likely to commit even more damaging mistakes in the future.

The manager was simply doing what he had been told to do by human resources in multiple training programs. Managers are told that they must carefully document the poor performance of anyone in a "protected class." Right from the jump, managers are given a not-so-subtle message that people of color, gays and lesbians, and women are more likely to be poor performers. There is no immediate, timely feedback; no friendly advice relating a similar experience of first assignment errors; no "It's OK, it's part of the learning curve" reassurances. Rather, the silence speaks volumes: "I'm not comfortable enough with you to tell you the truth. I have to regard you as a potential litigant and not a rising star."

On the other hand, Hudson, Kristen's colleague with a penchant for jumping in the wind of others' ideas and presenting them as if they were his own, had quite a different review experience. He walked into the room confidently and made a casual, collegial remark to the managing director about one of their mutual favorite sports teams. He asked if he could start by reviewing his accomplishments to date. The managing director smiled approvingly and said, "That's what I like about you—always ready to hit the ground running. But let me go through the prepared review first." When a couple of criticisms emerged from the peer review, Hudson pounded his fist on the table and said, "Look, if we cater to the whiners and mediocre performers who are just jealous, we're going to lose market share. I refuse to accept that those criticisms have anything to do with me." As positive accomplishments were being discussed, Hudson pointed out that several had been missed, and he ended the conversation by asking whether he'd be promoted soon or should jump to a competitor.

Proprietary surveys by Klein Associates—a consulting firm addressing workplace bias, discrimination, and harassment that I founded in 1987—tell this type of story over and over. People of color, out gays and lesbians, and women are far more likely to say that their performance reviews contained surprises than their heterosexual, white male counterparts. If a worker has to wait until an annual discussion to receive constructive communication, how can he or she compete favorably with someone who's getting regular and consistent guidance on how to be a company rock star?

SELF-PROMOTION

The relative importance of self-promotion in an organization has been well documented. That leaves most women and many cultural groups for which humility is highly valued at a gross disadvantage. Traditionally, men have been socialized to speak well of themselves to compete intrasexually for both economic resources and romantic attention from women. In contrast, women have been socialized to be communally oriented rather than self-centered.

Studies have found that too many individuals spend their careers trying to establish visibility, proving that they belong, and overcoming stereotyped ideas about their lives and work habits. The effort is exhausting and slowly takes its toll.

Two years after her review, Kristen recounted what she thought would be a year of triumphs. She had led a team that convinced a client firm to expand its work substantially with her firm. When the team members returned to the office, the managing director led them to a victory lunch. "To Kristen," he toasted.

"Thank you, but I never could have done it without all the help I got," she said, putting her best team foot forward, waiting for her colleagues to praise her.

"I stayed in the conference room until 3:00 A.M. two nights working on the PowerPoint presentation," said Dan Kirkland. He was right, but Kristen found him sleeping in his office for hours at a time and often had to correct his work.

"I did all the company research that really impressed the client," chimed in Jerry Evans. Before Kristen managed a second sip from her glass, every male team member had spoken up about the results he created. Like many women, Kristen wrongfully assumed others would notice her achievements and give her credit, without her needing to resort to self-promotion. "Well, then, I guess this toast is for Dan, Jerry, Brian, Mark, *and* Kristen," the managing director said. Kristen got a sinking feeling that her plan had sorely backfired, sabotaging her success.

Kristen remembered how during the project she asked Jerry to send the managing director an e-mail about a new development.

She favored e-mails with the managing directors because they were very busy, and she didn't want to bother them with small details. But when she never received a copy of that e-mail, as she had requested, she asked Jerry whether he had sent it. His reply: "Oh, I don't like using e-mail. I'd rather go to his office and talk to him face-to-face. It helps with the networking and being visible. You know." Kristen didn't know. She thought her strategy was best, but it also kept her anonymous and less visible to her managers, something her male colleagues had long ago figured out. The following week, she couldn't help but notice Jerry as he left the office to have lunch with the managing director. She had sent several e-mails trying to get on the director's schedule for lunch, but she had not received a response.

The answer to Kristen's dilemma was not as simple as delivering a message in person. While self-promotion and visibility are important tactics for any competitor, they posess special problems for women. On one hand, since women have been historically perceived as less competent and competitive than men, taking on an atypical, confident, and assertive demeanor can help counteract gender stereotypes in the workplace. However, women who engage in this way are not as well received as men with similar behavior. Kristen had heard enough stories to know that women who self-promote are ridiculed.

The nuances of self-promotion in American businesses today are a minefield for women and members of many ethnic groups. Many women aren't even aware of its insidious effects. Consider, for example, Heidi Roizen, a managing director of a venture capital firm with more than $2 billion under management. As is true with many prominent Caucasian businesswomen (she had achieved prior success as an entrepreneur and senior corporate executive), Heidi was hard-pressed to cite any gender-based obstacles she had to overcome—that is, until she sat in on a business school class discussing a case written about her. In one class section, the professor lectured on the case about Heidi Roizen; in the other, he lectured about the identical case but using *Howard* Roizen. Business school students were asked about leadership skills, likability, and a number of other factors. Across the board, Howard got higher marks. Heidi began to rethink hidden barriers in her own career.

Kristen considered her own barriers—particularly after she realized while drinking beers with the guys and discussing salaries that she was being grossly underpaid. While her starting pay had been the same as her idea-stealing colleague Hudson, he landed a bonus twice the size of hers last year. He also received a significant raise after he threatened to quit if he wasn't promoted.

Miguel also suffered from a lack of appreciation of his true worth. He did receive a raise and promotion—but only after he stopped resisting the box in which the firm was determined to keep him. Even though his heart was in technology, he carefully buried that part of his dream and climbed into the career casket that was artfully created for him. He decided that it was a fight he couldn't win. The company's limited views recognized only his race, so he capitulated. Six months later, he was made VP in charge of Latin market outreach, spending most of his time outside the United States, working with solid managers but having limited exposure to any influential decision-makers in the firm. The fast-track rotations were Asia and Europe, not Latin America.

THE LAST STRAW

The news about Hudson's bonus and raise were the proverbial "last straw" for Kristen. She never told her 10-Q lunch mates that she was quitting her job. At her exit interview, which had been outsourced to an HR benefits firm (further proof of the company's lack of commitment to employees), she wanted to talk candidly about the lack of flexible time and the long, antisocial, antifamily hours that all associates were expected to put in. Instead, she told the interviewer she wanted to work on personal projects.

Kristen knew that the company saw outsourcing exit interviews as a cost-saving maneuver and an unimportant part of the process. Each departing employee, like Kristen, hoped the exit interview would offer a chance to share concerns freely, but employees wanted to speak with someone who was invested in the company—someone with the power to change problems, who knew the players, and who could get their perceptions and experiences relayed to the right people. Kristen knew that voicing her true concerns would be fruitless. Speaking by phone to someone who is only trying to get the form filled out as quickly as possible (since his or her contract is on a cost-per-exit-interview basis) only added insult to injury.

The resolutions required by management to ensure that future employees do not leave for the same reasons are not as easily outsourced as the exit interviews. They require management to admit its mistakes and change its practices dramatically. In the absence of these steps, the concerns of exiting employees remain unresolved, and the holes in the leaking diversity pipeline continue to drip.

Eric's situation was classic: solid reviews, good performance, and no advancement. Something was wrong. When he asked his manager what steps he should be taking to improve his chances of advancement, his manager called HR and said that Eric was making allegations of race discrimination. The manager refused to speak to him without the presence of an HR representative.

"I never mentioned race to my manager," Eric said during his outsourced exit interview. "The only person who mentioned race was the manager himself." Eric knew that boutique firms would love to have him, but he would either be uncomfortable as a gay man at an African American–owned firm or perhaps suffer racial insensitivity in a gay-friendly business. "The firm mentality is a problem," he told his exit interviewer. "How hard am I going to work for the carrot of becoming managing director when I know that as soon as I get close to it, it will be snatched away? I need to find work that is meaningful to me, regardless of its monetary rewards."

Instead of being productive in the workforce, a growing number of employees—especially people of color, women, and gays and lesbians—have started writing pieces for Internet blog sites for ex-staffers. They anonymously rate their firms' performances. They blog about their negative experiences, and they warn friends and strangers against accepting offers. No standardized way exists to calculate the costs of their experiences and the costs of their sharing their war stories with others. But if we could factor in the actual costs for recruitment and training, along with the intangible expenses, the final tally would be financially staggering and socially sobering. This is the impact of the slights unseen.

CORPORATE LEAVERS

The Level Playing Field Institute has seen these hidden barriers with brilliant clarity via more than a thousand walking and talking case studies who breathe life into theory. We have tracked "corporate leavers": people who have voluntarily left their jobs to change their careers midstream, who participate in interviews and focus groups and passionately share their stories and their pain. The Level Playing Field Institute has gathered these stories through partnerships with non-profit and professional organizations, as well as multi-billion–dollar white shoe firms similar to the one Eric, Kristen, and Miguel left.

Indeed, it is at a corporate leavers' dinner and discussion event that our protagonists meet again—five years after they quit their jobs. The event was sponsored by their ex-firm at a restaurant not far from corporate offices. They arrived ready to share their stories in hopes of creating a new experience for future employees. The firm could now learn what it missed through its ad hoc exit interviews, how the little slights unseen that went unchecked grew into a workplace culture filled with hidden barriers to fairness for people of color, gay and lesbian professionals, and women.

As the group milled in the uneasiness of meeting old colleagues and mixing with unfamiliar faces, Kristen saw Eric from across the room and made her way over. Just as they were reminiscing and catching up, they were shocked to see Miguel walk in. After hearing of his promotions and Latin American successes, they were confident that he would be "the one" to tough it out. As Miguel later explained, he could no longer bear being someone he wasn't: pretending he didn't notice that everyone around him was heading to the golf course together after work, pretending it was funny when he was mistaken for a busboy, pretending that he was proud to be the company's Latino poster boy. He no longer chose to work for a company that promoted him based on stereotypes and assumptions, without a genuine understanding of his individuality. He proudly distributed business cards for his new startup consultancy. The firm's largest competitor was now one of *his* key clients. "You know, I could use a serious deal maker and someone with real marketing savvy," he said, eyeing Eric and Kristen for a response.

"Do you offer flex-time?" Kristen asked, patting her expecting belly.

"Do you have benefits for domestic partners?" Eric chimed in.

"Yes and yes," Miguel said.

CONCLUSION

Miguel, Eric, and Kristen set a date to meet at their old haunt and plan their careers. This time around, they were actually looking forward to going into the office, a place where their unique strengths and abilities would be appreciated, a place where they wouldn't be pigeonholed into roles based on how they looked or where they came from, a place where they could finally produce and create at their highest levels.

CHAPTER THREE

FROM THE TOP

Ninety-five percent of American managers today say the right thing. Five percent actually do it.
–JAMES O'TOOLE[1]

Consider the following headlines:

January 2007: GAP CEO steps down due to retailer's slumping sales

October 2006: McAfee chief steps down after options probe

September 2006: HP chairman to step down amid scandal

July 2006: Avaya CEO steps down due to substantial fall in earnings

May 2006: Toyota's North American CEO steps down amidst sexual harassment scandal

With surprising frequency, the business press includes news of CEOs losing their jobs due to scandals or disappointing earnings problems that extend beyond the executive's control. When is the last time a retailing CEO spent time on the selling floor? Still, we are accustomed to holding a CEO accountable for any major event that happened on his or her watch.

The character and culture of an organization is, undoubtedly, shaped from the top—that's why the level of the management's commitment and involvement is critical. In fact, it can be argued that there is no such thing as a bad workforce, just bad management. Good management can transform any organization.

In the wake of the ongoing rash of American business scandals, Malcolm Gladwell, journalist and author of *Blink: The Power of Thinking Without Thinking,* wrote in *The New Yorker* (2002), "The talent myth assumes that people make organizations smart. More often than not, it's the other way around." In other words, keen managers can make their organizations smarter (or dumber). But smart organizations happen through a committed training and development system that is implemented and supported from the highest levels of management.

Reams of management literature and research support this. Scan through leading management journals, surf the Web sites of the change consultants *du jour,* and you'll see that every piece of research and analysis repeatedly underscores the importance of commitment from the top in achieving any business objective— from Total Quality Management and strategic initiatives to innovation and environmental issues. The stronger the commitment level from senior managers, the greater the potential for success.

For decades, I have conducted surveys soliciting the opinions of employees on a range of worklife issues in their companies. Across this time period, across industries, and across the globe, the same dynamic unfolds: If one employee experiences, observes, or overhears disrespectful conduct, he or she has a significantly lower confidence level in senior management. If the inappropriate behaviors—be they bullying, racist jokes, or sexual harassment— aren't interrupted, the conclusion is drawn that the top at least tolerates such conduct, even if not directly engaging in it.

Consider two case studies conducted by Investors in People, a U.K.-based organization that has developed a standard for improving organizational performance. In both cases, new management completely turned around organizations that were seriously underperforming. At Company A, morale was low, absenteeism was high, and performance was weak. At Company B, staff turnover levels were through the roof, highlighting the discontentment and lack of motivation among the staff. This high turnover gave the company a reputation as an awful place to work, and managers found it difficult to recruit skilled replacements. As a result, the actual skill base within the company was dangerously low.

The key to the turnaround in both companies was a completely fresh management perspective, with visible commitment by the team leaders. For example, at Company A, the new managers got to know staff members personally, getting up at 5:30 each morning to meet with early morning shift workers. After winning the confidence of the staff, the managers moved on to the real substance of improving how the employees worked by offering training programs. In one case, to demonstrate her personal commitment and involvement, one manager underwent the training with supervisors that reported to her. By passing the same tests she required of her team, she gained their tremendous respect.

In Company B, a serious lack of communication between management and staff emerged as a key issue. Teamwork was poor, and virtually no cooperation existed among departments. The company provided no incentive for staff members to develop their skills and seek higher qualifications. To remedy this, management instituted a new approach based on frequent and regular communications, briefings, and regular employee reviews. The response was so overwhelmingly positive that even experienced employees were motivated to earn higher qualifications on their own. No longer was the company facing a shortage of skills; after correcting the problem, multiskilled employees made the workforce more flexible. By setting up enlightened systems of communication and training, and by being persistent and committed to them, the company achieved fundamental change. In both companies, the results were win-win.

As for diversity, workplaces will never be truly diverse and fair for all employees if the CEO does not establish and maintain a diverse culture. Employees are keenly aware of what does and doesn't matter to a chief executive; the tone set by the CEO has a tremendous trickle-down effect. What seeps down from the top can be a positive force for impacting the work experience of all employees, or it can be a potentially noxious force that drives talented employees out the door. Every time a manager is allowed to get away with harassing behavior, racially insensitive jokes, or sexually explicit comments because the management explains it away as "just Joe being Joe" or "he didn't really mean it," the employee cynicism index goes up. And strong anecdotal evidence suggests that cynicism levels are inversely proportional to productivity levels. Resigned employees are not productive employees. Furthermore, management can get it right only when sufficient time and attention are devoted to a full understanding of the subtle issues of its corporate culture and how they play out in day-to-day behavior.

PLAYING THE DIVERSITY GAME

Instead of focusing on creating fair workplaces that are truly diverse, too many CEOs are playing the diversity game, mastering the movements and strategies to erect a carefully constructed diversity facade. Winning this game isn't difficult. Have you hired a chief diversity officer recently? Move ahead two spaces. Don't worry if the budget for programs is anemic or this so-called "officer" does not directly report to the CEO. Those types of details don't matter in the diversity game.

Next move: Does your company Web site clearly state your diversity slogans with statements like this: "We believe diversity is a key driver of our success"? Jump ahead five spaces. Has your company experienced a diversity debacle, such as an embarrassing revelation of discriminatory practices à la Denny's restaurants or Texaco? Do not pass Go and go directly to jail! But don't worry, because you can quickly use your "get out of jail free" card just by paying a highly recognized public relations firm thousands of dollars to get your company on one of next year's "Best of . . ." lists and sponsoring a few high-profile minority events. Don't forget to write a check for Jesse Jackson's annual Wall Street Project, the Catalyst dinner, the local Martin Luther King, Jr. breakfast awards, or any number of local diversity job fairs, youth programs, or summer camps. You'll be out of the naughty chair and back in the diversity game in no time. (Of course, this is *not* to say that there is nothing redeeming about the organizations and events listed above. There is, however, an unfortunate and almost unwitting collusion at work: the advocacy organizations often come out with simplistic or unrealistic requests for a global business context. They produce shoddy research based on response rates that are appropriate for direct-mail, unsolicited advertising but not for a rigorous understanding of complex problems. And they frequently make demands and threats that stir backlash. Corporations regularly treat the situation as a game—they issue platitudes, sponsor community events, and engage in window dressing, all the while assuming that they really are meritocracies and that the problem of lack of diversity does not lie within their walls. This dance between the advocacy organizations and the corporations too often has the unintended consequence of very little real, lasting progress.)

This is the true commitment level of the majority of company CEOs. To be fair, however, it comes from unawareness rather than malevolence more often than not. Nevertheless, in other critical areas of business, being asleep at the wheel doesn't get the CEO off the hook. If diversity really mattered, a CEO whose company is hit with a major class action discrimination suit on his or her watch would resign, just as surely as CEOs now do for options scandals.

Consider a small private equity fund, housed in a Fortune 50 financial services institution, which has as its purpose investing in low-income community businesses. Not only are all members of the investment staff upper-middle-class Caucasian men, but they are also clueless about the link between diversity and the success of their business. After being asked to take a look at a startup whose mission was to serve healthy meals in low-income public schools, I asked the staff about the demographics of the company relative to the demographics of the neighborhood. With a combined defensiveness and hostility that was startling, the youngest member of the team shot back, "We don't have quotas. We only hire the most qualified people for the job." Given the ignorance of facts and laws, not to mention rudeness displayed to a prospective client, it was clear that this equity firm hired by other metrics than intelligence, business acumen, or civility.

PLATITUDES AND PROMISES

Obliviousness or hostility to diversity wouldn't be the conclusion drawn if you canvassed the Web sites of major corporations. There, diversity jargon runs rampant, along with what often turns out to be empty platitudes and even emptier promises.

A gaping chasm exists between what companies purport to be and the actual reality of the workplace. In July 2004, the business world woke up to this blaring headline: "Morgan Stanley agrees to pay $54 million to settle class action gender suit." The investment banking firm settled the suit filed by the Equal Employment Opportunity Commission (EEOC) on the day it was to go to trial. The EEOC accused the firm of discriminating against hundreds of female employees in its institutional equities division by denying them promotions and raises. The landmark case also claimed that Morgan Stanley tolerated groping, lewd comments, and male-only outings to strip clubs and golf courses with clients.

Since then, Morgan Stanley has done a good job in cleaning up its act, according to company officials. As a part of its settlement, the firm agreed to institute a range of programs and initiatives to improve the culture, as well as the promotion and retention of women and other minorities. Today, on its company Web site, Morgan Stanley positions itself as a diversity Goliath, valuing diversity as an opportunity for clients, people, and the firm. Here's the firm's diversity mission statement:

> By valuing diverse perspectives we can better serve our clients while we help our employees achieve their professional objectives. A corporate culture that is open and inclusive is fundamental to our role as a global leader constantly striving for excellence in all that we do. From our recruiting and career development programs, to our supplier diversity and work-life programs, our commitment to diversity is unparalleled. Over the years, our diversity and work-life initiatives have received numerous awards from publications and organizations. Our objective is to have an impact on diversity both internal and external to Morgan Stanley. This is what makes Morgan Stanley a premier employer of choice and a great place to work.

Sounds very convincing. But when you begin to canvass the multiple "water cooler" Web sites where current and former Morgan Stanley employees share their perspectives on company culture, a completely different picture emerges. Read the following comments that were posted at Vault.com:

A current Morgan Stanley vice president shares these thoughts: "Diversity is good—there are many varieties of white male. Advancement opportunities are excellent as long as you are white male and you extract as much money from client accounts as possible."

An organizational development analyst in New York writes, "The retail side of the firm is not conducive to growth because of specific close-minded preferences by the current managers. A more diverse culture is severely warranted for this white shoe firm. That is why I decided to leave for a more universally accepted and truly professional company."

A senior analyst writes this: "The firm is making noise about improving the corporate culture, but due to poor communication with employees, it comes off as false. Instead, opportunities for advancement are limited by hiring in senior people from elsewhere."

Other posted thoughts on diversity and the corporate culture at Morgan Stanley include these: "Diversity: There certainly is diversity, but it's there to meet the statistical ratios rather than people from all walks and races being fully embraced. Elitist WASPY environment." And "Advancement should be based on performance not friendship."

This type of honest employee feedback, devoid of agendas or marketing potential, illustrates the widening gap between how a company perceives and markets itself and the reality of the day-to-day experiences of its rank-and-file employees. All of this from a company that wins diversity awards and landed on *Working Mother* magazine's 2003 list of best companies and *Essence* magazine's best companies list for 2003, 2004, and 2005!

MAKING THE LIST

Business needs a reputation system to rival eBay's ratings of sellers or any major university's student ratings of professors. Indeed, a key part of the diversity game for any CEO is landing on the coveted "Best of . . ." lists, the annual rankings by *Fortune* magazine, along with *Working Mother, Black Enterprise,* and *Essence* magazines. In one 2003 study entitled "Shareholder Benefits of Diversity," the researchers noted that companies featured in *Fortune* magazine's former "50 Diversity Elite" (discontinued in 2002) average a three-day abnormal cumulative return of 1.57 percent around the *Fortune* publication date (Keys et al. 2003). Yes, good diversity press can boost stock prices, but that says nothing about whether there is, indeed, an effective diversity management strategy—only a good public relations strategy.

In fact, journalism insiders assert that the "Best of . . ." lists contain little quantitative rigor. Journalists who work on these lists—even at *Fortune* magazine—contend that the methodology is far from strict and that *Fortune* discontinued its "50 Diversity Elite" ranking for good reason.

Consider, for example, a recent survey mailed to one of the largest financial services firms in consideration for list inclusion at a national women's magazine. The firm provided glowing answers to the questions asked, but when pressed for backup to support its responses, the company said that the information was "highly confidential and could not be shared outside the firm" or "confidential/proprietary and could not be used for publication." Therefore, every key fact (for example, where minorities rank in the levels of pay, how many minorities are actually in the top 10 percent of wage earners, how minorities are faring throughout all management levels of the company) was not permitted by the firm to be independently verified by the writers and editors of the magazine. They were supposed to rely on the company's word. Nevertheless, the company made the magazine's list that year.

This is a continuous problem with "Best of . . ." lists. First, there is little journalistic rigor behind them. And second, a thorough analysis of which companies make the lists and which get slammed with eye-popping race and gender discrimination suits reveals a disturbing connection. Many of the same companies that are heralded in the most prestigious national business publications for being models of diversity and best companies for minorities are also facing the biggest and most expensive employee discrimination suits in history. Consider a few examples.

Wal-Mart is no stranger to criticism and employment lawsuits. In 2001, a sex discrimination lawsuit was filed against the mega-retailer and largest private employer in the United States, alleging gender discrimination. That same year, ironically, Wal-Mart ranked No. 80 on *Fortune*'s "Best Companies to Work For" list. The suit alleged that Wal-Mart created a system that frequently paid its female workers less than their male counterparts for comparable jobs and that Wal-Mart bypassed women for key promotions. In 2003, the Arkansas-based company established a new diversity office to serve as its driving force for diversity initiatives, according to the company's press release. But the office's attempts to add diversity programs when such programs clearly weren't a baked-in part of the Wal-Mart culture seemed too little, too late. In 2004, a federal judge approved the class action status for the case, making it the largest private civil rights case in U.S. history.

But a landmark sex discrimination case with 1.25 million pages of evidence and two hundred sworn depositions (and counting) didn't curtail the company's list presence. In 2005, Wal-Mart landed on *Black Enterprise*'s "Best Companies for Diversity" list under the flattering headline: "When it comes to minority representation, these corporations mean business."

Here's another example: in April 2005, Sodexho Marriott Services agreed to an $80 million settlement with thousands of African American employees after a federal suit alleged that it routinely discriminated against them. One year later, the company made a Herculean leap to No. 14 in the nation among the "Top 50 Companies for Diversity" in the United States by *Diversity Inc.* magazine. In 2006, Sodexho was also named one of *Diversity Inc.*'s "Top Ten Companies for Executive Women" and "Top Companies for People with Disabilities."

And then consider this: in 2000, Coca-Cola was facing a public relations nightmare of New Coke proportions. The headlines read, "Coca-Cola settles discrimination suit—soft drink giant shells out $192.5 million against racial bias allegations." The lawsuit, which had been ongoing for two years, claimed that Coca-Cola discriminated against African American employees in fair pay, performance evaluations, and promotions. The settlement also set up an independent task force to monitor Coca-Cola's employment practices and make enforceable recommendations. In the package, Coca-Cola agreed to pay $113 million in cash, $43.5 million in salary adjustments for African American employees over the next ten years, and $36 million for the independent oversight of employment practices and the initiation of diversity programs. That was enough for the company to land on *Fortune*'s "Best Companies for Minorities" list in the same year. *Fortune* attributed Coca-Cola's first-ever appearance on the list (Esposito et al. 2001) "in part to measures launched in the wake of its $192 million discrimination settlement. Among the improvements: more well-paid minorities and a greater number of minority suppliers."

To make such improvements and land on a "Best of . . ." list in less than a year must be a remarkable business turnaround story suitable for a case study in some of the top business schools. Clearly, making the list doesn't require a proven track record, and it's equally clear that having a federally mandated task force monitoring your activities doesn't limit your ability to be categorized as The Best. Does a company deserve commendation when its diversity accomplishments were court mandated and enforced by federal regulators? Apparently so, because in 2004, the soft drink giant made the cut again, appearing at No. 26 on *Fortune* magazine's "Best Companies for Minorities" list.

African American women looking for a great place to work often turn for guidance to *Essence* magazine, a trusted resource in the black community. In 2005, *Essence* compiled its "35 Great Places to Work" list by surveying 130 firms. According to the article, of the 130 surveyed, only 35 companies agreed to answer the questions. That means that every company that answered the survey made the list in some capacity—not exactly a rigorous process.

Among other "great places" on *Essence*'s 2005 list is delivery giant FedEx Corporation, which received an overall "good" ranking. That's not good news, considering that in September of the same year, the U.S. District Court certified a sweeping class action suit against FedEx, alleging that the delivery giant also served up an express discrimination service by denying opportunities to people of color and women, paying minorities less than their white counterparts, and giving minorities poor work evaluations. The suit, which was originally filed in 2003 by eight current and former employees, alleged discrimination against African American and Latino hourly workers and certain managers by the company's disproportionately failing to put workers of color on promotion tracks, providing less compensation for similar work, and discriminately disciplining minority workers.

Despite having a pending discrimination case that was directly tied to African American men and women, FedEx was able to land on a "Great Places to Work" list of a prominent African American lifestyle publication simply by answering questions. The *Essence* survey, designed by an independent consulting service at significant cost, perhaps neglected to ask whether the company had any pending discrimination suits on record.

These examples highlight how easy it can be for a company to get good diversity press while routinely discriminating against minority employees. Still, the "Best of . . ." lists serve as ideal fodder for company Web sites and marketing materials, where CEOs can boast of their accolades and "Best of . . ." achievements (in between critical meetings with their legal staff as they strategize their way through yet another discrimination suit or potentially litigious incident they'd rather keep quiet).

So what should a company do to earn favorable diversity press and rightfully "make the list"? Figure 3.1 recaps the misguided approach that so many companies take and offers a better alternative.

Trying to win at the diversity game will never yield sustainable results. In an environment where success entails improving your ratio of positive to negative press headlines and covering your hide to avoid litigation, there is no room for real change. Without a consistent and deliberate system in place to help them understand the role of daily slights, CEOs will continue to watch talented employees leave their companies' ranks.

WHAT DRIVES PEOPLE OUT THE DOOR?

It is typically not the headline-grabbing incidents that drive most women, people of color, and gays and lesbians out the door. Research conducted by the Level Playing Field Institute shows that the last straw is typically just another slight after an extended period of enduring daily micro-insults.

Consider an example: It's midnight at a prestigious law firm, and a Japanese American fourth-year associate gets called by the name of a first-year Korean American by a senior partner who is barking out an assignment in the elevator. As she deals with this insulting behavior, she wonders why she bothers to stay at the office until 3:00 A.M. on some nights, putting in long hours and sacrificing her own quality of life to put money in the pockets of the firm's partners who can't even make the effort to learn who she is and pronounce her name correctly.

For more than a decade, I trained new hires—both newly minted MBAs and senior vice presidents and managing directors—at one of the leading global investment banks. The firm made a major commitment to building and sustaining its culture, promoting ethical conduct, and implementing innovative training programs. Despite this commitment, the firm still tolerated the inappropriate behaviors of some senior male executives who brought in truckloads of money *and* truckloads of legal problems.

FIGURE 3.1 MAKING THE LIST

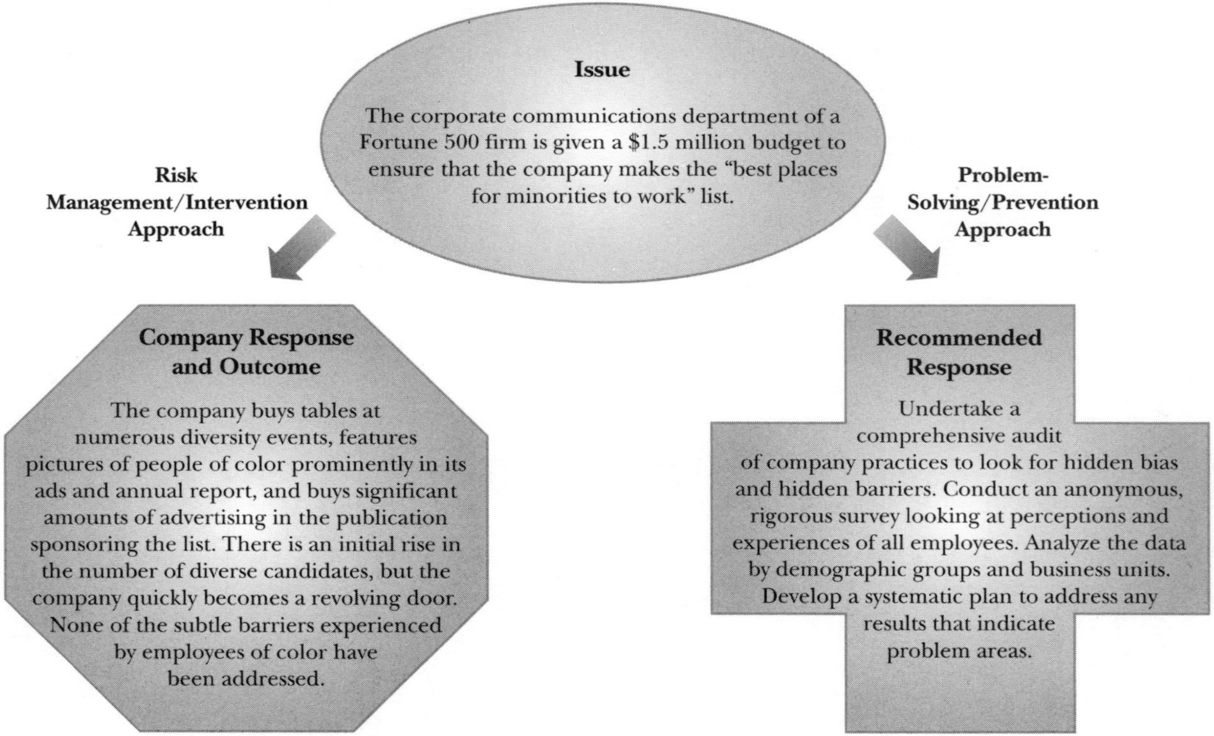

Issue

The corporate communications department of a Fortune 500 firm is given a $1.5 million budget to ensure that the company makes the "best places for minorities to work" list.

Risk Management/Intervention Approach

Problem-Solving/Prevention Approach

Company Response and Outcome

The company buys tables at numerous diversity events, features pictures of people of color prominently in its ads and annual report, and buys significant amounts of advertising in the publication sponsoring the list. There is an initial rise in the number of diverse candidates, but the company quickly becomes a revolving door. None of the subtle barriers experienced by employees of color have been addressed.

Recommended Response

Undertake a comprehensive audit of company practices to look for hidden bias and hidden barriers. Conduct an anonymous, rigorous survey looking at perceptions and experiences of all employees. Analyze the data by demographic groups and business units. Develop a systematic plan to address any results that indicate problem areas.

File drawers were filled with copies of the complaints leveled against them as well as the gag orders accompanying settled lawsuits. The gap between what was stated and what was practiced grew and grew, until one summer I was asked by an aggressive young Caucasian man, having graduated near the top of his Harvard MBA class, "If the firm really believes this, then why is *Mr. X* still here? Isn't this just a cover-your-ass activity for the company?" Although I could recite the laundry list of impressive efforts launched by the global bank, the simple truth of his question caught me off guard. I quickly considered and ruled out responding with "Well, *Mr. X* simply brings in too much money," so I pointed out that this was an excellent question, best directed to the senior person in charge of his division.

If the accounting books included the costs of distrust in senior management and the cynicism and disengagement resulting from these issues, none of the men who were being protected would be generating profit. Instead, they'd represent a deficit.

Chief Change-maker

American businesses needs more CEOs who recognize their roles as the chief change-makers in their organizations and who understand the cumulative impact of subtle bias—and then maintain a vigilant and adaptive stance, ready to engage in organizational change and redirection as required. Of course, the barriers to reaching this goal are many, and the primary one is an executive's own close-mindedness regarding change. A study by Geletkanycz (1997) at the Carroll School of Management at Boston College argues that while top executives are known to play a key role in strategic adaptation, evidence suggests they are not equally open to organizational change.

A CEO's decisions are also affected by his or her own biases. Without a deeper understanding of bias (including their own) and a working knowledge of how it relates to organizations, top managers can never be fully committed to diversity efforts that actually work. CEOs must first examine their own attitudes and beliefs about diversity and about people who differ from them. When a CEO understands his or her own weaknesses and challenges, he or she is better prepared to lead an organization. Leadership is the most important element for change, and that includes fostering workplaces that have an inclusive culture and that enhance cross-cultural awareness and skills through communication, training, and education. This is the starting point for any meaningful change in creating fair workplaces.

Growing recognition of the critical need for CEO commitment in any diversity strategy is beginning to take hold in the media. In 2006, *Diversity Inc.* magazine (Frankel 2006) modified the methodology of its "Best Companies for Diversity" rankings to give

> far heavier emphasis to the most important aspect of diversity management—CEO commitment. . . . Without a strong diversity champion at the top of a company, no diversity-management initiative can have long-term success. Therefore, we weighted the questions to give more emphasis to CEO commitment, followed by human capital, corporate communications and supplier diversity.

This new rubric radically changed *Diversity Inc.*'s 2006 compendium. This may also signal a sea of change for the "usual suspects" who traditionally and consistently land on the myriad "Best of . . ." lists without any rigorous accountability for their company systems. Hopefully, a deeper dive by more media outlets is on the horizon. That may compel otherwise reticent CEOs to do more than offer lip service to the diversity movement.

In the meantime, diversity management continues to need deep-rooted, publicly stated support from the top, including a CEO's signing off on executive compensation linked to diversity goals and chairing the diversity council. From there, businesses succeed by holding their executives accountable for meeting measurable, obtainable goals. Diversity management, as an integral part of the line operations of a business, cannot succeed without that same level of accountability. A CEO's vision for diversity is a critical first step, but no substantial progress will be made unless management has specific, quantifiable goals tied directly to rewards and penalties. Specific steps to assess fairness from the inside are presented in Chapter Six.

Measuring CEO commitment to diversity initiatives often isn't as clear-cut as measuring the number of people working in a specific job function. However, several methods to evaluate the support of C-level officers do exist. Perhaps the most important metrics are from the "customers" of diversity—that is, the employees themselves. What would a truly anonymous survey say about a CEO? Surveys that I have designed and administered over the years take each of the company's stated values, including diversity goals, and ask every employee to evaluate to what extent each level of management displays the value in his or her daily behavior.

CONCLUSION

The future of fair workplaces relies on the CEO and senior management creating real diversity systems that work. As Malcolm Gladwell (2002) said, companies "don't just create; they execute and compete and coordinate the efforts of many different people, and the organizations that are most successful at that task are the ones where the system *is* the star." Management has to set the proper tone, prove its commitment to employees, and create an environment in which employees believe their differences are welcomed, where they are allowed to make a constructive contribution, and in which management treats them as whole human beings, not fragments. Any CEO's greatest asset is the ability to inspire others and provide employees with a clear, consistent framework within which they can achieve their full potential. When the top actually reaches the bottom, then, and only then, will the diversity movement reach its full potential.

Chapter Four

The Cost of Bias

Flashback: it was an early Monday morning and Eric awoke to a subtle pain in his chest. Rising slowly from the bed, he began his morning ritual: six-minute shower, three-minute suit selection, and then anywhere up to ten minutes creating the perfect shirt and tie combination from his treasured collection of custom-made shirts and designer ties. But as he got closer to being ready to leave for work, he found that the pains intensified. By the time he stood before the mirror crafting the perfect knot in his tie, the sharp spasms were traveling down his arms and extending through his fingertips. By the time he began to pull the knot tight, he was feeling light-headed and having difficulty breathing.

At this point, Eric wasn't worrying about money. He was worrying about a heart attack. But the stress-related problems Eric was suffering would prove to be costly and just a small part of the incredibly high price tag that comes from hidden bias in the workplace. Every day, unfair treatment—as well as the subtle and blatant forms of discrimination—lead to a litany of expenses, from increased health care costs of stress-related illnesses, to the literal turnover costs of lost productivity and loss of client relationships.

The weight of bias in the workplace is a burden borne by three separate entities: First, the employees themselves, whose health and vitality suffer; second, their employer, who pays the price in lost motivation and absenteeism; and third, society at large, which takes a drubbing, further weakening our ability to compete in a global marketplace by enhancing stereotypes and shutting out talent. The magnitude of the hit depends on how the employee responds to the unfair treatment.

The costs of these hidden biases cannot be found in annual reports or social science journals. As reported in Chapter One, the Level Playing Field Institute and Knowledge Networks designed a nationally representative survey of professionals and managers to determine the costs of voluntary turnover due to unfairness. The Corporate Leavers Survey was primarily sponsored by Korn/Ferry International and a New York–based law firm ranked in the top half of the AmLaw100, which has chosen to be anonymous. Both the Executive Summary of the study and the detailed cost analysis can be found in Appendix B. This chapter looks closely at these costs and others. They begin at a very personal level.

PERSONAL COSTS: JOB STRESS

After sitting down for several minutes, Eric decided to try to make a stop at his doctor's office before heading into work, hoping for a quick fix and a helpful prescription. Instead of the sixty-second diagnosis Eric was expecting, he was asked a lengthy barrage of questions about his lifestyle and work habits. How many hours did he work on average per week? What were his sleeping patterns? Was he under stress at work? The answers: seventy hours in a good week, sleep was considered a luxury, and stress was a norm not worth mentioning. Eric began to contemplate his work habits and lifestyle. When had he changed from a happy, motivated man into this exhausted shell of a person? His doctor's next words, telling Eric that he was suffering from hypertension, were troubling.

Eric thought hypertension was a disease of older people, sedentary people who had poor diets and family histories of the disease. Eric was ordered to take off work for a week, scheduled for additional tests, and prescribed a costly medication for his high blood pressure. Eric studied the $269 pharmacy bill as he walked out of the drugstore and was surprised to find he was quietly crying.

For five years, Tene Lewis, a health psychologist at Rush University Medical Center, studied how the chronic stress of subtle, everyday discrimination (that is, "minor, everyday insults") impacted the health of 181 African American women. The findings? Women who reported higher incidences of everyday discrimination were two and a half times more likely to experience coronary artery calcification than their counterparts who experienced less discrimination (Lewis et al. 2006).

Now that Eric had become part of those statistics, he joined the disproportionate number of people of color, women, and gays and lesbians who share similar fates. Frequent headaches, insomnia, and the side effects of high blood pressure medication affected his productivity, forcing him to miss work, limiting his effectiveness with clients, and damaging his personal commitment to his employer and work responsibilities. While Eric's health and job satisfaction were compromised, his company also paid handsomely for having lost a productive employee. And we all pay the price eventually.

Hidden bias and hidden barriers account for substantial costs at the personal, company, and societal levels. Some of these are out of pocket and easy to measure: Eric's trip to the doctor, the executive recruiter's fees, job training programs, and unemployment insurance. Depending on one's accounting standards (what is actually valued), the hidden costs are even more staggering. For an individual who has spent his or her life believing that society is a meritocracy, what is the cost of dashed hopes, cynicism, and lost self-esteem? For a company that refuses to examine its hidden barriers, what's the cost of whole groups of employees who have diminished confidence in management? For society as a whole, what's the cost of a huge reservoir of untapped and underutilized talent, which translates to a lack of role models and a lack of varying perspectives at the table to design products, solve problems, and develop services? Society faces the mounting expenses—due to the effects on individuals, families, and communities—of the relentless pressure to increase productivity and control people costs.

PERSONAL COSTS: BEYOND THE OFFICE

Diminished health and battered self-esteem are merely by-products of bias in the workplace. Long before Miguel, Kristen, and Eric moved on, they began paying the literal price of their workplace experiences. Because they felt obligated to put in "face time"—to be seen at the office at all hours, whether or not their work required it—they began paying for housekeeping and laundry services to compensate for lack of personal time to spend on these tasks. Miguel took a class to learn golf, in hopes of being included when his managers hit the links. Kristen hired someone to teach her poker to help her fit in with her card-playing colleagues. And Eric, after spending $269 on hypertension medications, hired a career coach to help him navigate his department's bumpy terrain.

Kristen's marriage bonds were also affected. She began to take the stress of work home to her husband. She was irritable, frustrated, and on the cusp of depression almost on a daily basis. One morning, lingering over a cup of tea, Kristen wondered when she had crossed the line from intrinsically happy to basically miserable. As the daily pressures slowly transformed Kristen into someone she didn't know and didn't like, her marriage suffered considerably.

Numerous studies of workers, from police officers to surgeons, have shown that work-related stress can contribute to divorce. In a 2001 study reported in the *Journal of Marriage and Family,* University of California at Berkeley researchers had male police officers and their wives keep "stress diaries" for a month and participate in laboratory interviews. Study findings were not surprising: Stress from tension, or just exhaustion, at work brought stress to the marriage—more negative emotions or fewer emotions overall (Roberts and Levenson 2001). In an even broader sweep, social scientists at Penn State University documented in a widely recognized study that marital quality and job satisfaction are clearly linked. Using data from a twelve-year panel survey of a nationally representative sample of married individuals, the researchers found that both men and women who were troubled at work ended up being troubled at home (Rogers and May 2003).

Torn between an unfulfilling career with few rays of hope on the horizon and having healthy romantic and familial relationships, many women take the career off-ramp. A top-tier management consulting firm began investigating why white women, people of color, and gays and lesbians were voluntarily leaving after two years, a point in time at which they had not yet begun to make money for the firm. As it turns out, they were caught in a vicious downward spiral with the following implications:

Feelings of exclusion

Diminished self-confidence

Greater risk aversion

Reticence to ask for help or guidance

Slower development and growth

This, of course, becomes a self-fulfilling prophecy: Unfair treatment at work significantly impairs a person's ability to engage the very traits that are necessary to get ahead, such as self-confidence, willingness to take risks, and ability to ask for help. In a painful irony, those who are undermined by the chain reaction set off by experiences of exclusion or stereotyping end up acting out the substandard performance they were suspected of in the first place: "See, *they* really can't cut it," conclude senior managers. Yet these same managers are oblivious to what set the downward spiral in motion, noting only the outcome and holding responsible the individuals caught in the vortex.

Some of those who left the top-tier management consulting firm were in worse shape than when they started, despite having a prestigious entry on their resumes. They set their sites lower, believing that they had failed and that they really weren't good enough. Gone were the glamorous though grueling lifestyles, the outsized salary and perks, and the immediate name recognition of their past employer. Others, however, were empowered by their decision to get out. Here's what one senior manager told me in an interview:

> When I decided to quit, I was already launching my business. I already had clients who needed more of my time. I set up a meeting with my boss to give him the letter. We hardly ever met anymore. On this day he forgot the memo I had given him about the meeting. He said, "Well, I've only got a minute." I said to him, "Well, it's only going to take a minute for me to hand you this letter. But it might take you longer to read it." He just about fell out of his chair. It proved to me that I was doing the right thing. I was never going to go anywhere.

CORPORATE COSTS: IGNORING THE PROBLEM

Regardless of how employees choose to deal with bias, it continues to eat into company profits. Even for those who try to put up with it at the office, such as Eric, the numbers continue to add up. Although he made no complaints at work, his personal health costs increased and his work productivity and commitment levels decreased.

In addition to the personal costs absorbed by the individual facing bias, my research has shown that a drop in productivity is almost always the result while someone is desperately trying to ignore a bad situation, work around it, or strategize how to avoid the individuals dispensing the inappropriate treatment. As reported in Chapter One, the annual cost to U.S. businesses of managers and professionals voluntarily leaving their employers due *solely* to unfairness is an estimated $64 billion.

Just the cost of job stress alone has been conservatively estimated to top a staggering $300 billion per year—or $1,000 for each person in the United States—according to the American Institute of Stress (2004). This extrapolation, cited by the federal government and medical researchers who study job stress, includes the spiraling costs of lost productivity, absenteeism, employee turnover, and medical bills for on-the-job accidents. The legal costs, insurance fees, and workers' compensation awards aren't even included. Nor are the federal fines for workplace discrimination, which topped $100 million in 2005, according to the U.S. Equal Employment Opportunity Commission (EEOC). Those costs are expected to continue to rise. In 2006, Verizon Communications was required to pay a record $48.9 million to end a landmark government lawsuit claiming it had discriminated against female employees who were pregnant or on maternity leave (Joyce 2006).

Obviously, not all workplace stress is related to bias and barriers, but our national survey revealed that every year at least half of all professionals and managers experience some form of inappropriate behavior in the course of performing their job duties, and many are subject to chronic mistreatment in multiple forms. Some of this treatment is legally actionable, but much of it is not. However, all of it is stressful. Consider these facts:

- One out of every five employees who didn't show up for work today is probably home because of stress, according to the European Agency for Safety and Health at Work.[1]
- Nearly one out of five employees who quit is leaving because of stress, according to a survey by Integra Realty Resources.[2]

- According to the St. Paul Fire and Marine Insurance Co., health complaints are more strongly associated with work stress than any other life stressor, including family or financial stress.[3]

CORPORATE COSTS: USING A COMPANY COMPLAINT CHANNEL

When Kristen stepped into her manager's office to leave a note on his desk, only to find pornography on his computer screen, she shared the incident with a colleague in confidence. However, word that she was offended by the porn eventually drifted back to her manager, solidifying Kristen's reputation as "not one of the guys." In fact, just as she thought she was breaking down the barriers between her and the mostly male department, she found herself right back at square one. Recently, after a business dinner with a client, Kristen was sent home by car service while the rest of the team went to a "gentlemen's club" with the client.

The following week, at a networking lunch for women employees, she shared a few anecdotes from her experiences in the department with a well-respected senior woman at the firm. A few days later, she received a call from human resources summoning her to their offices. The company policy mandates an investigation anytime someone hears of behavior that could constitute sexual harassment or discrimination. Kristen feared being further ostracized by submitting to a formal complaint process, but because of the firm's rigid policy, if she did not comply, she would be categorized as a policy violator. (A 2006 Supreme Court ruling that trimmed the rights of whistle-blowers, while legally relevant only to public employees, is expected to have a chilling effect on the private sector as well.)

Even though the company has internal controls to try to stop any unfair treatment, the costs mount. If Kristen's manager (who makes $150,000 per year) and the HR director (who makes $120,000 per year) each spent three days dealing with her complaint, the loss of their time, plus the time of co-workers who would be interviewed, would equal more than $3,000. Once the consultant who charges $5,000 per day is brought in to investigate and mediate, the price tag grows. In the end, the real cost of Kristen's cab ride home is closer to $20,000. Even this figure is conservative, as it excludes the cost that comes from decreased employee morale and the company's tarnished reputation as the story spreads.

CORPORATE COSTS: TURNOVER

After Eric decided to quit the firm, he gave himself three months to wrap things up and try to look for something new. His company began paying the price for the unwelcoming environment he was subjected to long before he submitted his letter of resignation. His loss of commitment to the firm and wavering productivity affected his division's financial performance. He no longer bothered to share his innovative ideas, which weakened the company's competitive edge. He mentally checked out of his job. He marked the date he would submit his resignation on his calendar in red ink: March 21.

From that day forward, he was committed to doing only the minimal requirements for the job, while devoting the lion's share of his energy to creating new opportunities for himself. He stepped outside to chat with headhunters, studied the backgrounds of potential employers, took a morning off for a "get-to-know-you interview" at a nearby firm. At his desk, he dropped his weekly check-in calls with current clients and passed a promising client referral to a new colleague. One afternoon, scanning a report, he had a jolt of creativity. A complex restructuring of the project he was reading about could, potentially, save everyone a lot of time. He sighed. It wasn't worth the negotiations to convince his managers to allow him to try, and it wasn't worth the extra time he'd have to put into it. Eric signed off on the project and went home.

Companies are the biggest losers when the expense of bias is tallied, hemorrhaging billions of dollars' worth of lost time and productivity, coupled with the literal costs associated with paying for services such as online employment advertising or temporary staffing assistance. A joint 2002 study by the Rutgers University Graduate School of Management and the Saratoga Institute (a division of PricewaterhouseCoopers) found that the total cost of losing even one position to turnover can easily reach 150 percent of the employee's fully loaded annual compensation figure.[4] Highly paid managerial and sales positions can cost a company significantly more—200 to 250 percent of their compensation—according to

Bill Bliss, president of Bliss & Associates, Inc., in Butler, New Jersey, whose firm offers leadership development and talent management services.[5]

As reported in Chapter One, our national survey of professionals and managers asked the voluntary leavers to what extent, on a 10-point scale, unfairness played a role in their decisions to leave their jobs. Here are the rates by groups of those who indicated that unfairness was the *only* reason:

- People of color: 9.5 percent
- Gays and lesbians: 5.6 percent
- Caucasian women: 4.6 percent
- Caucasian men: 3.0 percent

If we add points 8 and 9 from the 10-point scale, indicating that unfairness was a strong contributor to their decision to leave their employer (but not the sole reason), the numbers increase sharply. Overall, 28.6 percent of the managers and professionals in our study ranked unfairness an 8, 9, or 10 in their decision to leave. Considering that unfairness, as perceived by salaried managers and professionals, can be identified and mitigated by employers, this staggering cost is controllable.

Our cost analysis (see Appendix B for full details) took a very conservative approach: we used U.S. Census Bureau data to establish the number of managers and professionals who fell into each racial/ethnic group. Since women constitute a majority of managers and professionals, we did not do a further breakdown by gender. White women voluntarily leave jobs solely due to unfairness at a rate that is 50 percent higher than the rate for white men. This number alone would substantially increase the total costs of turnover. After establishing the number of managers and professionals in each racial/ethnic category, we then multiplied it by the percentage of those who left solely due to unfairness, as uncovered by our nationally representative survey.

For annual compensation, we also used a conservative approach: we took the average salary and benefits for professionals and managers as calculated by the U.S. Department of Labor, Bureau of Labor Statistics. This figure is $97,677 per year.[6] Thus, the cost of turnover of one professional or manager at this salary equals $146,516 × 435,030.2 who leave each year solely due to unfairness, for a grand total cost to U.S. businesses of $63,738,884,783 per year.

CORPORATE COSTS:
DAMAGED REPUTATIONS

Eric's manager had good intentions when he made Eric the company's unofficial diversity outreach coordinator. Eric was sent to diversity recruitment fairs, community dinners, and alumni events, but he was burdened by working the extra hours and devoting his personal time to attending work-related social events. Furthermore, the deeper his dissatisfaction with the company became, the more leverage he had to damage the firm's reputation through these same channels. At recruitment fairs, his pitch about the company's commitment to diversity grew less and less persuasive. At the African American Professionals Leadership dinner, he regaled a table full of his colleagues and competitors with accounts of his boss's insensitivity. "And then he asked me again if I played basketball," was a typical punch line. When his fellow Ivy League alumni approached him about possible employment at the firm, he warned them off. "It just isn't the best place to work." The trickling costs of Eric's frustrations became a flood, threatening to raise company costs even more through damage to the company's reputation.

In recent years, we've surveyed workers at a number of high-tech firms, quantifying the costs of hidden bias. These companies, even more than most in corporate America, are hungry for cutting-edge employees. They're desperate for the innovators, the risk takers, the smartest, the most creative, the hardest working. Although these firms have human resources offices, most new hires are found by referrals, especially from current employees. But we found in our surveys that employees who experienced, or even observed, any form of inappropriate conduct on the job (from bullying to unsuitable comments) within the past year were significantly less likely to recommend their company both to clients and potential hires. Those in-house naysayers can do an inordinate amount of expensive damage.

Reputational Risks: Unfairness

Notably absent from many calculations of employee turnover is the financial impact of lowered reputations among consumers and potential employees due to turnover. Given the widespread experience of perceived unfair treatment at work and its strong impact on voluntary turnover, we were curious about the impact, if any, this could have on a company's reputation. We asked respondents whether their experiences affected the degree to which they recommended or discouraged consumers from purchasing their previous employers' products or services, and the degree to which they recommended or discouraged others from seeking jobs with their previous employer. Specifically, we asked the following two questions:

- "Thinking of the unfair experiences you mentioned happening to you in your former position, did these experiences encourage or discourage you from recommending others to buy your company's products or services?"
- "Thinking of the unfair experiences you mentioned happening to you in your former position, did these experiences encourage or discourage you from recommending others to seek a job from your company?"

Respondents were asked to answer these two questions based on the following scale: "strongly encouraged," "did not encourage or discourage," "strongly discouraged," and "does not apply."

Recruitment-Related Reputation Costs

Of those respondents who experienced any form of unfairness within a year prior to the survey, 27 percent indicated that their experience strongly discouraged them from recommending others to seek a job from their former employer. More than half, 58 percent, indicated that unfairness led them to some degree to discourage others from seeking a job at their former employer. Across all forms of unfairness about which we inquired, respondents who experienced unfairness indicated that they would strongly discourage others from seeking employment with their previous employer at significantly higher percentages than they would discourage prospective clients or customers. Interestingly, having been treated poorly as an employee had a stronger impact on referring prospective employees than it did on referring prospective customers or clients—a notable finding when one considers the shortage of qualified candidates.

We found that certain, specific forms of unfairness were strongly correlated with whether or not an employee encouraged others to seek a job from his or her employer. Nearly three-fourths of respondents who were bullied discouraged others from seeking employment with a former employer—as did 71.4 percent of those who were compared to a terrorist, 71 percent of those who were publicly humiliated, 70.2 percent of those who received unwanted sexual attention, and 70.1 percent of those who were passed over for a promotion due to their personal characteristics.

Figure 4.1 demonstrates how another source of employee anger and frustration—inappropriate comments or behavior by clients— can lead to reputational damage. Two different approaches to the problem are presented. One will end up costing the employer, while the other nips the problem in the bud.

Of course, the scope of reputational damage varies. A single employee such as Eric, with strong ties to his Ivy League alumni community, can tap those personal connections to draw top performers and clients to a firm. Or he can choose to discourage other top-flight candidates from working for his employer. A more public assault from a highly publicized discrimination lawsuit, such as the barrage of Wall Street bias cases (Smith Barney [now part of Citigroup Inc.], Merrill Lynch & Co. Inc., and Morgan Stanley), which together cost the firms more than $150 million to settle, would tell hope-filled graduates, "It's hard to get ahead here."

Intuition tells us that a strong link must exist between employee satisfaction and customer satisfaction, partly causal and partly stemming from both feeling recognized and valued by the same organizational culture. The popular business book *The Loyalty Effect* (Reichheld and Teal 1996) asserts that companies could be far more profitable if they paid attention to employee retention. For example, they found that a trucking company could increase profits by 50 percent if it cut driver turnover in half and that increasing a stock broker's retention by 10 percent would increase that person's value 155 percent.

FIGURE 4.1. WHEN THE CUSTOMER ISN'T RIGHT

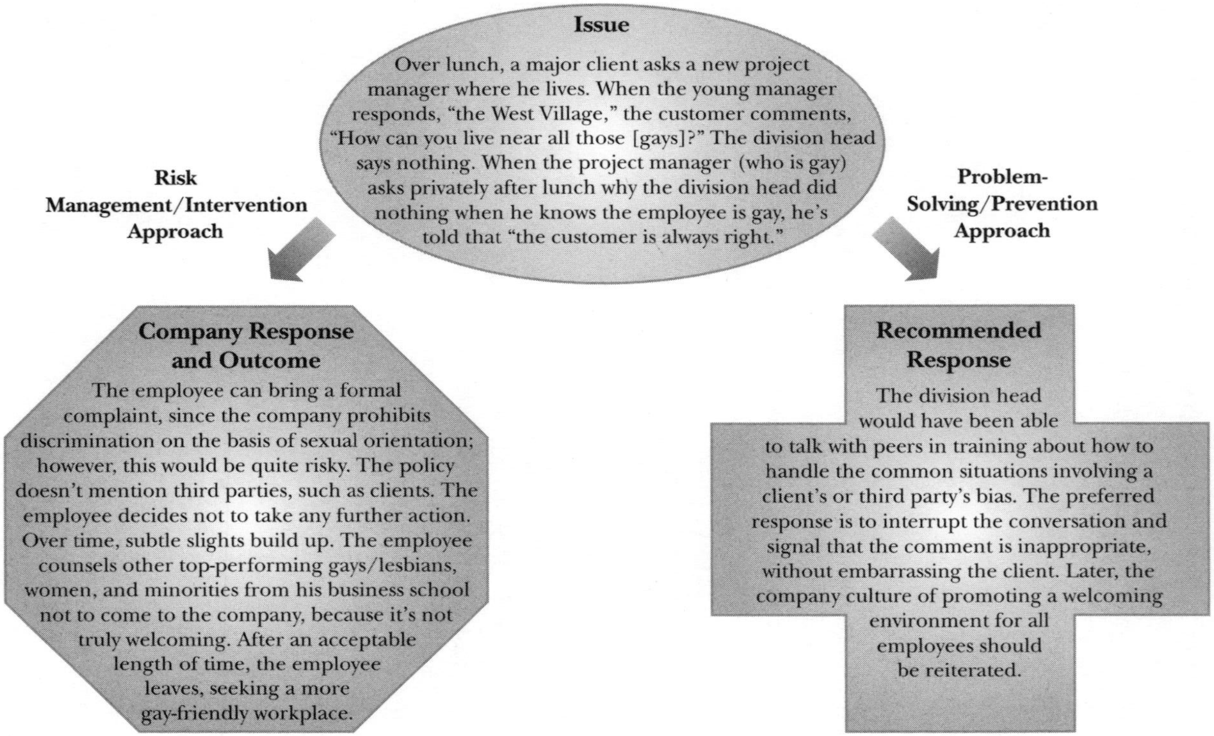

Issue

Over lunch, a major client asks a new project manager where he lives. When the young manager responds, "the West Village," the customer comments, "How can you live near all those [gays]?" The division head says nothing. When the project manager (who is gay) asks privately after lunch why the division head did nothing when he knows the employee is gay, he's told that "the customer is always right."

Risk Management/Intervention Approach

Company Response and Outcome

The employee can bring a formal complaint, since the company prohibits discrimination on the basis of sexual orientation; however, this would be quite risky. The policy doesn't mention third parties, such as clients. The employee decides not to take any further action. Over time, subtle slights build up. The employee counsels other top-performing gays/lesbians, women, and minorities from his business school not to come to the company, because it's not truly welcoming. After an acceptable length of time, the employee leaves, seeking a more gay-friendly workplace.

Problem-Solving/Prevention Approach

Recommended Response

The division head would have been able to talk with peers in training about how to handle the common situations involving a client's or third party's bias. The preferred response is to interrupt the conversation and signal that the comment is inappropriate, without embarrassing the client. Later, the company culture of promoting a welcoming environment for all employees should be reiterated.

CONSUMER-RELATED REPUTATION COSTS

Of those respondents who experienced any form of unfairness within a year prior to the survey, 13 percent indicated that their experience strongly discouraged them from recommending their previous employer's products and/or services to others. A majority (51 percent) indicated that unfairness led them to some degree to discourage others from purchasing their previous employer's products or services.

We also found that certain, specific forms of unfairness were strongly correlated with whether or not an employee discouraged others from purchasing the former employer's products or services. More than 56 percent of respondents who had been compared to a terrorist strongly discouraged others from purchasing their former employer's products, as did 48.8 percent of respondents who had been publicly humiliated, 48.7 percent of respondents who had been bullied, and 48.4 percent of respondents who had received unwanted sexual attention.

Management and marketing literature are overflowing with studies about the importance of retaining customers to a business's bottom line. The analyses are complex and multifaceted, varying industry by industry. Many point out that "customer retention" reflects both the more obvious repeat business from loyal customers as well as the reduced costs of acquiring other customers. For example, a Domino's $5 pizza represents $5,000 over the ten-year life of a franchise. Or to Ford, a loyal customer is worth $142,000 in the combined value of repeat business and reducing the acquisition cost of a new customer (Payne 2006). Frederick Reichheld and W. Earl Sasser (1990) concluded that an increase of 5 percentage points in customer retention leads to an increase in profits ranging from 35 percent in software to 75 percent in credit cards—and even as high as 125 percent for one credit card provider. The University of Michigan's National Quality Research Center found that increasing customer satisfaction by 1 percent correlated with a 3 percent increase in market capitalization (Peppers and Rogers 2005).

A company that is ranked 1,000 on the Fortune 1000 list would have similar annual revenues and market capitalization—roughly $1.5 billion. A 3 percent increase in market capitalization is $45 million. The company has around 13,000 employees. We'll assume about one-third, or 4,333, are professionals or managers. If 5.5 percent of them quit in one year due solely to unfairness, that's 238 people; 31 of them will be strongly discouraged from recommending their previous employer's products and/or services to others. The company's turnover cost will be $23,247,126. If we believe that 238 people leaving due solely to unfairness can decrease customer satisfaction by 1 percent, the company has foregone $45 million in market cap, plus $23 million in turnover. Whether or not you believe any specific assumptions, it is clear that companies are forfeiting substantial sums that they may never have realized were in their grasp.

Recently, I was contacted by an international law firm that had just lost its last remaining woman litigator in its New York office. Given that more than half of all law school graduates are currently women, a firm has to make a concerted effort to drive *all* of its women out. As part of being signatories to the Diversity Principles of the Association of the Bar of the City of New York, general counsels at major New York–headquartered corporations are now routinely asking for overall demographic information about the prospective law firms they are auditioning to do their work; they are specifically inquiring about who will populate the team that might be assembled to handle their cases or matters. Having no lawyers of color or women lawyers in a courtroom to connect with jurors puts clients at a serious disadvantage, and the law firm would have a difficult time asserting that it is able to act in the best interests of its clients. How many multi-million–dollar lawsuits will this firm not even be able to participate in because it has not addressed the chilly climate for its own female lawyers?

Corporate leaders, whose focus is necessarily the bottom line, are often stunned when the costs of hidden bias are laid out for them. Suddenly this moves from a human resources, touchy-feely issue to an item that must be resolved. Sadly, it frequently takes a reality check—a lawsuit or federal fine—to bring about real change in a corporation.

SOCIETAL COSTS: WORKERS, JOBS, AND THE ECONOMY

When all of the personal costs and business costs of hidden bias and hidden barriers are calculated, we might conclude that this is "merely the cost of doing business." The annual compensation of many CEOs dwarfs the amount it costs companies to deal with the bias lawsuits, turnover, and other items that are inevitably going to turn up when bias is left unchecked.

But what about the intangibles? Current estimates from David Reibstein, professor of marketing at the Wharton School of the University of Pennsylvania, indicate that 80 percent of a company's value is now classified as the "intangibles" tied up with people, in contrast to the 80 percent that used to be tied up in tangible assets such as factories, equipment, and inventory.[7] Although annual reports are littered with lofty statements like "employees are our most important asset," most employers have yet to figure out how to unlock the true value of that 80 percent. For the businesses that get it right, the rewards will be enormous.

And what about the opportunity costs? The U.S. Treasury defines these as "the difference between the yield that funds earn in one use and the yield they could have earned had they been placed in an alternative investment generating the highest yield available." What's the cost of the foregone opportunity? What's the cost to society of demoralizing and demotivating people like Eric, Miguel, and Kristen?

The American Electronics Association is a non-profit organization that has been supporting high-tech companies since 1943. Its 2005 report *Losing the Competitive Advantage? The Challenge for Science and Technology in the United States* (Kazmierczak et al. 2005) produced seven key recommendations; two of these are directly tied to hidden bias and hidden barriers in U.S. schools and workplaces:

- Champion dramatic improvements in the U.S. educational system: "To increase the number of science and engineering students, the United States first needs to provide *all* [emphasis added] students an adequate foundation in math and science."
- Support high-skilled immigration: "For the past 60 years, America has been the beneficiary of an influx of many of the most talented minds on the planet. That period could grind to a halt given restrictive immigration policy, tremendous opportunities abroad and the perception of not being wanted."

Many thought leaders, from every sector of society and every part of the political spectrum, have pointed out that the United States is in danger of a reduction in its standard of living if it cedes its competitive advantage to developing nations such as China and India. Said Thomas. L. Friedman, foreign affairs columnist for *The New York Times* and a best-selling author on globalization, "I think we as a society have an obligation to public policy and tax programs and subsidies and wage insurance and health care to find a way to cushion people who are in white collar jobs, just as we did— or tried to, to some extent—with blue collar, so they are not going to get steamrolled by these phenomena. We're talking about four million jobs that will be outsourced to India probably over the next 10 years. And that's not an insignificant number."[8]

The impact of globalization on jobs in various countries is a complex issue. Most important, it is dynamic, not static. Globalization means that new "winners" and "losers" are constantly emerging as the pace of innovation and technological development increase. Good jobs will go to the best-educated and -funded talent pool, while jobs that can be routinized will go to the lowest-cost provider.

Business leaders need to examine their assumptions and ask whether clinging to their hidden biases and refusing to identify and remove hidden barriers are more valuable to them than the upholding the standard of living Americans have come to enjoy. They have a wonderful opportunity to turn things inside out: The very employees who have been marginalized, written off, and assumed to lack brains, talent, and drive may hold the key to restoring the country's preeminence in innovation. Indeed, some of the greatest global challenges stir the passions of people within these groups.

At the Level Playing Field Institute, we tackle the spiraling corporate costs of hidden bias from both ends: working with management to find and solve problems and working with promising young students who can provide those firms with the diverse talent they need. From our Initiative for Diversity in Education and Leadership (IDEAL) Scholars program at the University of California at Berkeley, we meet bright, inspiring, dedicated students every day who want to make the world a better place.

In 2001, I interviewed a fifteen-year-old high school senior who was born in Nigeria and transplanted to Oakland, California, after being orphaned. His parents had been in a car accident, taken to the emergency room, treated for bruises, and released. The next day, they were both dead from internal injuries. After living with his grandmother and caring for her until she died from breast cancer, he was adopted by an Oakland family. He managed to learn English, take the right courses, and sustain the grade point average required for admission to the best public university in the world. During his interview for our program, he matter-of-factly stated that he wanted to earn both medical (M.D.) and doctorate (Ph.D.) degrees to be able to reform health care systems so that the fate suffered by his parents would never be suffered by anyone else. He has since graduated with a double major in biology and public health, already has his first academic journal publication, and is enrolled to earn a master's degree in public health before pursuing medical school. Is he safe from hidden bias and hidden barriers? Hardly.

During his first week in the dormitory, a freshman approached him seeking to buy drugs. Our student replied that he could be of no help since, as a Muslim, he doesn't touch drugs. The young white man persisted, "Oh c'mon, every black kid knows where to get drugs." Countless times through his undergraduate experience, he was assumed to be a thug, not a scholar. It happened on the bus, as passengers would move their purses away from him; while shopping for school clothes, as store detectives followed him; or in the hallways of the offices of his summer internship, when instructors would ask whose laptop he was carrying. Somehow he has kept his eyes on the prize, but there is no way of knowing whether the buildup of subtle slights is approaching a toxic level.

Surfacing hidden bias and removing hidden barriers have always been matters of fundamental fairness. But now these issues have become economic imperatives. Just as we're barraging young, talented, enthusiastic people of color, gays and lesbians, and women with stereotypes and assumptions of inadequacy and driving them from the corridors of higher education, corporations, and professional services firms, the United States is facing an unprecedented talent shortage.

Catherine C. Candland, founder and CEO of Advantage Human Resourcing, gathered these facts about the looming crisis (2003):

> The Bureau of Labor Statistics (BLS) estimates that there will be 10 million more open positions than available workers in 2010,

and the Employment Policy Foundation (EPF) projects that this gap will grow to 35 million by 2030. . . .

As the "knowledge economy" continues to evolve, jobs will require more education and specialized skills. Occupations requiring post-secondary training or a college degree will increase to 42 percent by 2010 according to BLS, and to 65 percent by 2030 according to EPF. Currently, only 38 percent of the American labor force has a two-year college degree or higher. Therefore, unless there is a dramatic shift in educational attainment ratios, the situation is even bleaker than the population statistics indicate.

CONCLUSION

With the anticipated labor shortage, draining talented and motivated people like Miguel, Kristen, and Eric out of the workforce goes beyond bad corporate ethics, or even bad corporate fiscal planning. Too many people are paying for counselors and blood pressure medication, tossing their education and training, and struggling with their marriages. Too many businesses are opting to ignore bias, shunting the problems to weak internal complaint mechanisms, hemorrhaging cash due to employees who quit, and scrambling to repair their reputations. And this is more than our society can afford: we are losing talent, losing belief in the meritocracy of our institutions, and risking our way of life and our coveted high standard of living. This is the wrong way to live, it's the wrong way to run a company, and it's the wrong way for our society to advance. And it doesn't have to happen.

CHAPTER FIVE

DOES BLINK = BIAS?

Stare at these words for a moment.

Did you read *THE CAT*? Most people do. Now look again. Notice that the symbols for *H* and *A* are not actually letters—they're identical, nonspecific symbols. You probably didn't notice this at first glance. Your brain filled in the information you needed, using pattern recognition based on past experiences. This is an inherent part of being human. At one time, this pattern recognition was a survival mechanism: *Red mushrooms make you sick. Red mushrooms make you sick again. Stop eating red mushrooms.* In the starkest Darwinian system of natural selection, you either figured it out by recognizing the pattern or you died.

When people consider the patterns by which they live, most would deny that those included stereotypes. And it's true—after hundreds of years of the most egregious racism imaginable, most people in the United States today are not overtly biased. It's true in the corporate world, too. Ask a group of CEOs, and they'll tell you that they can find genuine talent regardless of gender, race, or sexual orientation.

But consider the example at the top of this page when your brain automatically filled in the information that was missing.

And then consider this: What information is your brain implicitly providing when you walk into a conference room and see a person dressed unusually, a person whose skin is darker or lighter than that of others, a person whose hair or size or style or age is different than what you normally experience?

Researchers have refuted the notion that only racists use stereotypes and instead confirmed the uncomfortable fact that stereotypes are an inherent part of how we all relate to each other. In the workplace, the science is clear: unconscious bias routinely creeps into those split-second decisions in the office and elsewhere, impairing our ability to make intelligent, intuitive judgments.

What happened to Eric one cool, fall day was neither overt bigotry nor an anomaly. After spending the weekend in the office wrapping up an intense but creative project, Eric shrugged off his coat as he stepped into his manager's office to talk about his next assignment. He was hoping to be given a lead role with a new initiative that looked like a sure moneymaker. He was more than hoping, really.

Eric's patterns continued to be influenced by his childhood in Detroit, when his parents taught him to live in shifts. He saw his life in strict time blocks for both his personal and professional goals. He knew life wasn't fair, and he'd seen how the ups and downs of the auto industry—the epitome of big business—impacted his and his parents' day-to-day existence as he was growing up.

But now he was playing that corporate game, fueled by career ambitions, and working to understand it, tame it, and win it. Eric knew that his success on his prior project, coupled with his track record for hard work and creativity, put him at the top of a small heap to head the new assignment. So he was stunned when his manager told him he had already decided that leadership spot should go to Mark, Eric's white male colleague—a man with slightly lower productivity and fewer accomplishments than Eric but a chipper man, a good worker, and a positive and friendly person.

When he made this decision, Eric's manager wasn't blatantly thinking, "Eric's black, so I can't put him in charge." In fact, he considered Eric to be a talented and motivated team player; it's just that he wasn't all that comfortable with Eric. Not that any perceptible tension or discomfort was present when he dealt with Eric. Indeed, Eric's manager prided himself on his open-mindedness.

He made sure that Eric was given assignments he could handle and that if they slipped a day, it wasn't mission critical. Yet Eric's manager never stopped to reflect that Eric had *never* missed a deadline and was often completing assignments early and offering to help out his colleagues. Completely unconsciously, Eric's manager assumed that Eric had been an "affirmative action hire" (someone who wasn't as qualified as his peers and was hired only because of his race) and acted accordingly.

"It's nothing against you at all, Eric. You're doing great. Just stay focused on your current projects. Mark is a better fit: he's worked with many of these business units before and went to the same school as Chip, the big boss. Since they're both such loyal alums, I thought it would actually help all of us," his manager explained.

IMPLICIT ASSOCIATIONS

The Level Playing Field Institute has an exclusive partnership with Project Implicit, a collaborative research initiative aimed at examining the thoughts and feelings that exist either outside of conscious awareness or outside of conscious control. The project's key tool is the Implicit Association Test (IAT), an online exercise (take it yourself at www.implicit.harvard.edu) that measures how quickly a person responds with positive or negative words to photos of people. This striking research, which is gaining widespread attention for its provocative findings on unconscious bias, is one of the most objective systems devised to date to quantify prejudice. We all have prejudices based on learned patterns—that is, we prejudge a situation or a person based on cues from our past experiences. Not all prejudices are bad, however. Some are simply preferences, such as favorite colors, songs, or art.

Psychology professor Mahzarin Banaji, who helped develop the IAT, was surprised to discover her own biases when she took the test. But, in fact, her experience was typical. Almost all of the people taking this test describe themselves as unbiased at the onset, yet a whopping 88 percent of white people who take the test show some bias against African Americans, and a majority of people who take the test show bias against photos of people who are overweight, gay, elderly, or Arab/Muslim.

So how does this impact the workplace? Actually, the better question might be this: How doesn't it impact the workplace? From letters of recommendation, resumes, and hiring interviews, to promotions, wages, and job assignments, the unintended but inherent biases of our corporate leaders put up barriers that are not the blatantly discriminatory practices that can be fought in the legalistic framework. These barriers are, perhaps, even more insidious, since they remain the largest impediment to success for people of color, women, and gays and lesbians in the United States.

RESUMES

In 2004, researchers at the University of Chicago Graduate School of Business sent close to 5,000 fictitious resumes in response to help-wanted ads in Boston and Chicago newspapers. They randomly assigned very white-sounding names (such as Emily Walsh or Greg Baker) to half of the resumes, while using African American–sounding names (such as Lakisha Washington or Jamal Jones) on the other half. The results? White names received 50 percent more callbacks for interviews, regardless of occupation, industry, and employer size. "Taken at face value, our results on differential returns to skill have possibly important policy implications. They suggest that training programs alone may not be enough to alleviate the racial gap in labor market outcomes," the researchers wrote in their conclusions (Bertrand and Mullainathan 2004).

Theirs was one of a large number of sociological resume studies conducted in recent years. In 2003, for example, a sample of 236 undergraduates (most of whom were white women) rated resumes having equal qualifications in which gender, masculinity and femininity, and sexual orientation were apparent. Overall, the participants—especially those who described themselves as "religious"—rated lesbian and gay male applicants less positively than straight men but more positively than straight women (Horvath and Ryan 2003).

The bias is at least as pervasive in academia. In 1999, in a study still widely cited, University of Wisconsin–Milwaukee researchers sent altered curricula vitae with the names Brian Miller or Karen Miller on the top to 238 academic psychologists. Both men and women were more likely to vote to hire the man rather than the woman, even though their records were identical. Similarly, both genders reported that the fictitious Brian Miller had adequate teaching, research, and service experience compared to Karen Miller, who, they suggested, needed to accomplish more (Steinpreis et al. 1999).

LETTERS OF RECOMMENDATION

As with resume consideration, bias can play a part in letters of recommendation. Kristen's letters of recommendation, for example, showed inherent bias. Her scholarly prowess had launched her from thrift-store poverty on a farm to an academic scholarship at Harvard University, where she earned her BA and MBA. Graduating among the top in her class, she was juggling multiple awards and job offers, but she still needed letters of recommendation, which she sought from several of her key advisers.

Their responses were sincere and supportive, but they were also patronizing. They described her as "an earnest farm girl" and said that she had a "traditional hard work ethic." These professors, both men, knew Kristen well, so they referred to her by her first name: "Kristen is an intelligent young lady," and "Kristen works hard, but is able to maintain balance in her life."

Inadvertently, those professors were sending all sorts of unwritten messages in their letters, and managers who had already decided to bring this promising MBA into their departments read between the lines while making their assignments. Key phrases, like "balance in her life," were translated as "Watch out, she might want a family and may be less inclined to work long hours." "Intelligent young lady" translated to "She's very smart, but not a leader." The phrase also signaled "not threatening." "Earnest farm girl" meant "naive, not a shrewd negotiator."

These professors wanted the best for Kristen, but their letters led her new manager to steer her toward smaller clients—children's hospitals, nursing homes, and retailers—while several newly hired male counterparts were assigned to high-revenue-generating accounts like oil and gas and financial services firms.

These types of gender-based assignments are not unusual and have prompted sex discrimination litigation in recent years, including claims against Morgan Stanley, Costco Wholesale Corporation, Boeing, and retail giant Wal-Mart. In Kristen's case, as for many women, being assigned to less lucrative clients meant her chances of being made a senior manager were greatly diminished. At the end of her first year, as Kristen was listening to her first, in-depth performance review, she tried to identify what misstep had set her behind several men in her hiring class. It never occurred to her that it could possibly be a few phrases in her initial letters of recommendation that had set her on a slower track.

But Kristen's situation is shared by many women and people of color who depend on letters of recommendation to swim up their professional streams. The leading research on recommendation letters (Trix and Psenka 2003) studied three hundred letters submitted for faculty positions at a large American medical school in the mid-1990s. At the time, despite a greatly expanded pool of female applicants and students, women accounted for only 32 percent of the assistant professors, 21 percent of the associate professors, and 10 percent of the full professors. These Wayne State University researchers found that recommendation letters for women were consistently shorter and were far more likely to include what they termed "doubt raisers": phrases like "lacks confidence at times" or "has been limited by personal issues."

Their findings made it clear that if you're writing letters of recommendation, you must take care not to include biased or stereotypic language. And if you're reading letters, consider the implicit biases within. Consider a specific expression from a letter of recommendation, imagine changing the gender or race of the applicant, and then ask yourself, "Would that same expression still be used?" For example, are men ever described as "perky"? (This term found its way into a significant number of reviews for women at one top-tier professional services firm.) Similarly, how often do we use "qualified" as the adjective in front of anything but "minority"? Do we even mention race at all if the person is Caucasian?

Job Interviews

For those who do make it to the job interview stage, the implicit biases are even more of a challenge. A great deal more than education, experience, eloquence, or even clothes and makeup can impact a hiring decision. And only some of these factors are within an applicant's control.

Studies of orchestra auditions have repeatedly shown that women are more likely to be chosen if the conductors doing the hiring can't see them. One such study indicated that blind auditions have accounted for 25 percent of the increase in female orchestra musicians (Goldin and Rouse 2000). Because of this, most orchestra hopefuls now audition behind curtains. An accomplished violinist could be dressed in pajamas at her audition and still be hired. All that matters is her music.

In most workplaces, however, the hiring decisions are far less objective. Research conducted at the University of Toledo shows that individuals formulate opinions about a candidate within the first twenty seconds of the interview and that these first impressions will likely determine one's final evaluation. In the study, naive observers watched the first few seconds of fifty-nine job interviews, which included the candidates as they were greeted by the interviewers and escorted to a seat. The clip ended before the first prepared interview question was even asked, and yet the ratings given after watching this "thin slice" of behavior were similar to those made by interviewers after a twenty-minute structured interview. The researchers suggested that our immediate, snap judgments become self-fulfilling prophecies that influence our behavior toward an individual and cause them to appear in a manner consistent with our initial impression. It appears that these snap judgments are "the most obvious threat" to the legitimacy of the interview process (Prickett et al. 2000).

Miguel, the business school success who had fought his way out of a crowded barrio apartment toward a corporate career, was ready for snap judgments during his first job interview, but he faced an unexpected challenge. His awkward moment came when the interviewer switched to Spanish for a friendly question.

"*¿Dónde nació usted?*" she asked.

Miguel wasn't fluent in Spanish, but he understood enough to know that she was asking where he was born. But was there more to this question? Was she wondering if he was an immigrant? Or was she testing his Spanish-language skills? Perhaps she was just being friendly or trying to develop a bond. If he told her that he was born in an apartment in Harlem because his mother didn't have medical insurance, would that work against him? Wasn't it equally honest to say Manhattan? Or perhaps this was an opportunity to explain that he wasn't Mexican. Miguel assumed that Mexican Americans were considered less ambitious than Cuban Americans.

Miguel was quiet for an awkward moment and then answered in English with a polite smile, "I'm from New York." The interviewer didn't delve further. She made her own assumptions, never asking if he spoke Spanish. Nor did she ask if he would be interested in working on Latin American projects. Those unwanted assignments simply came his way after he was hired.

INCORRECT ASSUMPTIONS

Miguel's experiences facing stereotypes at work are typical. It happens all the time.

An African American speaker and Harvard University graduate, with whom we have worked at the Level Playing Field Institute, is routinely introduced as having attended Howard University, even though she has written her alma mater's name in bold letters on her introductory bio. What connections do our brains make when they see an African American and a university name that begins with *H* and ends with *ARD*? This process of filling in the *OW* instead of the *ARV* that distinguishes the names of the schools is exactly the same as what we filled in at the beginning of this chapter when we read *THE CAT*. Our brain fills in that African Americans go to Howard, not Harvard.

Last year, one of the top CEOs in the country—a woman—arrived early at a meeting and was asked by an executive secretary who was setting up the room to fetch coffee "for the men who will be here soon." She laughed, got the coffee, and later said that the experience happens at least once a year—although usually it's someone soliciting her investments who makes the mistake.

An African American partner from a prestigious international law firm was sitting in a conference room prior to a negotiation that would determine whether her client's corporation would emerge victorious in a multi-billion–dollar acquisition. The lawyer for the target company arrived and asked her to make copies, assuming she was a secretary or paralegal. She made the copies, reviewing the documents her opposing counsel was bringing to the negotiation. She then introduced herself and took the lead in the meeting. She later charged him the appropriate portion of her $800-per-hour billing rate for the photocopying time.

These are gaffes. But as we've seen in earlier chapters, the hidden biases reflected in these awkward moments have staggering personal and corporate costs. The impact is far greater than that of a minor slip. Effected individuals will eventually leave the job. Corporate reputations are eventually damaged.

It's important to emphasize that the inclination to use stereotypes is not limited to white male managers. As a diversity researcher and trainer, I was running a focus group comprising white male partners at a top international law firm. Information gathered from this and other focus groups would be used to design a questionnaire that would be sent to all lawyers and staff at all the firm's offices. At the end of the focus group session, a litigator approached me and said, "You didn't ask us about work-family issues." I responded, somewhat defensively, telling him that the women's partner group spent most of their time on this issue, and I had gleaned plenty of information about the firm's approach to juggling work and family.

As it turned out, this partner was a single father who had foregone a substantial amount of compensation by refusing to travel. He wore a beeper at all times, in case one of his children needed him, and he was known to drop out of meetings if family issues came up. "If you don't ask everybody the same questions, you don't know what people's experiences really are," he said. "You're basing what you know on stereotypes."

He was right. In fact, this is a fundamental principle built into employee surveys. We expect different rates of agreement by race to a statement such as, "People of color are given the same opportunities as comparably qualified Caucasians at our company." However, the most enlightening survey results come from looking at how different groups respond to neutral statements, such as, "My manager helps me solve work-related problems," or "My co-workers frequently seek my opinion on their work projects."

In another unfair assumption, I barely mentioned a description of the Level Playing Field Institute's programs for underrepresented students of color while engaging in premeeting pleasantries with a hedge fund president. He began the conversation by discussing a fund-raising dinner he had attended the previous night for a prominent, private university that was not distinguished in any way when it comes to diversity issues.

I wondered, "Why would he care about issues facing students of color?" I assumed that he wouldn't be interested, and it wasn't worth my time to explain them. But I was wrong again. And I was stunned as he told me that he believed his portfolio managers (who each make tens of millions of dollars a year) had numerous unfair advantages to get where they are. These were precisely the types of advantages to which our students would never have access. This hedge fund president did, indeed, "get it."

Addressing Implicit Bias

A common misperception is that if bias is implicit, not much can be done about it. This is simply wrong. When seeking to improve diversity, break glass ceilings, and empower the Erics, Kristens, and Miguels, managers can take some simple steps. The most important part of eliminating stereotypes is to understand "blind spots." Taking the Implicit Association Test is one quick and easy way to recognize your own biases. Asking your managers to take the test can begin a conversation with significant, positive consequences.

Frank and direct conversations about topics such as race, age, and appearance can be difficult with friends and colleagues, but if you can find a safe environment in which to address these issues—perhaps by explaining that you are trying to understand your own blind spots—the discussions can be important and enriching. Applicable exercises are presented a bit later in this chapter.

These conversations, however, are safe only if they take place among peers. Being asked to reveal sensitive information to someone who controls your paycheck is an unfair request. Many early diversity training efforts were unsuccessful for precisely this reason. Ironically, their design was oblivious to the power dynamics in the room, even while it purported to heighten participants' awareness about the power differences between women and men or between racial minorities and Caucasians.

The facilitators would ask people to disclose the first person of color they ever knew or every stereotype they had ever heard about women, Jews, blacks, Italians, and on and on. How would *anyone* feel comfortable being the "only" in a room, hearing your boss and co-workers use every hateful and hurtful slur they could think of to describe those who share your heritage?

Stanford University Professor Claude Steele incorporated weekly "rap sessions" about race as part of a racially integrated "living and learning community" within a dorm at the University of Michigan. "Participation in these sessions reduced students' feelings of stereotype threat and improved grades," wrote Steele in his conclusions. (Stereotype threat is discussed in Chapter Nine.) How great was the improvement? The grades of African American students who participated in the living and learning community program were 15 percent higher than those who did not participate. "Our research bears a practical message: even though the stereotypes held by the larger society may be difficult to change, it is possible to create niches in which negative stereotypes are not felt to apply," said Steele (Perry et al. 2003).

Every corporation has some of these niches: the productive, upbeat, and diverse departments or teams where relationships just seem more easygoing, with less personal and professional tension.

Diversity training can also be an excellent way to examine the stereotypes we use that lead to unfair judgments about others. These should not be boring, step-by-step PowerPoint lectures; nor should they be led by managers who might themselves need to recognize their own implicit biases. Instead, these should be provocative and interactive sessions, conducted without accusations or finger-pointing. I frequently use small group discussion and larger group debriefing about situations (gathered through focus groups and surveys) that have actually occurred at the specific company where I'm conducting training. Another option is to use challenging situations that have occurred at another employer in their same industry (see the following example). Setting the right context, communicating the importance of understanding and mitigating biases from the top down, and making sure no one is in a class with his or her boss are important preconditions.

The following is a sample hypothetical used in professional services firm training. Such case studies are compiled based on data from focus groups with current and former employees and/or with data from employee surveys.

Jessica is a well-regarded fourth-year associate. She is a tireless employee who routinely works late nights and weekends in her office. She has become increasingly trusted by a growing client. Everyone agrees that the client's satisfaction with Jessica's service has greatly contributed to bringing more business to the firm.

After the birth of her first child and some time off for maternity leave, Jessica returns to work on a full-time basis, but she now leaves the office as early as feasible to spend time with her family, and she is in the office on weekends only occasionally. She informs her colleagues and the client that she is available by e-mail throughout the night, since she logs on to her computer after the baby's feedings. She also stresses that she's willing to come back to the office after her baby is asleep.

The partner/senior manager with whom she works, and who has been very supportive of Jessica's career, now stops in to see her. He states that while he is happy for her personally about the birth of her child, he also thinks that Jessica should give some thought to working part-time until she can spend more time at the office. The partner/senior manager explains: "It's clear that the focus of your attention is changing. Things happen here in the evening and weekends on many occasions, and e-mail just doesn't cut it."

Jessica says she'll think about what he's said. The client, before this encounter, had intimated that there was always an opportunity for her in-house, if she'd consider it.

If Jessica came to you for advice—as a trusted friend and colleague, not a fellow professional—what would you recommend? Should she move to the client's business? Is Jessica being realistic about her time? Was it wrong for the partner/senior manager to express his concerns? What if it had been his experience that several women associates had changed their life focus when they had children, and he was merely trying to protect the firm's interests? How could the partner/senior manager have expressed his concerns differently? What's wrong with working part-time for a certain period? What's the best resolution of this situation for the firm? For Jessica? How should this conversation be rescripted?

TARGETING BLIND SPOTS

To recognize your own stereotypes, you might opt to walk yourself through this simple exercise, being as honest with yourself as possible:

Write down several labels or categories you use based primarily on appearance or surface characteristics—for example, Wall Street trader, firefighter, corner grocery store owner, hairdresser, nurse, judge, and so on. What are your assumptions about the race, gender, and sexual orientation of these people? Write down a handful of adjectives related to each of the categories. Now ask yourself this: Do those adjectives apply to all members of that group? Would members of those groups agree with those adjectives? How do your assumptions affect your behavior toward members of those groups?

Once you have recognized your own blind spots, you can consciously mitigate your own stereotypes. Let's say that you're heading off to a marketing campaign pitch meeting with an Asian woman and a gay man. For the sake of this discussion, let's assume that you've examined your biases and you're aware that you tend to think Asians are typically good at engineering and gay men are creative and artistic. Walk into the meeting consciously ready to mitigate your own biases. These stereotypes are conditioned ways of thinking, based on pattern recognition. With awareness and deliberate practice you can consciously change your patterns.

BROADEN THE DISCUSSION

While acknowledging and addressing personal stereotypes, it's also important to go beyond people. Apply your efforts to eliminate implicit bias to product decisions, design issues, investments, and other aspects of business that make the discussion around diversity and people decisions easier. This can be as simple as the caterers you choose or the photos you opt to include in a newsletter.

Does it sound too simple? Consider this study: a team of researchers from four different major universities decided to test how quickly they could "socially tune" a group of students. They asked the students to take tests that would reflect automatic racial bias. They weren't asking the students directly if they liked white people or people of color; they simply showed students photos of people of different races and noted their reactions. Students who were given this test by friendly researchers wearing T-shirts that said "Eracism" were far more likely to react with less bias than those being tested by a researcher wearing a shirt without a statement or by an unfriendly researcher (Sinclair et al. 2005).

These findings suggest that something as simple as a poster of African American heroes, a screen saver of leading Asians, or a T-shirt that says "Eracism"—a simple slogan—can begin to sway implicit bias. They also show how a manager's subtly conveyed attitudes could potentially have great influence.

Intriguing new research suggests that the presence of diversity influences how we think. Tufts University psychologist Sam Sommers conducted a study reported in the *Washington Post*:[1]

> Sommers asked all-white and diverse groups to read short passages and then asked them to answer SAT-style questions about the passages. When the topics touched on race—affirmative action, for example—whites who were part of diverse groups answered more questions correctly than people in all-white groups.

The groups had no verbal interaction before answering the questions, so it wasn't that people of color raised issues that prompted white participants to remember the material more clearly. Rather, the mere act of sitting around a table with a diverse group of people seemed to improve the performance of white participants.

While such changes could be deliberate—white people forcing themselves to be more alert when people of color are around—Sommers thinks the changes are largely unconscious. "It is not just the minority group members who are responsible for the diversity—something happens to all the members in a group when the group is diverse," he said. "White people behave differently and have different cognitive tendencies in a diverse setting than in a homogenous setting."

CONCLUSION

Recognizing the existence of implicit bias can be inherently uncomfortable. Few of us want to acknowledge that we carry, and use, stereotypes. Yet understanding and accepting what is now a broad field of peer-reviewed and published research that confirms implicit bias creates a new and important opportunity. Corporate leaders, who for decades have sought to create a facade of diversity, primarily by trying to broaden the color of the people they hire, can now recognize an unprecedented opportunity to say that bias exists, whether or not they know about it.

This turns the diversity argument inside out. We start out on common ground. We are all biased, and many of our biases reflect familiar stereotypes in our culture. If we don't learn about them, we will continue to hold on to them and act on them. Biases that we do not acknowledge will create hidden barriers for others. An employer who doesn't take steps to understand and mitigate hidden bias and the hidden barriers that flow from it will come to be seen as negligent.

CHAPTER SIX

DISMANTLING BARRIERS FROM THE INSIDE

*Lincoln is the first white man I ever spent an hour
with who did not remind me that I am a Negro.*
–FREDERICK DOUGLASS[1]

It has been 150 years since abolitionist Frederick Douglass made this observation after sharing time with the president. His mission to end slavery was successful, but the daily reminders of racial bias continue today in major organizations around the world.

No one is leaving nooses on Eric's desk, calling Miguel derogatory names, or slipping a hand up Kristen's skirt. Yet, in subtle ways, each day in the office they are reminded of their "differences"—race, sexual orientation, and gender.

Eric's manager, for example, stops by his office for a daily "hoops update." Eric knew nothing about NBA basketball statistics until landing this job. Now he finds himself reluctantly studying the NBA All-Star rosters so he'll have something to talk about. Meanwhile, Miguel has become the office go-to guy for Mexican restaurant tips, even though he's Cuban American and eats only organic health food. And Kristen is frustrated that she keeps getting the consumer goods, health care, and retail accounts—low-margin areas that offer only limited growth and don't fully leverage her finance skills.

The managers at this organization would argue that this is a workplace without bias, a fair and comfortable space to work that is clear of race, sexual orientation, or gender barriers. But as the people working there will tell you, the hidden biases are omnipresent.

Picture a row of buckets, each ready to hold a category of bias discussed in earlier chapters: an unwelcoming environment, stereotyping gays and lesbians, balancing work and family for women, bias in hiring, and more. Each of these buckets is gradually filled, drop by drop, with slights, incidents of favoritism, and bigotry. Eventually, the contents of each bucket are solidified into hidden barriers. Now an organization that had a few biased individuals or policies has itself become a biased organization: a place where an African American man can no longer become a manager, where a woman cannot receive an international assignment, and where a gay man cannot work with a prominent client.

As emphasized in Chapter Three, both the problems of hidden bias and barriers, as well as the solutions, are in the hands of business managers. Leadership is crucial in creating an equitable workplace. What follows are pragmatic steps, lessons, and systems; however, without commitment from the top, the entire process of finding and eradicating hidden bias and barriers becomes a charade.

DOING IT THE WRONG WAY

Before you read about the right way to find and eradicate those barriers, you should be apprised of the wrong way to do it: First, tell all of your employees via a meeting, e-mail, or memo that you want to avoid litigation and you want a safe, bias-free workplace. Then require that anyone who experiences anything perceived to be bias in the workplace take concerns to a manager or human resources. Unfortunately, a person subjected to bias who does not follow this protocol, ironically, becomes the one violating the policy!

This is standard operating procedure, and it doesn't work. Sometimes a manager is the source of the problem. Even if that's not the case, complaining to your manager is rarely a good way to move up in a company.

Down the hall from Kristen's office was a senior individual contributor she knew only as Mr. Miller. He had been employed at the office for several decades, had climbed a few rungs up on the corporate ladder, and was now working in what clearly was his last assignment. White-haired, fastidious, and soft-spoken, Mr. Miller always provided Kristen the materials or answers she needed, but he didn't offer more.

One day she stepped into his office to ask for some data for a project she was completing. She sat down to discuss her request, shrugging off her blazer. At that moment, their manager opened the door and poked his head in. "Stripping down behind closed doors?" the manager laughed. "Be careful you don't give old Miller here a heart attack!"

As he stepped back out, Miller and Kristen looked at each other. "I can't believe he still has his job," sighed Miller.

"Oh, I've been to business school. I'm used to it," said Kristen, shaking her head.

"You shouldn't be," said Miller. "My daughter is in business school now. The last thing I want is for her to get a job and be treated like this."

His comment gave Kristen pause. Was her silence perpetuating the problem? Perhaps. But her own interests had to come first. She didn't see how she could complain about this manager without damaging her own career.

"Have you ever complained?" she asked her colleague.

"Again and again," he said. "Which somewhat explains why I'm still on the rookie floor."

For most corporate human resources offices, unless inappropriate behavior is so overt as to be illegal, action is rarely taken. Taking a complaint to a manager or human resources is, in effect, putting a company on notice. For employees willing to risk their job over the issue, it's the right channel. But what if you want to stay at the job? What if the problem is more subtle?

The bottom line is that the corporate standard—waiting for problems to be reported—falls short in three key areas: confidentiality, inclusiveness, and early warning signs. Several important methods can be used to overcome those shortfalls and find and resolve hidden biases in any workplace before they become barriers and blow up on the front page of the *New York Times*. These include focus groups, surveys, and systems audits.

FOCUS GROUPS

Miguel received his invitation in an e-mail routed through human resources: "Please attend a Diversity Focus Group session, Monday, 9 A.M., Conference Room B-1." His manager told him he should make this meeting "a priority," meaning, "Be there." On Monday morning, somewhat nervously, Miguel made his way to the session. Who would be there? What would they ask? How candid could he be?

Focus groups are supposed to be objective research tools, where groups of people are asked their opinions about a particular issue or topic. The individuals in the group are screened to be part of a subgroup—in this case, minority employees on the leadership track. When used as tools to discover hidden barriers, focus groups can be extremely productive when conducted with clear guidelines of openness and confidentiality—a sort of workplace immunity.

The group leader, an in-house consultant Miguel had not met before, explained that the goal was not to target individuals in the focus group itself but to learn about hidden bias and barriers in the workplace. Miguel looked around. Who would have thought that so many Latinos worked at this firm? And all of them are on the leadership track? He was impressed. The consultant broke the ice by asking them to introduce themselves and explain their ethnic background and their positions in the firm. She told them that they had been selected both because of their race and because of their strong work performance. "You are better positioned than most to help us learn about bias in this firm," she said. "We're asking for your help." Then she asked provocative questions: "How are your own job assignments impacted by your race? Did you hear racist jokes, and what were the reactions? In what ways have you been reminded of your race in the workplace?"

The conversation rolled. Participants laughed, argued, considered, and agreed. They ended the session on a high note when they all realized that they'd had run-ins with a notorious bigot and legendary tyrant in their department. One person said he first heard about this man when he was in graduate school. Another said he knew firsthand of a half dozen complaints to HR. Still another said that she had heard about an out-of-court harassment settlement.

"If this place is serious about diversity, why is he still here?" wondered Miguel out loud. And yet it was a catharsis to have this and other issues in the open, confirmed by colleagues, recognized by someone in the firm who at least appeared to be in a position to bring about change.

Miguel left the focus group feeling inspired and motivated. Perhaps this would be a turning point. Two weeks later, the man they had all discussed in the focus group quietly retired. There was no going-away party, no roasts or toasts. Miguel quietly considered his departure a victory.

Focus groups are an evolving process. They are increasingly used in the workplace, and their benefits are twofold: they can help eek out otherwise hidden information, and they can bring positive attitudes to participants. In this way they are similar to surveys.

A note about the effectiveness of focus groups versus surveys: Both can be effective, depending on the tone that is set, whether their findings result in actions, and the expertise of the design and analyses. However, focus groups need to be carefully constructed so that no single participant chills or dominates the discussion. Each focus group participant should be given information on how to contact the facilitator independently and confidentially, in case he or she has something to say and doesn't feel comfortable saying it to the group or if lingering thoughts are troubling the person. For instance, I often send a follow-up e-mail to focus group participants thanking them for their thoughts, reminding them of the agreement to respect their colleagues' confidentiality, and inviting additional comments. Focus groups can be the only source of data collection—which is limited—or the first step toward designing a survey.

SURVEYS: AN OVERVIEW

In general, surveys are the most reliable way to gather organizational data because they eliminate the sources of bias associated with other forms of collecting information. This is why researchers have used them for generations. In the workplace, surveys solve the inherent problems found in the standard "call us with your problem" method. Here's how:

- **Confidentiality:** The office door is closed. The manager and employee are speaking in serious, low tones. Both are taking careful notes. The employee walks out confident that the discussion was confidential and thorough. She believes her problem was heard and will now be addressed. But what happens next? The manager takes the problem up the chain of command, to a director perhaps, who might take it to a vice president. The information is filtered as it makes its way up the organizational hierarchy. And when asked for the name of the employee who raised this concern, the information is readily shared. As a result, the problem that the senior management team hears about has probably been "sanitized," and the complaint was anything but confidential. This hinders realistic planning.

Since some information is extremely sensitive, employees will express their opinions honestly and fully only when they believe that their confidentiality will be protected. They may be reluctant to tell their supervisor, members of the senior management team, or even external consultants their true feelings about the organization in a focus group—especially in front of colleagues who may not honor their confidence. However, when sitting at their own desks, facing a survey that doesn't ask their name but does ask about their impressions or experiences, employees are more likely to respond truthfully. A survey may not pinpoint an individual or incident, but it will provide honest, valid information to use as a basis for clarifying the current strengths and weaknesses in the organization. These data then become the basis for designing an effective training program, formulating specific ongoing structures, and assessing the impact of training and organizational changes after they are completed.

I cannot stress enough the importance of complete confidentiality on surveys. Eric saw his reputation and his performance rankings plummet after a would-be confidential survey. At the time, he was the only African American in his fund accounting department. He was well regarded, doing a wonderful job by all accounts, and enjoying the work. Then an upward feedback survey was sent out asking him to rate his superiors. It was supposed to be confidential. Although he knew that not everyone was going to be honest, he decided to tell the truth. But when the administrative assistant brought him the form, she wrote a number on it.

"This is supposed to be confidential. There aren't supposed to be any numbers on it. Why are you doing that?" asked Eric.

"I was instructed to do that by the controller," she said.

"Wipe that off," said Eric. "This is supposed to be confidential. You're not supposed to be tracking anyone's forms."

The number was covered over with correction fluid. But that spot on the survey remained, and it was enough of a sign for his managers to track the comments back to him. Eric's manager came back from a retreat devastated by the negative feedback. The backlash was swift.

"All of a sudden everything was wrong with my performance," he later said. "Any mistakes my supervisors were making were suddenly my responsibility."

Because of the lack of confidentiality, a survey that was supposed to find hidden barriers became one itself. In this case, Eric went from being a leader to a possible leaver, thinking about quitting as the pressure became extreme.

- **Inclusiveness:** Your company probably has a diversity committee. New employees are probably asked to sign a copy of the antidiscrimination policy, and they might attend a requisite diversity training session. A system may be in place to handle issues of overt bias. But not all voices are being heard. Do you really think a closeted gay employee frustrated with routine homophobic jokes is going to come to a diversity committee meeting to complain? What about the pregnant executive whose key accounts were recently given to a subordinate? Since surveys systematically gather information from all employees, the organization has the opportunity to hear both from those who do and those who do not use other organizational communication channels. With full participation, employees have a greater stake in the outcome of the process. In addition, the views of each individual are given equal weight; characteristics such as articulateness and degree of power or influence are controlled. Thus, selection biases are eliminated, and managers can get a more accurate check of their corporate pulse. Employee resource groups (ERGs) can serve this function as well. When someone can meet with others who share his or her background and ask for practical advice and problem-solving help, that person is much more likely to believe that the company has a place for him or her.

• **Early Warning Signals:** Eric is certainly not going to complain because someone is trying to talk to him about basketball. That would probably just be regarded as "whining." But those daily "hoops updates" may be an early warning sign, an incremental drip that could point to an impending torrent of larger problems.

Miguel also noticed signs of things to come. For example, at a recent meeting, a group of clients mistook him for an executive assistant and then asked him, before he had opened his mouth, if anyone more senior and proficient in English was available with whom they could work. He told them that he would be making the initial presentation, followed by a colleague. Later that day, Miguel's colleague, a Jewish man, stepped out of the room, adjusted his yarmulke, and smiled ruefully at Miguel.

"They don't like my people any more than yours," he said.

Problems like these are bias now, not yet barriers. But word of such problems isn't likely to reach useful information channels until they become major issues—definitely costly and possibly litigious. By this point, it's too late to resolve them and have everyone work together effectively. A survey can identify small but significant issues that might otherwise be ignored. These can be addressed before they grow.

Just imagine if one of my consulting clients, a global bank, had been conducting surveys regularly or had a safe, confidential, effective, informal complaint channel. They could have avoided a huge mess that involved the firing of two senior top performers. As it turns out, these two "gentlemen" had been calling a senior woman a "fat pig" and "fat bitch" for quite some time. When she finally couldn't take it and summoned the courage to complain, plenty of corporate machinery revved into action. Human resources had to work with an outside employment counsel who informed them that the senior managers had to be fired, since there was a risk that the woman would claim that they were creating a hostile environment.

Later, the investigation discovered that the woman was widely regarded as a bully, and she had not been held accountable for unrelated policy violations, such as arriving late for work. The company had overlooked her violations since she had a fabulous track record of revenue generation, was professionally well regarded in her field, and was one of the few women at her level at any investment bank.

Once news of the firing of the two men traveled through the ranks, a huge backlash ensued. Was the bully being protected because she was a woman? Was there a double standard, or was the employer just worried about a possible legal claim? Although her behavior was at least as unprofessional and demoralizing as that dished out to her, none of her employees could sue the bank over her bullying. The outside counsel decided that, for further protection, the bank should hold mandatory training for everyone in the business unit on what constitutes a hostile environment. However, given the uproar over the terminations, senior management (also on the advice of counsel) decided that the senior woman shouldn't be present during training. In fact, she was offered a buyout package, since no one believed that she would ever be treated decently by her co-workers.

Let's add up the score here: by ignoring the unprofessional and demoralizing conduct of three senior people because they generated huge revenues, the bank lost all of them. Further, they demotivated everyone and fueled cynicism that the bank's senior management cared only about the short-term bottom line, not about treating people fairly or creating a respectful work environment. Training was the final insult, reminding everyone that the first order of business was for the bank to protect itself from its employees, those people the bank's Web site referred to as "our most valuable asset." Had the bank conducted a well-designed, well-executed survey at any point during this escalating disaster, senior management would have had the opportunity to step in and address it. But design, execution, and effective follow-up are all key.

Surveys: What to Ask

If you decide to use an anonymous survey, what should you ask? And whom should you ask? Following are sample survey themes that could be effective in finding hidden barriers in your workplace; they'll need to be customized, vetted by employees, and then turned into precise questions appropriate for quantitative analyses.

Questions to Ask All Employees
- Are you treated differently from others in the workplace based on your race, gender, or sexual orientation?
- Have you had negative experiences based on your race, gender, or sexual orientation? If so, did those involve advancement opportunities, employment practices, or other personal experiences?
- Have you observed bias, including ridicule, teasing, insults, stereotypes, derogatory names, or pejorative language, at this workplace?
- How frequently are these acts interrupted by someone pointing out that they are inappropriate?
- Do you believe that management engages in practices that benefit members of their own race, gender, or sexual orientation?
- What do you believe will happen if you report unfair treatment in this workplace?
- How often do you discuss diversity issues with someone at this organization of a different race, gender, or sexual orientation?
- If you completed an earlier survey, do you believe that any concerns were addressed in an appropriate manner?

Questions to Ask Individuals Who Turned Down Job Offers from Your Organization
- Why did you turn down this job?
- Where are you going to work instead? What's appealing about that work environment?
- What is the reputation of this work environment?
- What do you know about the diversity of people working here?
- Would information about the race, gender, or sexual orientation of the people working here impact your decision about this position?

- Were considerations about your own race, gender, or sexual orientation a factor in your decision to turn down this position?
- Would you consider future job offers here?
- Did reasons of corporate culture, inclusion, or bias have anything to do with your reason not to accept this position?
- Please complete this thought: if the job offer and/or this company had the following characteristics, I would have accepted the position.

Questions to Ask Individuals Who Left Your Organization Voluntarily

- In what ways do you think your race, sexual orientation, or gender impacted your opportunities here?
- Have you observed bias, including ridicule, teasing, insults, stereotypes, derogatory names, or pejorative language, at this workplace?
- Have you been directly impacted by bias in this workplace?
- Have you seen efforts to eliminate bias in this workplace?
- What role, if any, did your race, sexual orientation, or gender have in your decision to leave?
- Did reasons of corporate culture, inclusion, and bias have anything to do with your leaving?
- Are you going to a competitor or changing industries/fields?
- What could the company have done to help you stay?

Systems Audits: Questions to Consider

A systems audit is a crucial part of a comprehensive examination of organizational bias. This is a behind-the-scenes look at your firm, from performance reviews and candidate pools to assignments and promotions. It's a look at numbers, but, more than that, it's a look at the actions taken by the decision-makers in power.

First consider these questions:

- **How diverse are your candidate pools, and is that diversity mandated?** In 2002, the NFL adopted its so-called "Rooney Rule," requiring that at least one candidate of color be interviewed for each head coaching vacancy. Four years later, the

University of Central Florida's Institute for Diversity and Ethics in Sport credited that rule for the record seven African American head coaches in the league (Binette 2006).

- **Where are positions advertised, and where are candidates recruited?** Employee referral systems have long been identified as a double-edged sword: while they produce candidates who are likely to be a "good fit," they also produce candidates who are demographically the same as the majority of current employees.
- **What is the race and gender breakdown of new hires?** The answer to this question can narrow down the source of problems. Perhaps more outreach is needed or better training is needed for those doing the hiring. It might mean that a screening exam is, unto itself, a source of bias.
- **What is the breakdown by race, gender, sexual orientation, and age of your entire organization?** It's a simple question, and probably the most likely one to be examined. But don't be misled. The simple percentages of African Americans, Latinos, Asians, women, and forty-somethings in your organization do not tell the complete story and in some cases could be very misleading. You must look deeper by asking these follow-up questions:
  - What is the race and gender breakdown in management?
  - What is the race and gender breakdown in senior management?
  - What is the race and gender breakdown of your domestic staff?
  - What is the race and gender breakdown of your various international offices? This is an important question for two reasons: first, the numbers can be deceiving. A major financial firm might proudly boast of a very diverse employee pool. However, when the Bangkok, Taipei, Tokyo, and Beijing staffs (made up mostly of local hires) are taken out of the data, the firm is shown to have remarkably few Asian employees.

    International hires are also important to review because, in many organizations, an assignment abroad is the only way to climb up the corporate ranks. Hidden biases may determine how these assignments are made. Some can include a reluctance to assign women to Saudi Arabia, Japan, or other countries where the assumption is that they will not be respected. In the same vein, an inclination to assign Latino employees to Latin America or Asian employees to Asia can also be an indication of a hidden bias. If you're operating on assumptions alone, you're missing opportunities. Without asking, you will never know that the Asian American Harvard graduate you hired grew up in Kuwait as the daughter of a petroleum engineer and speaks fluent Arabic.

- **What is the breakdown by race, gender, and sexual orientation of employees who are voluntarily departing?** A key point here is to review whether disproportionate numbers of minorities are leaving the firm. If this is the case, it's a crucial indicator of a problem.

- **What is the breakdown by race, gender, and sexual orientation of terminated or laid-off employees?** Again, this can be a key indicator of a problem. By breaking down the specific demographic details, you might be able to target a particular issue.

- **What assignments are your employees of color, women, and gays and lesbians receiving, and how do those compare to the full range of assignments?** Certain accounts, clients, and projects are inherently more high profile, prominent, and revenue generating. Those accounts are the path to promotion and success. Other assignments are going to keep an employee busy and provide a necessary service to the organization, but they are not likely to move anyone up the corporate ladder. It's important to monitor who gets what type of developmental assignments (over the course of a quarter or a year) to see who is being pushed or stretched and who is getting face time with the big clients.

Kristen quickly saw that she was receiving safe and doable, but low-profile, assignments compared to her white male workmates. Her unit operated under what they called "a free market system": Employees were supposed to approach managers, let them know they were available, and ask for projects. Kristen tried to do this once—just once—with a manager she didn't know. She had sent an e-mail and made an appointment, but when she walked in, the manager glanced up from his desk and mistook Kristen for a secretary. "Just put the file on that table," he said. She was mortified. Then she came up with a new strategy.

When the star Caucasian men were taking their vacations, Kristen knew she had a two-week period to get a decent assignment. It might mean working through the Christmas holidays, but it was worth it to get an opportunity at a good assignment. On one hand, the strategy worked. Kristen did get a high-profile assignment when her male colleagues were out of the office, but it was a lousy way to get a good project—unfair and biased. She missed her traditional family gathering, missed her husband, and resented her job demands.

PERFORMANCE REVIEW AUDIT

I have singled out performance reviews here because they are frequently overlooked and can be a significant source of hidden bias. Look for loaded language that can appear in reviews, as in letters of recommendation (as discussed in Chapter Five). Words like "perky" or "loud" or "aggressive" carry negative implications, while "enthusiastic" or "clear" or "assertive" can mean the same thing but carry more positive implications.

When comparing the performance reviews of minorities versus those of the broader swath of employees, I see that minorities often receive somewhat useless performance reviews because appraisers are worried about liability. Minority employees receive comments like "nice to have around," "good team players," and other generally positive feedback. But they aren't given useful, constructive criticism, and they aren't given specific issues for improvement, which makes it difficult for them to better their performance.

After his first evaluation, Miguel thought about quitting. His evaluation didn't raise any concerns and didn't mention any specific issues, except for a confusing criticism about managing perceptions. But when bonus time came around, Miguel's bonus was reduced to two-thirds of what he'd expected.

"Well, what happened? I've had a great year, and you've reduced my bonus by two-thirds?" he asked. No one could explain why. He received no feedback. Nothing. He had been willing to make a huge sacrifice by offering to relocate to serve growing business requirements. He had volunteered to do over and above what was expected and was told that he would be compensated accordingly. But not only was Miguel *not* compensated for his performance, he also wasn't compensated for his willingness to relocate. Miguel took his complaint to human resources, but the HR manager was defensive and said that this matter had nothing to do with his race. "I didn't say it was a racial issue," Miguel later told Eric and Kristen. "I didn't bring in race at all. I just said I wasn't being treated fairly based on my performance."

An experience similar to Miguel's is documented in Figure 6.1. A better approach to manager-employee interactions across demographic differences is also presented.

WHAT ARE THE SOLUTIONS?

The preceding questions are starting points—a means to an end but certainly not a solution unto themselves. The mere act of conducting a survey, a focus group, or a systems audit sends a message to an organization that diversity is an issue that matters; that bias, discrimination, and harassment are on the agenda; and that your organization wants to be proactive about these issues. It's a strong start.

In some cases, solutions become evident in focus group or survey findings. Bayer Corporation, the international health care organization, regularly surveys the one hundred CEOs of the fastest-growing science and technology companies in the United States as part of an ongoing annual public opinion research project. The company's 2006 survey found this stark dichotomy: four out of five CEOs polled said that they are concerned that the United States is in danger of losing its global predominance in science and technology due to people shortage issues. Data from the Commission on Professionals in Science and Technology (cited in the survey) indicates that women make up only 25 percent of the science and technology workforce, with racial minorities representing a much smaller percentage. Yet, at the same time, just over one-third of the CEOs surveyed said that their companies participate in precollege education programs designed to promote girls', young women's, and minority students' interest in math and science.[2]

The survey showed both a problem—the worker shortage—and a solution—an opportunity to participate in education programs

FIGURE 6.1 MAKING RACE AN ISSUE

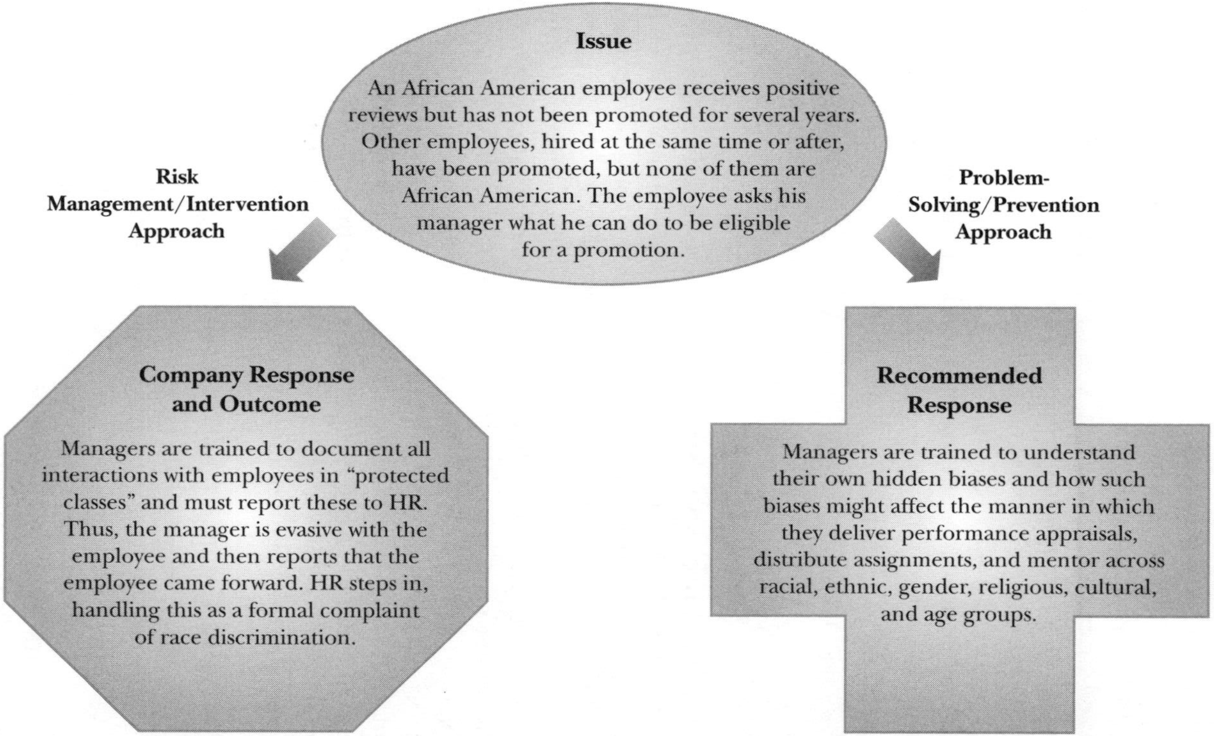

Issue

An African American employee receives positive reviews but has not been promoted for several years. Other employees, hired at the same time or after, have been promoted, but none of them are African American. The employee asks his manager what he can do to be eligible for a promotion.

Problem-Solving/Prevention Approach

Recommended Response

Managers are trained to understand their own hidden biases and how such biases might affect the manner in which they deliver performance appraisals, distribute assignments, and mentor across racial, ethnic, gender, religious, cultural, and age groups.

Risk Management/Intervention Approach

Company Response and Outcome

Managers are trained to document all interactions with employees in "protected classes" and must report these to HR. Thus, the manager is evasive with the employee and then reports that the employee came forward. HR steps in, handling this as a formal complaint of race discrimination.

tapping minority students. However, more than twice as many of the science and technology CEOs saw the problem as those who are currently engaged in efforts to solve it. Apparently, chief financial officers across an array of industries don't share these CEOs' views. A recent *CFO Magazine* survey of 210 CFOs uncovered their view that the lack of racial diversity within the profession isn't a problem. In spite of the ongoing disparity in racial representation, "the vast majority [of CFOs surveyed] said diversity efforts were not a high priority; even more troubling, many respondents (20 percent) at companies with $1 billion or less in revenues said diversity efforts were not a priority at all" (Stuart 2007).

CORPORATE LEAVERS: WHAT MY EMPLOYER COULD HAVE DONE TO HELP ME STAY

Surprising overlap exists among the top factors that would have caused each of our groups of survey respondents to reconsider leaving their employers. For example, a strong percentage of all groups (24 to 41 percent) indicate that they would have been very likely to stay if their previous employers had offered to pay them more fairly. However, that is the most important concern only for heterosexual Caucasians, both men and women. For gay and lesbian workers, pay is a close second to "offering better benefits." In contrast, people of color put concerns about pay tied for third place, giving it equal weight with "offering a more positive work environment"—yet pay and work environment fall behind "better management, which recognizes one's abilities" and "having a flexible schedule." Full details are described here.

People of Color: Very likely to have stayed if employer had . . .

- offered better management that recognized your abilities (34 percent)
- offered schedule flexibility such as flex-time, alternative working hours, or telecommuting (30 percent)
- offered to pay you more fairly (29 percent)
- offered a more positive work environment (29 percent)

Gays and Lesbians: Very likely to have stayed if employer had . . .

- offered more or better benefits (43 percent)
- offered to pay you more fairly (41 percent)
- offered schedule flexibility such as flex-time, alternative working hours, or telecommuting (35 percent)

Caucasian Women: Very likely to have stayed if employer had . . .

- offered to pay you more fairly (24 percent)
- offered schedule flexibility such as flex-time, alternative working hours, or telecommuting (20 percent)
- offered more or better benefits (20 percent)

Caucasian Men: Very likely to have stayed if employer had . . .

- offered to pay you more fairly (28 percent)
- offered more or better benefits (20 percent)
- offered better management that recognized your abilities (18 percent)

Reviewing the top three or four factors that would have encouraged leavers to stay yields one perspective. A different perspective emerges when we look at which aspects of worklife held strong appeal for just one group. Although the percentages may not be high in the absolute sense, these are the aspects of worklife that each group felt substantially more strongly about when compared to other survey respondents. In other words, two of the demographic groups identified several steps their employers could have taken to keep them that did not have the same appeal for the other groups. The details follow.

People of color felt more strongly about several aspects of worklife than did their colleagues. Employers should have . . .

- made assignment and promotion decisions based on who was most qualified (26 percent)
- had a more diverse workforce (15 percent)
- offered mentoring programs (13 percent)

- offered a confidential way to make *and act on* complaints (13 percent)
- had better diversity policies (12 percent)
- offered to become a stronger corporate/social citizen (11 percent)

Gays and lesbians also felt more strongly about several aspects of worklife than did their colleagues. Employers should have . . .

- taken steps to make the work environment more respectful (27 percent)
- offered more meaningful work (23 percent)
- offered to change your manager (21 percent)
- offered counseling or training to deal with difficult people or situations (17 percent)
- offered to change your work group (14 percent)
- offered a better geographic location for you (14 percent)

Interestingly, neither Caucasian women nor men felt more strongly about any efforts their employers could have made than did their colleagues who were people of color, gay, or lesbian. Important conclusions can be drawn from this look at the data. Specifically, it appears that current workplace dynamics, in general, are more geared to heterosexual Caucasians—both men and women—than they are to people of color or gays and lesbians. In addition, employers need to involve different retention strategies for different groups.

So far in this chapter, I've explained the methods for revealing hidden barriers and why it is essential do to so. What follows next is a three-part comprehensive approach to dismantling those barriers.

DISMANTLING BARRIERS, PART 1: POLICIES GOVERNING INAPPROPRIATE BEHAVIOR

A standard policy usually begins like this: "It is the goal of this organization to promote a workplace that is free of all types of harassment." Many people see the word *harassment* and immediately think of sexual harassment—which is, of course, only one part of a much broader picture. Usually policy language is crafted by attorneys who cite previous cases as they write the policy. This strategy is fairly effective for limiting liability, but it does little to prevent the costly, hidden barriers that drive women, people of color, and gay and lesbian workers from the workplace. Having a policy is usually a defensive, check-the-box exercise rather than a carefully thought-out, customized document designed to offer real guidance.

Effective Policies Take a Zero-Tolerance Stance

A "zero-tolerance stance" is different from the typical "zero-tolerance rule." A zero-tolerance stance conveys that the behaviors governed by the policy are taken seriously and are understood to have a deleterious effect on individuals, workgroups, and the organization as a whole. In contrast, a zero-tolerance rule requires rote application of a policy (and, presumably, disciplinary procedures if the policy is violated) without any room for nuance or judgment regarding how to achieve the best outcome consistent with the principles. Ironically, zero-tolerance rules may in some ways be antithetical to diversity, because they treat everyone and/or every behavior the same rather than understanding the individual, subjective experience, nuance, and context of behaviors. Take a strong, consistent, principled stance and make sure that it is modeled by top management.

Policies should emphasize principles rather than rules. A few years ago, a Fortune 500 company implemented a new comprehensive antiharassment policy after settling a costly lawsuit. In its attempt to minimize liability, the company offered employees a detailed list of do's and don'ts. Included were rules such as "No comments on dress or appearance," "No sexual jokes," "No touching." Smart, preventive steps, right? Not a chance! Who wants to work somewhere that expects you to make million-dollar decisions when interacting with customers but to become a grade school kid following orders when interacting with colleagues? Not long after this policy took effect, a formal complaint from an administrative assistant in marketing was filed; she observed the department's senior manager hugging his executive assistant in her cubicle, in view of everyone on the floor. Human resources sprang into action, calling outside employment counsel, who sent over a twenty-page checklist on how to investigate complaints. After a flurry of activity and shortly into this most serious endeavor, the accused manager was asked whether he indeed hugged his assistant. His answer? Yes, he had; they had been working together for seventeen years, and she had just received a call that her mother was the victim of a hit-and-run auto accident and she was in a coma. A hug was the most appropriate, most human gesture a boss could engage in, but it violated company policy. Should he be reprimanded? Fired? After all, the company was proud of its "zero-tolerance policy."

EFFECTIVE POLICIES ADDRESS ALL FORMS OF INAPPROPRIATE BEHAVIOR

It is imperative to include all forms of conduct that have a negative impact on individuals (because of group characteristics) and workgroups and the achievement of the organizational mission and business objectives. Focusing only on behaviors deemed illegal in one or more locations in which the entity has offices will be seen as concern for protecting only the organization rather than a positive goal of creating a respectful work environment.

Also, don't create separate policies governing different forms of harassment. This makes matters confusing, and dealing with harassment issues in different documents forgoes the opportunity for the organization to state its larger view—that inappropriate conduct undermines the organization's business and/or mission. Separating the types of harassment can also be divisive. Groups that could see their common interests in a unified policy and program to educate about and eradicate prohibited behaviors often believe they must compete for resources and visibility when issues are segregated.

EFFECTIVE POLICIES ARE JUSTIFIABLE

Link the policy and specific behaviors to the type of culture the organization seeks to create, as well as the organization's mission and core values. For example, you could say that inappropriate behavior, as outlined in the policy, makes it impossible to attain the company's aspiration of being the employer of choice in your field. Show how various forms of conduct contradict how the organization defines itself. For example, if the organization delivers high-quality services, becomes a trusted business partner, or operates with transparency, point out that tolerating inappropriate behavior undermines the company reputation and credibility with all stakeholders.

EFFECTIVE POLICIES ARE SPECIFIC

Clearly articulate the range of behaviors that are prohibited by the policy. Provide multiple examples in plain language that reflect the kinds of day-to-day situations encountered by employees. Examples should include behaviors that are clearly prohibited by the policy, those that may be prohibited under certain circumstances, and those that are clearly outside the range of the policy. Describe who is covered by the policy, where, and when. For example, does the policy apply to all behaviors that transpire on company premises, including those that may occur during official breaks, lunch hours, or dinner hours? Does it cover off-site interactions as well? Does the policy articulate when an employee is representing the employer and when the employee is considered to be "off duty"? Especially confusing situations include business-related socializing, work-required travel, and organization-sponsored social events. Describe how the policy does and does not govern the behavior of third parties, including clients, vendors, consultants, temp workers, and business partners.

EFFECTIVE POLICIES TALK ABOUT POWER

Context always matters, with the most important element being the power relationship between the parties. Power relationships include official rank or status in organizational hierarchy, as well as cultural variables, such as who is expected to defer to whom based on gender, age, or other factors. If an individual who is the target of unwelcome behavior is especially vulnerable due to employment status (an intern, for example), the person's position may change how a situation is viewed. A person's ability to speak up about unwelcome and/or inappropriate conduct should be weighed as well. Employee comfort level in speaking up is a function of many factors, including culture and perceived risks and consequences.

DISMANTLING BARRIERS, PART 2: PROBLEM-SOLVING AND COMPLAINT CHANNELS

Many employees don't know where to turn when facing an uncomfortable workplace situation. They take it home with them, perhaps share their concerns in confidence with a co-worker, or just start looking for another job. An effective organization has a clear, simple, and sophisticated complaint process that is both transparent and fair.

EFFECTIVE PROBLEM-SOLVING AND COMPLAINT CHANNELS PROVIDE MULTIPLE OPTIONS

Organizations should provide a range of ways for employees to handle situations of perceived inappropriate behavior; these are both informal and formal problem-solving and complaint mechanisms. Employees should be given a clear "road map" of all channels and how to access them. These should be easily obtainable by employees through multiple media. Employees should be able to access information on their own, via intranet, kiosks, handbooks, or anonymous hotlines. They should also be able to consult a manager or go through official organizational resources. It should be clear which channels provide confidentiality and which channels have the power to investigate and discipline.

The best problem-solving and complaint options recognize power differences between parties to a dispute and seek to create a level playing field for everyone involved. Informal channels (that is, those that take action only when requested) allow the employee to retain control of the situation and can offer strict confidentiality. Informal channels allow for obtaining information about how other options work, seeking advice, gaining another opinion or perspective, and role playing. Informal interventions can also include voluntary mediation or shuttle diplomacy. Often used in international negotiations, *shuttle diplomacy* describes when a trusted, empowered neutral goes between the direct parties in a conflict. For highly charged situations, this approach often achieves an effective resolution more quickly than bringing the parties face-to-face. For example, after meeting with Miguel about his bonus concerns, this third party could meet with the manager, engage in fact-finding with HR, and propose a successful outcome.

Formal channels, on the other hand, provide for quasi-judicial proceedings, such as making formal statements, conducting an investigation, and having a person or governing body review all relevant information and render a decision. Formal channels should have written, clear processes, including the names and roles of the decision-makers, a timeline for each step, and the availability of an appeal process. Formal channels should explicitly describe what constitutes retaliation against the complainant and how it will be dealt with. An organization may not be able to quell social ostracism, but it can prevent someone from being deliberately passed over for a well-deserved promotion.

EFFECTIVE PROBLEM-SOLVING AND COMPLAINT CHANNELS ARE PRACTICAL

Provide practical tips on "what to do if you feel unfairly/inappropriately treated," including actions employees can take alone, seeking assistance outside the organization, and seeking assistance within the organization. Be sure that employees understand that a range of interventions is available, some of which can be taken in combination and some of which rule out pursuing others. For example, filing a formal complaint that is investigated and has the possibility of discipline being imposed rules out subsequent pursuit of a self-help approach.

DISMANTLING BARRIERS, PART 3: TRAINING

Bias, discrimination, harassment, and diversity training must be interesting, engaging, provocative, and relevant. It must also be mandatory in order for everyone in an organization to take it seriously. All new hires should be trained, and periodic updates are productive not only to keep the issue fresh but also to raise issues that might be quietly developing. Here's a warning, though: poorly designed/delivered training is not only a waste of resources, but it can evoke great cynicism. "Off-the-shelf" materials frequently include unrealistic or overly generic examples. Platitudes about "zero tolerance" and "diversity is a business imperative" can exacerbate the gap between what is stated and what is actually practiced in the organization. "Check the box" exercises that are merely designed to protect the organization from liability often are met with resentment.

Effective training offers four qualities: it is customized, broad, sensitive, and creative.

EFFECTIVE TRAINING IS CUSTOMIZED

Training should be customized for your company's managers, complaint handlers, and employees. Content should be a balance between top-down and bottom-up approaches, including imparting organizational messages, policies, and procedures. And it should answer concerns raised by employees in surveys or focus groups. Customization should be based, in part, on employee perceptions and experiences of unwelcome, inappropriate conduct. Be sure to address issues specific to your own organization's mission and practices.

EFFECTIVE TRAINING IS BROAD

Cover all forms of inappropriate conduct as globally defined, from "moral harassment" (repeated or prolonged exposure to embarrassing and humiliating situations) to negative behaviors based on specific demographic characteristics. Include a range of behaviors from subtle to blatant, with emphasis on any particularly problematic behaviors gleaned from focus groups, surveys, or pending problems.

EFFECTIVE TRAINING IS SENSITIVE

An insensitive trainer who conveys an attitude that the entire policy is a joke or a headache will do more damage than good. Training techniques themselves require cultural sensitivity. Expectations vary based upon whether one is to be a passive participant in a lecture from an internal or external expert or whether one is expected to learn through participation, application of policies, and/or brainstorming improved organizational approaches with others. Articulate the ground rules about the confidentiality of what is said in the session and the degree to which the session may or may not to be used for problem solving of current, real situations.

Effective Training Is Creative

Interactive training provides an opportunity for participants to explore their views, assumptions, and approaches as they compare to those of their peers. Case study and vignette-driven training is generally agreed to be the most effective, provided that the situations are realistic, allow for some disagreement, and are debriefed with clear guidelines to apply to future situations. Small groups allow for greater ease of interaction and provide a higher degree of safety for openness. Examples used should be sophisticated, nuanced, and subtle. They should focus on gray areas, blurred boundaries, and issues that require discussion rather than issues that can be gleaned by oneself from written materials and lists of do's and don'ts. Always close the loop and clarify the recommended action(s) for specific situations.

Conclusion

The firm in which Eric, Miguel, and Kristen worked conducted its own bias audit. The reviewers were stunned when they came to Kristen's unit and saw, without a doubt, that the manager who had made Kristen and her colleague Mr. Miller so uncomfortable was a continuing source of distress. Human resources had heard reports about this man for years. There had been talk of a sexual harassment lawsuit, which was quelled when the manager agreed to go through sensitivity training and counseling. It was assumed that he had changed. Obviously he had not. And this time, with his track record, there was no way his productivity could balance the costs he was incurring to the company.

As a result of the bias audit, the manager was asked to leave. No one told Kristen and Mr. Miller why their manager was replaced. No one needed to. His departure was a relief to them both—in fact, to their entire department. And for the time being, both of these intelligent, committed employees decided to stay.

What happened next was equally inspiring. An ombudsman was appointed. An ombudsman (also known by the gender-neutral term "ombuds") is, as the Ombudsman Association explains, "a designated neutral or impartial dispute resolution practitioner whose major function is to provide confidential and informal assistance to managers and employees and/or clients of the employer. . . . When providing assistance, an ombudsman uses a variety of skills which include counseling, mediation, informal fact finding, and upward feedback mechanisms that offer a range of options. . . . The ombudsman functions outside the ordinary line management structure and has access to anyone in the organization, including the chief executive officer."[3]

It all seems simple, right? Employees should be asked in an objective way what issues of bias they face, and then these issues should be tackled (or better yet, prevented) through policies, problem solving, and training. It sounds simple, but it's a lesson missed by many major organizations that opt instead to use superficial solutions that are costly and counterproductive in the end. Corporate America's widespread diversity programs are missing the point, leaving a troubling void between their practices and the proven, effective solutions that can lead to true meritocracy in the workplace.

CHAPTER SEVEN

KNOW THE SIGNS FROM THE OUTSIDE

The average American manager works forty-two hours per week, and a substantial number of managers and professionals (three in ten, or 10.8 million people) work forty-nine or more hours per week (Heathfield 2000). A person who spends many hours at work can thrive only in an environment that is welcoming, supportive, collegial, and comfortable. A good work environment will provide a positive return on a worker's time and energy investment, in addition to the financial investment represented in each worker's education. For example, a recent estimate on the average cost of earning an MBA (tuition, living expenses, and so on) runs as high as $100,000 (Weiss 2006). Add remaining debts from the undergraduate years, and the financial liability is even more staggering.

Despite all that is riding on the decision of where to work, many prospective employees, such as Kristen, Eric, and Miguel, don't spend the necessary time or effort to vet a potential employer properly. According to one survey (Beagrie 2003), 52 percent of job applicants spend less than two hours researching a company and preparing for an interview. Most job seekers are overly focused on pay and how soon they can be promoted. Search firms and employment agencies also seek quick placement so they can collect their fees.

Before Kristen landed her current position, she felt intimidated by the competition for available jobs. The career advice Web sites that she scoured for weeks during interview season told her to think only about broad-based industry and company questions, not whether the company she chose for employment was the right fit for her. And she learned, hands down, the answers to all the "right" questions, according to the career gurus—"What role does the company play in its industry?" "What are the company's key products, and what is its market share?" "What skills are in demand at the company—marketing, engineering, finance, sales, product development?"

She jumped at the first offer from a top-tier firm, thrilled that someone wanted her, but she gave no real consideration to the firm's culture and whether it would be a good match for her values. She had also put too much faith in the recruiting system itself. Just because a particular company was recruiting on her campus and had hired past graduates of her program didn't mean that the company would be a good choice for her.

Most company's screening techniques, such as psychological aptitude tests and skill assessments, are designed around narrow criteria and traditional job descriptions. And companies tend to focus on test scores and GPAs, making virtually no effort to examine a prospective employee's values and preferences—the very factors that will actually determine a person's fit or misfit within an organization.

In a desire for clear metrics about hiring "the most qualified" or "the best" employee, companies often look for any kind of ranking to help rate prospective employees. In recent conversations with an international law firm—one that often defends America's largest employers charged with discrimination suits—I witnessed a hiring rating situation gone too far. The law firm usually hired directly from law schools and focused almost exclusively on numbers: law school rank, class rank, grade point average, and whether a student was on law review. (In fact, the firm interviewed the top 50 percent of Harvard Law School graduates and only the top 2 percent of Howard Law School graduates.) The unwarranted confidence in these metrics was taken to an absurd extreme when the firm brought in a lateral partner. He was highly successful with an impressive client roster and reputation; however, the firm, which desperately wanted him to join its ranks, still insisted on seeing his law school transcript—which dated back nearly forty years!

Kristen, Eric, and Miguel—like thousands of other potential employees—quickly discovered that their company's hiring process was brimming with problems. The types of assessments being used didn't get to the root issues of what environmental concerns caused employee dissatisfaction and frustration and what actually made for a good employer-employee "fit." Consequently, they made hasty decisions, and job mismatches occurred. The typical outcome of such a situation is disappointment. A survey conducted by Jandl and Associates, an outplacement counseling firm, found that more than 40 percent of respondents reported mismatches as a key reason people get fired.[1]

With so much misguided thinking among prospective employees and an equally generous portion of misguided advice from so-called career experts, it's no wonder that job dissatisfaction rates are soaring across multiple disciplines—even among highly coveted professions, such as the legal field. Many job seekers fail early on to invest in a self-assessment of their values and priorities before beginning a rigorous search for employment. Truth is, taking time at the start to inventory your abilities and priorities, while educating yourself about the environment of potential employers, can help you avoid future career frustration.

Signs of a company's overall environment can appear as early as the interview process. Eric discovered one blatant indication after he interviewed at a top-tier "bulge bracket" investment bank. He was quite pleased with how the interview unfolded at first. He thought he exuded confidence, showed a clear understanding of the various business units, and had all the right academic credentials to land a coveted spot. He thought it was strange that he spent more than half of his interview time answering questions about diversity, his views on the most influential racial minorities in financial services, what factors he thought needed to be changed in inner-city public schools to encourage kids to pursue careers in business, and his favorite Martin Luther King, Jr. Day celebration. At the time, he thought it was a good indication of the company's interests in diversity-related issues.

But later in the week, he began to wonder if something else was at play. While meeting with some business school classmates to commiserate over the intense week of interviewing, one study group partner—a white man who had interviewed at the same company for a position in the same department—talked vividly about the various people to which he was introduced, how he was given a case study to critique, and was asked to share his ideas about effective and ineffective product marketing strategies. His friend had a multifaceted interview that allowed him face time with senior managers and an opportunity to demonstrate his analytical skills and marketing know-how. Eric was offered no such chance. He began to wonder if the interviewers saw him only as a diversity hire—a necessary staff addition for diversity roundtables, award dinners, and promotional materials.

Interview sessions can be a good opportunity to gauge a potential employer's "squirm factor." When asked questions about their company's diversity goals, initiatives, and employees, hiring managers may show signs of discomfort. For example, they may show a reluctance to answer sensitive questions, such as the overall turnover rate by racial and ethnic groups. And if the interviewer is willing to respond to such a question, consider whether he or she can produce a reasonable answer.

To heed the full breadth of the subtle signs and blaring signals at any potential employer, job seekers must engage in a comprehensive evaluation involving key areas: daily worklife; assignment, development, and mentoring; the company/firm culture and values; the gender, racial, ethnic, religious, and cultural climate; inappropriate conduct issues; corporate citizenship; and other diversity issues.

DAILY WORKLIFE

It's not called the "daily grind" for nothing. Managing the day-to-day demands at work can be one of the most difficult aspects of any job. Getting a real sense of the frustrating aspects of the daily experience and how they can differ for various demographic groups is crucial. These are elements of the work experience that have the potential to erode job satisfaction if they are overlooked or ignored. To judge our daily worklife, we must include both the intrinsic and extrinsic rewards of our job. Intrinsic rewards are judged by answering questions such as these: Is the work intellectually challenging? Are there opportunities to improve my skills and abilities? Extrinsic rewards are commonly compensation, benefits, and recognition, but they might also be whether colleagues frequently seek our opinion on business matters or whether we feel included in important social networks.

Often, daily worklife can be enhanced or ruined by the cumulative effect of seemingly small things: how easy or difficult it is to obtain the information we need to do our job, whether adequate mechanisms are in place to deal with concerns raised about the company, and especially whether and when those concerns are acted upon.

ASSIGNMENT, DEVELOPMENT, AND MENTORING

Choosing who gets what work assignment can be a subjective process, but it's critical for determining how women, people of color, and gay and lesbian workers fare. Companies employ various methods to assign work on plum projects, which often involve varying levels of objectivity, randomness, and even favoritism. When access to good assignments equals access to opportunities to excel, to be noticed, and to move ahead, every employee needs to understand how this process plays out at work.

After Miguel accepted his current job, he felt lost in the sauce for months as he tried to figure out the methodology for getting good assignments. The managers listed clear criteria for assigning work, but it was obvious to Miguel that the criteria weren't being applied across the board. Whenever he questioned the system, he heard another explanation for the exceptions to the rule. Eventually he realized that no system was in place at all.

For new employees like Miguel who don't yet know the ropes, mentors can be indispensable in career planning and success. Research in both educational settings and the workplace indicates that students and employees are more likely to succeed if they have a mentor. In an academic setting, for example, a mentor of a potential graduate student could help crack the code regarding what fellowship review committees look for in applications. Thankfully, Miguel found a good mentor at work. As he learned, a mentor is often the most valuable resource for helping a new hire decipher the less obvious information in the workplace—such as who are the real decision-makers and what is the most effective way to land plum assignments. He learned that a good mentor can also speak up on your behalf at important career junctures, such as when you are being considered for a promotion.

Not all mentoring programs are equal, however. Depending on how the program is structured, results can be mixed. For example, a voluntary mentoring program may not take into account the personalities and commitment levels of those involved. Some who volunteer as mentors underestimate the time and commitment that such an obligation can involve. Some voluntary programs run by companies are based on matching the experience of the mentor with the announced interests of the person to be mentored. But a busy litigator and an overcommitted associate may find that they don't have the time necessary to cement this relationship. Also, if the pair doesn't find immediate chemistry at the first meeting, the mentor-protégé relationship can fade before it has a chance to grow. While mandatory mentoring programs address some of these issues, most agree that the best mentoring relationships involve chemistry, an element that can't be produced on demand.

When volunteer or assigned mentors don't understand the hidden biases and barriers that may be in the path of a young professional, the relationship can be disastrous. Not long ago, I witnessed a mentoring "accident." A prominent venture capitalist from a marquee firm had agreed to be a mentor to a few entrepreneurs who were starting businesses with a "double bottom line"—that is, not only did they aspire to build profitable enterprises, they also wanted to create well-paying, stable jobs in low-income communities. One of these entrepreneurs was a Latina with an impressive resume of business achievement and community involvement. As she presented her current options for scaling her business, she matter-of-factly noted that an obstacle to date had been the racial and gender bias of lenders. Her experience indicated that the terms under which she could obtain financing were not nearly as favorable as those offered to businesses headed by Caucasians and/or men. The seasoned venture capitalist exploded with a tirade along the lines of "that has nothing to do with anything. Lenders and investors only care about the quality of the business and the management; it's absurd to think they're biased." A dedicated entrepreneur might be better off without a mentor who denies her experience and won't believe that she is being treated differently.

THE COMPANY/FIRM CULTURE AND VALUES

Every organization has a culture—a personality. And while every business may share common objectives such as serving clients or generating profits, every business will go about accomplishing these objectives in different ways. Within each work culture is a collective staff behavior (sometimes referred to as "the way we do things around here"), along with a set of values and beliefs that shape that behavior. The importance of company culture should never be underestimated. It is often powerful and pervasive. At times, a particular value can be so entrenched that it becomes part of the company's social fabric. When such a situation occurs, most employees aren't aware of, or aren't able to articulate, the assumptions influencing their behavior. The culture will drive what is done and what is left undone, and it will determine what actions and outcomes are rewarded or punished.

Quite literally, a healthy culture can spell the difference between corporate success and failure. Library shelves are full of case studies and research documenting how often companies develop brilliant strategies yet find themselves unable to execute them. Equally, many companies have invested millions of dollars in innovation initiatives, only to see creative ideas and novel plans stymied by cultural problems. In most cases, the root causes of these failures are incompatibility between management's objectives and the prevailing corporate culture.

Understanding a culture is not as simple as understanding a business principle such as "The client always comes first." A company's culture is multilayered, like the proverbial onion, with both observable and unobservable layers that when pulled backed reveal another opaque layer. When you peel back the layers of the onion, you eventually realize that the layers *are* the onion, and there is no core. Similarly, at a company, the layers *are* the company; only by peeling away those layers can you come to know what the organization is really about.

THE GENDER, RACIAL, ETHNIC, RELIGIOUS, AND CULTURAL CLIMATE

Sometimes, in true onion fashion, one layer of company culture exists for white males and another one exists for women and people of color, minority race/ethnicity, religion, or sexual orientation. Eric slowly began to discern that "the game" was different for him as an African American—and even more different as a *gay* African American. He was concerned, and rightfully so, that he couldn't play both the black person's and the gay person's game and win at both. So he had to play the game from which he couldn't hide, and he tried his best to conceal the other.

At one point, Eric tried (in a roundabout, totally clandestine, please-don't-let-this-backfire kind of way) to seek out a person in human resources to speak to as a sounding board. He was looking for a channel to express his concerns about "coming out" that offered him anonymity, if possible, or at a minimum complete confidentiality, to get some practical advice from other gay employees at the firm. He found nothing, so he did nothing. But every day, his feeling of isolation did its damage. Every time he reached another milestone at work—scoring a big client or nailing a presentation—he thought he was getting closer to fitting in, and he thought "things will be better now." But they weren't.

Later, when Eric heard of yet another office legend, he knew that he would never be able to come out to senior managers, only to trusted colleagues and a smattering of individuals who were perceptive enough to figure it out. A senior manager at the company had invited his team to bring their spouses and join him for a private, celebratory dinner at his home after the successful completion of a major milestone. The senior manager was a close-minded, naive man who had no idea that one of his team members was gay and would bring his partner to the gathering. On the night of the dinner, after the senior manager was introduced to the gay employee's partner, the manager quickly left the room to try to compose himself. Upon returning, he told his guests that he suddenly felt ill and was going to bed but that they should stay, enjoy the food (which had already been delivered by caterers), and see themselves out once they had finished.

Eric couldn't shake the sinking feeling that he had been duped by the company's claims of its large-scale diversity efforts. He was disappointed in himself for not quizzing insiders before accepting the job offer, for failing to ask deeper questions about company culture.

INAPPROPRIATE CONDUCT ISSUES

Inappropriate conduct takes a multitude of forms, along at least two axes. Along one axis is a continuum from subtle to blatant, from hidden to obvious. Feedback from a senior manager to the single representative of a particular group that he or she isn't a good fit may be a form of hidden bias, whereas a job posting saying "No blacks, no Jews, no women" doesn't leave much to the imagination. The other axis is whether or not the inappropriate conduct is covered by local discrimination laws. In the United States, managers are free to engage in bullying and public humiliation according to the law, despite the fact that these behaviors are as demoralizing as blatant discrimination.[2]

In contrast, French laws prohibit "moral harassment" (that is, behavior considered bullying in the United States) but do not provide a cause of action for a sexually hostile environment (that is, when unwelcome sexual behaviors such as comments, jokes, or gestures become sufficiently pervasive as to alter one's work environment). Although we traditionally focus on highly publicized matters of illegality, any inappropriate conduct, whatever its form and whether or not it is legally acceptable, has a chilling effect on the workplace, creating exclusive cultures that leave some out in the cold.

When Kristen accepted her job at the firm, she had heard about several gender discrimination lawsuits filed against prominent corporations, and she couldn't fathom that women were still being blatantly and obviously discriminated against in the 21st century. She was relieved to know that no such lawsuits had been filed against the firm where she would work, but eventually she would realize that inappropriate comments and conduct, short of discrimination defined by the law, were alarmingly prevalent—and the effects were no less profound—at her office.

Even on her first day during a welcome reception for new associates, a vice president introduced Kristen only as "the type of young lady I'd like my son to marry—smart and attractive," while introductions of her male colleagues included their academic and professional accomplishments. She smiled uncomfortably as the others let out friendly laughs. At the time, she brushed the incident aside, recognizing it was well intentioned and not wanting to seem too sensitive or to create waves during her first day on the job. The days on which Kristen experienced inappropriate conduct—whether it was her being scolded in front of her team by a manager who said, "If you can't handle the work, go home and play with your dolls," or enduring the tirades of a director whenever he was having trouble at home—passed into months. Although she wanted desperately to seek advice and counsel, she had learned of a female colleague who had reported similar incidents and was later chastised and labeled a "ball-breaker."

The inappropriate comments and conduct soon began to affect Kristen's physical and mental well-being, the quality of work she was receiving (after all, being the "prettiest associate" isn't exactly a ringing endorsement of her professional qualifications), and her career trajectory. Although Kristen had learned early on that no discrimination lawsuits had been filed against her firm, she eventually realized that she should have done more research into the company culture to determine how it treated female employees in particular. She regretted that she did not dive deeper than major, public sources to inquire about the presence or lack of civility, respect, incidents of public humiliation, explosions of anger, and demeaning comments that were routine at this firm.

Whatever form inappropriate conduct takes and wherever it lands along either axis, the effect of such conduct is the same: it is demoralizing to employees, counterproductive to work, and costly to employers.

CORPORATE CITIZENSHIP

Miguel was trapped in a Latino nightmare. Every time a senior manager came by his office asking for a recommendation of a good Mexican restaurant, or asking how to say something in Spanish, or to share a Latino revelation ("Hey, Miguel, did you know that the president of Nike is Latino?"), Miguel wanted to disappear into the woodwork. He was often asked to sit in on company meetings related to business interests in Latin America, and there he quickly realized that his co-workers and the company as a whole had little awareness of Latino issues or values. He participated in discussions about working with Latino civic groups, but nothing ever materialized. Miguel had simply assumed that this large company, which supported programs such as the United Negro College Fund and the Urban League, would also put money into programs serving the needs of the Latino community as part of its corporate citizenship. Miguel thought of creative ways to introduce meaningful organizations, such as the National Council of La Raza, to the managers for possible sponsorships, but he realized after several rebuffed attempts that they were only giving lip service to their support.

Like other potential employees, Miguel had failed to research whether or not this employer put its money where its mouth was. Prior to accepting the job, he had failed to examine the programs, foundations, and civic events this company supported. Had he done so, he would have known that the company had no real interest in him or his community.

In the current climate of declining public trust of corporations, heightened surveillance, and more informed and empowered consumers, corporate citizenship has become critical to business survival. For example, the *2006 Annual Edelman Trust Barometer* (Edelman 2006) found that "if respondents lose trust in a company, they are highly likely (70 percent to 80 percent) not to purchase its products or services. Worse, people do not simply internalize their doubts; they talk to others and spread distrust—with up to 33 percent now using the Web to post their views." Investigating a possible employer's corporate responsibility track record is not only imperative in helping to determine your "fit" as an employee, but it is increasingly becoming a key indication of an organization's ongoing business success.

OTHER DIVERSITY ISSUES

Kristen was racking her brain. One day, after an insensitive comment from a manager who teased her as likely to be "off having babies soon," she realized she could not remember meeting one working mother during her interview process. "I would have definitely noticed not meeting any mothers," she said aloud to herself, wondering how she could have missed something so important. However, as she scanned her memory, she kept coming up short.

She had begun to read through the company's employee manuals with more interest these days, looking at policies for maternity leave, unpaid leave, paid sick days, and breast-feeding support. Her findings weren't encouraging. She found little in the way of support for new mothers or support for employees with families.

A 2007 study by Harvard and McGill University researchers (Heymann et al.) found that the United States lags far behind virtually all wealthy countries with regard to family-oriented workplace policies such as maternity leave, paid sick days, and support for breast-feeding. The study by the Harvard-based Project on Global Working Families said that workplace policies for families in the United States are weaker than those of all high-income countries and many middle- and low-income countries. Notably, it says the United States is one of only 5 countries out of 173 in the survey that does not guarantee by law some form of paid maternity leave; the others are Lesotho, Liberia, Papua New Guinea, and Swaziland.

Kristen eventually met a working mother at the firm, but she seemed constantly frustrated. She never received meaty assignments, regardless of how the so-called rules of rotation should have spun her way. On one occasion, this woman had been working hard on a project and putting in long hours. The day before the client presentation, one of her children became very ill and she called in to say that she was in the emergency room but would arrive at work later in the day. Her manager quickly assigned the presentation to someone else. The woman arrived later, as promised, only to find all her hard work handed off to a single, childless subordinate, who would be making the presentation the next day.

When Kristen began to seek out mothers in other departments to meet for lunch and coffee, she learned that many women in the company quit their jobs after having children. Every woman she met could rattle off the names of two or three former colleagues who left their jobs because they did not believe that the company supported them as mothers. Kristen had missed the signs during her interview, and she realized too late that she should have asked more questions.

MAKING AN ASSESSMENT FROM THE OUTSIDE

With so many signs to read and so many signals to discern, potential employees can become overwhelmed by what they need to know before saying "yes" to a job offer. The following comprehensive checklist can help you make a real assessment from the outside before you step in. If possible, find a person at the company with interests and a lifestyle similar to yours, who is working at a job similar to the one you're seeking, and ask the following questions in each key area.

DAILY WORKLIFE

- What are the most rewarding aspects of your day-to-day job?
- What are the most frustrating aspects of your day-to-day job?
- What does it take to be successful here? Do criteria for success differ for different departments/divisions/practice areas/specialties? For different tenure? For men and women? For different racial, cultural, religious groups? For straights and gays/lesbians?
- If your best friend were applying for a job here, what would you advise? Would it be the same advice to someone who was considering a position as a manager/professional versus a member of support staff?
- Do you have to check yourself at the door here? Can you talk about your background, family, and outside interests?

ASSIGNMENT, DEVELOPMENT, AND MENTORING

- Different companies/firms adopt differing ways of assigning work and projects. They have varying levels of objectivity, versus randomness, versus perceived favoritism. How would you characterize the assignment process here? How widely does it vary from department to department? Does someone verify that opportunities are fairly apportioned, or do assignments go to those who have the self-confidence to ask a manager/partner to work on them?
- When comparing your experiences to professionals/managers in other departments, do you receive opportunities to develop your specific talents at earlier, the same, or later tenure? How about when comparing the opportunities at this company/firm to those available at other organizations?
- Do you have a mentor? If so, how did that relationship develop and evolve? Is this a real mentor who looks out for your career, assignments, and reputation? Is your mentor of the same demographic group(s) as you?

The Company/Firm Culture and Values

- How was the company/firm described to you when you were being recruited/interviewing? In what ways has that turned out to be accurate? In what ways is that inaccurate? (For example, were you told that the company helps people juggle work and family obligations, but the only way to get ahead here is to work eighty hours per week and be seen in the office at all hours?)
- If you were writing the company's/firm's values statement—not the platitudes but the accurate descriptors—what would be the key values? How would you characterize the behaviors/characteristics that the company/firm really values?
- What are the top three reasons you came to this company/firm?
- What are the top three reasons you stay at this company/firm?

The Gender, Racial, Ethnic, Religious, and Cultural Climate

- What are the greatest supports and obstacles for women being successful at the company/firm?
- What are the greatest supports and obstacles for people from different backgrounds being successful here—such as U.S. racial minorities and people from other countries/cultures?
- Is it safe to raise issues of "diversity" here? Can you use a person or committee as a sounding board, with complete confidentiality/anonymity, to get some advice? Does that person or committee have any power over what really happens here?

Inappropriate Conduct Issues

- How common are nondiscriminatory forms of harassment? How are they best characterized: Incivility and disrespect? Rudeness? Unprofessional conduct?
- How common are the following types of behaviors: explosions of anger, public humiliation, abusive language, demeaning comments, overcritical attitude?
- Do these behaviors usually cross lines of power or authority? Are they present among peers? Across departments/functions?

- Does the company's/firm's current culture support challenging inappropriate conduct?

Corporate Citizenship

- What is the company's/firm's reputation in the city in which it is headquartered? Does it donate money to local organizations? If so, what types—opera or after-school programs?
- Does the company/firm have a philanthropy program? What are its areas of interest? Are employees involved in decision-making? Are products/services donated or just money? Can employees take time off to be involved with non-profit work? If so, are they seen as exemplary workers or as slackers?
- Does the company/firm have policies/guidelines on environmental stewardship? Are they meaningful or just a public relations maneuver?
- What is the company's/firm's history with respect to ethical issues? For example, has it been fined or investigated, or is it seen as rewarding ethical conduct?

Other Diversity Issues

- Is it safe to be an "out" gay or lesbian here? Does the company/firm offer domestic partner benefits?
- Does the company/firm value parents? Does the organization help or hinder balancing work and family obligations?
- Do other divisions exist among groups in the company/firm? If so, what are they?
- Does the company/firm accommodate crises, maternity leave, family emergencies, and disabilities? How is this accommodation displayed? Are the "rules" applied fairly?

Overall Sentiment

- All in all, do you think that there is a level playing field here? Is the company/firm a meritocracy?
- If you were writing this employer's values statement—those that are practiced in the daily behavior of senior management—what would they be?

- Lastly, find someone who is different from you in terms of demographics, but has similar skills and interests, and ask the following:
  - With whom did you interview (position, race, gender, background)?
  - What were the questions he or she (or they) asked you? How was your time spent?
  - Did the topic of the company's/firm's commitment to diversity ever come up? If so, who raised it?
  - Re-ask any of the questions from above and compare notes.

CONCLUSION

If the reality-based picture provided by speaking with current insiders doesn't meet your needs and standards/values, you should think twice about accepting a position with a new company. You should especially be wary if your demographic characteristics determined the content of your interview. If that was the case, know that the stereotypes about you and your affiliations will have as much to say about your career progression in the organization as your performance.

CHAPTER EIGHT

BIAS AROUND THE WORLD

Kristen awoke with a start and looked at the clock—3:30 A.M. After quick mental calculation, she realized that it was 9:30 P.M. back in New York. Ah, yes, the glamour of international travel, she thought. Looking over at the other bed in her hotel room, she realized that her assigned roommate had never come in. Having seen her at the reception last night, Kristen assumed that the rumor must be true: she's having an affair with an executive vice president. Risky for both of them. After trying every trick she knew to get back to sleep, Kristen finally got up and sent Eric an instant message: "R U awake?"

Here they were, the entire original training class, reunited in Frankfurt for their international training program. Some of them would be identified as rising stars, plucked from the group and put on the express train as it traveled upward through the corporate structure, darting around the globe, as proving grounds and grooming opportunities greeted those hoping to reach the rarified air as senior manager in any of the major global offices.

Then Eric's reply appeared on Kristen's screen: "Yeah, what took you so long? I've been up for hours =). Ready for breakfast? Call me."

As they sat in the hotel's casual restaurant watching the comings and goings of delivery people, Kristen made fun of some of the English translations on the menu while Eric remarked on how he felt simultaneously unwelcome and welcome in this country. So many people blatantly stared at him, yet he noticed that multilingual signs appeared and English was spoken almost everywhere he went. He recalled past conversations with Jerome, a senior manager he had met on a task force during his first few months with the firm. Eric rarely encountered a senior white employee who was enlightened about the dynamics of race and didn't shy away from a real conversation. Jerome explained to Eric that his international assignments had opened his eyes—the experience of being an outsider, of not knowing the informal rules, of always being stereotyped as the gauche American. Jerome vowed to keep the vantage point of observer—not just of insider, where all the assumptions are unquestioned.

As Eric thought about his conversations with Jerome, Kristen was mulling over what she had learned from her classmates in their Cultural Differences in Business workshop. Business dilemmas and cases were presented and small groups were charged with creating solutions. Many of these revolved around the well-known framework presented, in the book *Riding the Waves of Culture* by Fons Trompenaars and Charles Hampden-Turner (1997); they asked people to assess, for example, when it would be appropriate to cancel a business meeting in various cultures: (A) Never, (B) For a family celebration, or (C) Only for an emergency.

Most of the cases presented in the workshop were real stories from her own company's trenches. In essence, they begged the question of whose culture and norms prevail in a business deal where many nationalities are represented. Kristen's favorite case was the following:

> A professional who grew up in a different country is now working in the United States. He often uses endearing or familiar terms with women and initiates frequent touching of both men and women. Some employees object, while others dismiss it or find it acceptable. When challenged, he becomes quite defensive, explains that this is his cultural heritage, and charges that he is the victim of discrimination.

The discussion in her small group, made up of international colleagues, was lively. Many people objected to the Americans' way of bringing their own assumptions and laws to dominate, no matter where they are. Americans are crass and prudish, they said. They file too many lawsuits. Kristen became defensive, explaining to her international colleagues that the United States might have its shortcomings, but the country still leads the world for including women in business.

"How ironic," she told Eric over breakfast, "that I was defending American corporate culture after the deluge of bias I've faced."

"It was the oddest thing," responded Eric, remembering his group discussion. "I heard a lot of anti-American sentiment, too. At one point, Charles, the Parisian, said, 'I detest it when I have to work in New York!' Then Azihiko, the guy from Kyoto, blurted out, 'Me, too!' We were all shocked since none of us had ever heard him speak up critically about anything. Answering a chorus of 'Why? Why?' Charles said, 'Every morning I walk into the office and I have to steel myself and remember not to greet people as we do in France, by kissing both cheeks. I feel so stifled and cold.' But then Azihiko chimed in, 'Everywhere I go in New York, especially in the office, everyone touches me, grabs my arm, stands right in my face. I feel invaded.' After both men had spoken, everyone else in the group just looked at each other, stunned. Then we burst out laughing. That was a real 'Aha moment' for everyone."

Invigorated by the discussion and the caffeine, Kristen laughed. "My head is spinning with Aha moments. I ended up leaving the dinner at the same time that Joshua did—remember that kid with the really thick New York accent who was always telling jokes? Well, walking back to the hotel, we passed a store with the sign 'Schmuck' in the window. I cracked up, since I had learned that word from him. Joshua looked more serious than I've ever seen him. He said, 'Being in Germany gives me the creeps. See all that antique jewelry in the store window? It was probably stolen from my relatives before they were herded off to concentration camps and killed.' I was shocked and clueless about what to say. I've never thought about Nazis and the Holocaust and World War II as anything but remote history. I had to consider what it means to live with these legacies. But I guess none of this is news to you, Eric."

Kristen then spent a moment mulling over the presumed affair going on between her roommate at this event and the EVP. It seemed trivial in the face of genocide and slavery. If no one was being coerced, was it really a problem? Was she a prudish farm girl after all? But what if this woman had been promoted only because she was having the affair? Perhaps Eric or Miguel, or even she herself, was the most deserving candidate. Maybe this isn't about sex at all—maybe it's really about favoritism and a conflict of interest. She recalled the lively debate about whether loyalty to one's family or friends is a higher value than loyalty to the company. As Kristen tried to sort out her conflicting thoughts, she began to get a headache.

THE NEW CULTURE OF GLOBAL BUSINESS

Global business is a fixture of our modern landscape; it brings with it new winners and new losers. Most U.S. companies of any size have international offices, connections, or assignments. U.S. employees who are sent abroad can experience more false assumptions than real understanding about doing business in other cultures. For example, it's assumed that European businesses (known for their long lunch breaks, reasonable work hours, and five-week summer vacations) are bastions of ease and comfort. This is not exactly the case, however, and an American who arrives at the European office expecting to "take it easy" may be considered a slacker and handed a demotion. Another (false) assumption: women can't be leaders in Muslim cultures. Of course, you need look no further than Pakistan or the Philippines, both countries with large Muslim populations, to see that this is not the case; both countries have had women presidents. These cross-cultural misunderstandings can and do lead to financial and personal costs for businesses that make such assumptions.

It is important for U.S.-based companies to understand different corporate cultures abroad. It's also important that employees sent overseas are trained in both the legal and social differences when it comes to bias.

No matter how culturally sensitive U.S. organizations become, political systems, occupations, and standards of living will continue to shift in the hierarchy of fortunate versus unfortunate. The book *Many Globalizations* (Berger and Huntington 2002) examines trends in various countries, including Chile, Japan, South Africa, Germany, Turkey, Hungary, Taiwan, India, and the United States. The authors conclude that a global business culture is forming, which bears a strong American imprint; however, they point out that it looks neither like the worst imperialism of the past nor a "metastasized Disneyland."

One particularly problematic export from the United States is its legal approach to issues of difference. Over many years, I have conducted surveys around the globe asking employees about experiences and perceptions of behaviors that they believe constitute *harassment*—using the term in its largest international context of misuse of power. *Harassment* is a construct that covers a multitude of interactions, ranging from blatant favoritism based on nepotism to subtle ostracism based on one's mother tongue. This construct meshes with a framework of respect and dignity. By definition, engaging in any form of harassment is disrespectful.

However, the U.S. framework is rigid, declaring some of these behaviors (which logically fit on a continuum) illegal, while other behaviors, which might seem equally inappropriate, are legal. A wedge—the threat of legal action—is driven between the employee and employer, thus preventing them from being on the same side and working together to identify and correct a problem that precludes both from pursuing their objectives. And the issue doesn't disappear when a U.S. citizen leaves the country: Congress made the 1991 Civil Rights Act "extraterritorial," meaning that a U.S. employee working anywhere in the world for a U.S.-based company brings his or her rights along.

Here's an example of how this looks in practice: An American associate, Monica, is working in the Italian office of her American-based global investment bank. She observes a local male vice president—extraordinarily successful and well regarded—occasionally touch and hug one of the local administrative assistants. The behavior appears to be welcome. However, Monica believes that the behavior is inappropriate and violates her firm's policies, so she contacts a U.S. employee relations representative whom she knows and with whom she feels comfortable.

Now everyone is in a difficult position. If the company's primary approach to these issues is mitigating legal risk, appeasing Monica becomes the first priority. But demanding that all employees forgo customary and comfortable interactions because they make Monica uncomfortable won't do much for morale or company commitment, and transferring Monica back to the United States may constitute retaliation. Regardless of how the situation unfolds, Monica's career will be relegated to the slow track because of her actions, at least within this company.

The backdrop of global business has particular implications for trying to create more inclusive and welcoming work environments. The opportunities to learn about other cultures abound, as do the opportunities to be inadvertently offensive.

A study published in 2000 examined eight large, U.S.-based multinationals and found that all were planning, implementing, and evaluating a significant number and range of diversity initiatives in the United States and around the globe (Wentling and Palma-Rivas 2000). Yet the CEOs who lead (or at least endorse) such efforts are not uniformly committed to change. An international study concluded that cultural background may be a major determinant of an executive's willingness to adopt change efforts (Geletkanycz 1997). As with any organizational initiatives, the personal experiences of a leader will guide his or her commitment, which will, in turn, convey a powerful message to employees. Action and inaction both send a message, and employees will observe and draw their own conclusions as to whether creating a welcoming work environment for people from diverse backgrounds really matters.

CONFLICTING ROLE OF WOMEN

Many companies have struggled with the conflicting roles of women in different cultures. I worked with a top-tier international law firm that was a finalist for a major bank privatization effort. The prospective client let it be known that the successful firm would be expected to engage in the customary lavish entertaining. In this context, "entertainment" included hiring prostitutes, which is not illegal where the deal was taking place. A top-performing U.S. associate, working out of her firm's Asian office, had hoped to solidify her slot on partner track by working on the deal. Instead, she offered an ultimatum: "Go forward with the customary entertainment and I'll add my name to the ranks of ex-associates."

How should her employer respond? All too often, the legal framework, once again, dominates the response. Since she is a U.S. citizen employed by a U.S. firm, her rights follow her around the globe. This complicates the situation greatly. If she is sent home because she genuinely objects to local business customs, that could be construed as retaliation for speaking out about perceived discrimination and would, therefore, be illegal. Similarly, if she is removed from a deal that has the highest visibility or the most vexing legal challenges, this, too, could be seen as retaliatory.

Unfortunately, this situation can be characterized as a double negative: opening with an ultimatum doesn't invite creative problem solving, nor does acting out of fear of being sued. If the associate and her firm had been able to avail themselves of an ombuds or another third-party neutral, a workable compromise could likely have been identified.

GLOBAL TENSIONS

Dilemmas that mirror global tensions or conflicts can also emerge in the workplace: consider the Chinese woman who asks not to be staffed with any Korean businessmen. She says (based upon her experiences) that she will be discriminated against by them and that her input will be ignored. Therefore, if she were to work with Korean male colleagues, she would find it impossible to be effective.

Or consider the professional from India, who, because he possessed an impressive track record and relevant industry experience, was nominated for a high-profile assignment. However, the senior manager who needed to sign off on the assignment rejected his nomination, observing that it would be highly insensitive to have an Indian working with a vice president from Pakistan.

Should either of these decisions be honored? Both are operating on the basis of stereotypes, whether or not they've emanated from experience. The culture of each employer will define the parameters of how these solutions are approached: Is there meaningful dialogue about differences? Can conflicts be aired and worked through, or are they ignored? In the first example, a wise manager can monitor team dynamics and assure the woman that she will be treated fairly. The company can help the colleagues articulate expectations of working together and can require that neither will succeed without strong peer reviews. In the second instance, however, the decision was made by the senior manager. If the Indian professional challenges the decision, he may win the assignment, but he may incur consequences from the manager who was overruled. Once again, organizational culture will determine the array of available options and the outcome. Companies with a strong meritocratic culture and safe, effective complaint options will end this tale quite differently from those whose cultures strongly value hierarchy and following the chain of command.

WHICH COUNTRIES ARE "BETTER" AND WHICH ARE "WORSE"?

It's nearly impossible to address an international group of managers— even those who work for the same company—without encountering judgments about which society is more enlightened, who is more backward, who is the Neanderthal when it comes to gender issues, and who is puritanical about sexuality in the workplace. Although you may find the competition amusing, taking a superior stance and judging other societal norms are counterproductive activities. Such judgments reflect precisely what needs to be "fixed" if we are to establish a bias-free work environment. International businesses do best when they strive for a single set of unifying principles that allow for cultural differences. If the major dividing line is between welcome and unwelcome, we should not waste time trying to figure out which culture is intolerant, versus more tolerant, versus too tolerant.

EXPERIENCES OF EUROPEAN CORPORATE LEAVERS

This book has focused on U.S.-based companies, including those that are global. Stories from U.S. citizens have addressed the complexity of building welcoming, inclusive work environments within a demographically diverse society. But how different are these experiences in other developed countries?

I have gathered stories of corporate leavers from European countries, which demonstrate that the dynamics are the same— although with important cultural nuances.

In every country, some groups are considered insiders and some are outsiders. Some workers have to underperform repeatedly before they get sidelined, while others have to perform perfectly time and time again before they are noticed. Here is a smattering of experiences from colleagues based in various countries. All names have been changed.

• **Anique:** According to my employment contract, I was supposed to receive an Audi A6 as a corporate car. Initially, I was told that I would have to wait for my car because of budget constraints. When the car finally arrived, it was an Audi A3—a meaningfully smaller car than the A6 my contract had stipulated. When I raised this discrepancy, I received the following feedback: "It's not important for you. Your husband has a corporate car, hasn't he?" When I insisted on receiving an A6, I heard: "Anyway, a woman would look strange in a car like that; I doubt that you'd be able to maneuver it." I never did receive my A6, which gave me new insight on my employer. I quit shortly after having my first baby.

- **Florine:** I was a senior brand manager—one of nine in the company, most of whom were women. My track record was the best in the organization and so, accordingly, I received the highest bonus. My boss then told me, "You should have a child now. I already have a female head of team, and I can't promote you to that level and risk both of you being pregnant at the same time." A man was promoted instead of me. Unfortunately (but ironically), this man was in a ski accident shortly after receiving his promotion. The accident kept him away from the office far longer than my maternity leave would have. I decided to quit.

- **Dafina:** At a consulting firm where I worked, nine other women and I all received the same feedback on our review: "Must improve your style." We all requested a more detailed explanation regarding this point of "self-improvement," since it was quite vague. When we asked what, specifically, we needed to change, we were told: "I don't know. The problem is, you're not like us."

- **Beatrice:** I had just become the sole female member of my company's executive committee and was given an assistant's office. When I asked why, I was told: "This is the best that we can do—there's no other available space. But look on the bright side: at least you can access the ladies' toilets easily." I later found out that the company had decided to put a woman on the executive committee simply to avoid negative publicity. The location of my desk was of no importance to them whatsoever.

- **Ramona:** I was a partner at a major consulting firm and had just arrived at my first meeting with a team from another firm with which we were merging. I noticed—out loud—that no other women were present at the meeting. A senior partner from the other firm responded, "But of course! We only promote based on performance."

- **Yasmin:** While working at a global company headquartered in the European Union, I quickly found out I that needed a master's

degree if I wanted to be promoted. For five years, I juggled everything: I have a small daughter, a job, and I took classes at night, on
Saturdays, and during my vacation. For all those years, my life was
between parentheses. While I was still working on my degree, my
company started to have financial problems and was asking for vol-
unteers to take a severance package. I told them that I was interested, because I was concerned about my future at a company that
was in difficult financial straits. They informed me that I was not eligible because I was a single mother. So I was more or less forced to
stay. After I'd completed my degree, a position matching my profile
and goals opened up. It required a few years of sales experience and
a master's degree. I said to myself, "That's me!" The position, however, went to a blue-eyed blonde with a college degree and much less
experience than I. No explanation was given for the choice. Then it
dawned on me that a pattern had emerged: whenever I had taken
the time and effort to pursue something, it was denied me—for no
plausible reason. No one ever said to me, "You can't do X because
you're black." But what else am I to conclude at this point?

• **François:** One of my co-workers is an Arabic woman from
northern Africa. One day she asked me, "Have you noticed that
there are no executives here who are not white and French? No
French Arab. No French black. No French Chinese. Only white
French people. If you don't have the right complexion and family
name, you'll never be promoted here."

• **Makim:** Following an interview at a bank in a European capital city, I felt really, really badly. During the course of the interview,
I was told that it would be very difficult for me to work there
because, as a foreign-born black man, I would never be accepted
by any team and would face problems in my dealings with clients.
"Our clients want their sensitive financial interactions handled by
people like them—people from this country," I was told. Then I
said, "But how will the clients know that I wasn't born here? My language skills are impeccable." The interviewer responded, "They'll
see your name."

• **Nathan:** I'd been asked to find a senior executive to run
a FTSE 100 company. The perfect candidate happened to be a
woman. She was very well suited for the job, and she landed the
position based on her solid skills. On her first day at work, she

announced that she was six months pregnant. The client called me in a rage and demanded to know why I hadn't warned them that she was expecting. Evidently she'd made it through the entire interview process without anyone noticing that she was pregnant.

- **Markus:** I was working for an international consulting firm for a senior partner who is gay. Whenever anyone mentioned him, they all used the same formulaic expression: "Everett—you know, the gay guy." It used to drive me crazy. No other senior partners at the firm were named Everett. When they were talking about other senior partners, I wondered why people didn't say things like, "Paul—you know, the bachelor," or "Margaret—you know, the single mother." Those types of characteristics were just as irrelevant as Everett's sexual orientation.

- **Trent:** I worked for a conservative charity for one year in between positions with two high-powered global corporations. I had just designed a series of tests to help them select new hires based on their skills alone, and I tried them out to recruit my assistant. I ended up hiring a brilliant young woman who performed marvelously in the tests and was clearly the best candidate. My colleagues, however, were shocked to discover that my new assistant was a lesbian who wore dreadlocks. I told them that if they were serious about recruiting only the best person for a given job, based only on his or her skill sets, then they needed to overlook other traits that might make them uneasy initially—like hairstyle and sexual orientation.

CONCLUSION

The increasing globalization and interconnectedness of modern business leads undeniably to a range of challenges: employees working outside of their homelands often have false assumptions and a lack of understanding of legal and social differences in their new countries. International and multicultural offices face tensions and conflicts related to present-day and historical world flash points. Senior management is faced with the daunting task of establishing welcoming, inclusive workplaces capable of eclipsing international misunderstandings or hostilities that, in many cases, have existed for centuries. Global businesses must balance creating a unifying, worldwide company culture while accommodating and respecting local customs and cultures.

Companies that get it right have to encourage speaking up, debating, and separating what's nonnegotiable (for example, bribes, even if they are customary in a country where business is being done) from what's negotiable (for example, in what countries is it acceptable to tell a co-worker that he or she has put on weight or is too noisy or too quiet?). Given the right message from management, these conversations can be illuminating and fascinating and can greatly aid global business.

CHAPTER NINE

TEN STEPS BACK

"How's that report coming?" asked Eric's manager as they brushed elbows while balancing their lunch trays in the cafeteria. "You might want to get a double espresso. I guess you're going to be here pretty late."

Thirty minutes earlier, Eric had received an e-mail from this same manager, a hard-driving mentor who was alternately supportive and cutting. The e-mail demanded that Eric produce a new report analyzing a complex set of forecast figures: "Pls drop everything and get this to me ASAP. Definitely before morning," read the e-mail. "Sorry about the short notice. You're going to have to be flexible."

Eric knew he was being considered for a promotion. He also knew that to do this right, he was going to be working all night. First he was angry and then a little panicked. But Eric knew an opportunity when it arose. And flexible? That was the story of his life.

His manager could never know from reviewing his resume, his grades, or his recommendations that Eric came equipped with a rare set of highly developed skills: flexibility, doggedness, and resiliency. These weren't skills he was directly taught; these were the lessons learned from poverty, from blatant discrimination, and from the more subtle hidden barriers he had overcome, which started early in his life.

At nine years old, Eric loved third grade. He loved the neat notebooks, the sharp pencils, and his teacher's clear, crisp directions. He even loved the free lunch—usually a hot dog, chips, and soda—that he and the other children from low-income families ate every day in the noisy cafeteria. Eric was a hand raiser, a volunteer. So when his teacher asked if anyone might be interested in participating in a three-person team for the county science fair, of course his hand shot up. So did three other hands—a group of friends from a better neighborhood, whose mothers were home with them after school. It's not that Eric's teacher didn't see his promise. He was a gifted kid, smart and motivated. But she didn't choose him. After all, who would take him to the library to do the research? Who would buy the expensive office supplies to spiff up his presentation? And even if he did participate, how was he going to get to the event? The entire prospect was daunting, his teacher reasoned, so why encourage a kid in a direction that was never going to be possible for him?

Although he was just nine, this wasn't Eric's first impediment on a path to a successful corporate career. Those barriers were actually erected before he was born and continued wave after wave, pushing him back throughout his childhood. Now in his thirties, with his polished speech, initiative, efficiency, and professionalism, his managers and colleagues would never imagine that each of those traits was a deliberately learned skill, carefully designed to overcome the struggles he had been through.

In corporate America today, managers can't possibly know the experiences that have shaped their employees in the most profound ways. Yet, by understanding the complex possibilities and by considering the challenges and advantages those might bring, managers can better motivate, encourage, inspire, and mentor the people working for them.

So far in this book, I've written about ways to reveal and eradicate hidden barriers and hidden biases in the workplace. To understand those issues fully, however, it's important that we explore the early sources of obstructions and the impacts they have in the workplace. Businesses with a genuine commitment to diversity will see that they have a vested interest in removing barriers and biases— not just once an employee has arrived at the job but at much earlier stages. Simply put, those early hindrances limit the number of potential diverse applicants who can ever reach an interview.

When do hidden barriers begin? Historians will tell you that they started generations ago. Epidemiologists say they begin before we're born. Economics, health care, and housing play key roles in separating the Haves from the Have-Nots. Once you're on the Have-Nots team, it's a tough scramble to get onto the playing field.

Low-income women receive less prenatal care and, therefore, have more birth complications. Those complications can lead to children with learning disabilities, attention deficit disorder, and other problems. Low-income housing in all parts of the United States is more likely to have air pollution, dust, and mold (not to mention violence, noise, and chaos), which lead to children with higher rates of asthma, as well as more traumatic childhoods.

School is another issue. It's well documented that public schools in lower-income, predominantly minority districts have fewer funds, poorer teachers, and less technology. Broken assessments, such as the SATs, reflect as much about a student's upbringing as they do about his or her ability. In a *Wall Street Journal* article, Princeton University President Shirley M. Tilghman attested to this: "The best predictor of SAT scores is family income. Affluent families can enrich their children's high-school experience, providing private schools where class sizes are much smaller, summer programs in Spain and so on."[1]

The college admission process is a smooth and clear system for children whose parents have maneuvered the system before them and those who have guidance counselors and support. But getting into college—from knowing where to apply, to paying fees, to writing application essays—can be an overwhelming obstacle course for a young man or woman tackling it alone. Even once they've made it in, stepped over that line, and joined the Ivy League, privileges such as unpaid internships and challenges like work study requirements create longer distances to the revolving doors of corporate headquarters.

THE EARLIEST BARRIERS: HOUSING, HEALTH CARE, AND INSTABILITY

Miguel's mother struggled to keep their apartment serene and comfortable, but after the death of her husband she struggled to make ends meet and buy enough food, let alone help her children with homework. When Miguel was eight, he and his mother moved into his aunt's one-bedroom apartment with his maternal grandparents and a string of his aunt's boyfriends. The house was chaotic, so Miguel learned to focus on homework despite the ever-present noise. On days when he needed extra focus, he studied at the library.

Years later, when a massive deadline loomed over the office and people were shouting across the room at each other, Miguel smiled benignly at a stressed-out colleague who moaned, "How are we supposed to work in here? It's chaos!"

Miguel could focus in any situation. College dorms? Crazy day at the office? Not a problem. He had learned to do his homework with a baby nephew pulling on his hair, where his "desk" was whatever corner of the floor that he could clear. Colleagues would later remark on his ability to tune out noise, gossip, and arguments, and Miguel would just shrug. Growing up poor had been miserable at times, but perhaps he'd benefited from some of his experiences.

U.S. Census Bureau data show that 17.6 percent of American children under age eighteen were living in poverty in 2005 (DeNavas-Walt et al. 2006) The United States also has the highest childhood poverty rate among the sixteen wealthy, industrialized countries that belong to the Organization for Economic Cooperation and Development, according to the Economic Policy Institute (Allegretto 2004). Poverty brings a torrent of problems to children, negatively impacting their health, education, emotional well-being, behavior, and their ability to attain success as adults in the job market.

Low-income children are more likely to be exposed to cigarette smoke, alcohol, and drugs prenatally, leading to potential health and learning problems. Their homes are more likely to be in polluted neighborhoods, triggering a host of medical conditions. They are less likely to receive vaccinations and other preventive care, making it more likely that they will become seriously ill. A number of recent studies concluded that children raised in low-income families are more likely to begin school with health problems, emotional problems, and limited language skills.[2] All of these issues interfere with learning.

EDUCATIONAL BARRIERS: DISPARITY IN THE SCHOOLS

Kristen was smart, driven, and, like her farming parents, extremely tenacious. During high school, she worked part-time at a bank, saving money for college. School was not a great place for Kristen. In seeking out a "better" public school, Kristen's parents enrolled her in school in a university town twenty miles away from the family farm by using a relative's home address as their own. At the "city" school, Kristen always felt like she stood out: her thrift-store or homemade clothes were plain, and children made fun of her rural drawl. Although she was intelligent and hardworking (earning A's in every class), Kristen's teachers rarely noticed her. Her classmates were the children of the town's professors, doctors, lawyers, and bankers. They received all of the attention and were encouraged by the teachers to meet the high expectations set for them in the classroom.

In repeated studies, educational researchers have shown that teachers' expectations are reflected in their students' performance and achievements. In one famous study (which ethicists would no longer allow to be repeated), teachers in South San Francisco were told, falsely, that a particular group of elementary school students was on the brink of a period of rapid intellectual growth. At the end of the year, those students who had been randomly selected were found to have gained more IQ points than the rest of their classmates (Rosenthal and Jacobson 1968).

Since then, dozens of studies have examined the issue and found that teachers form expectations for student behavior and achievement early in the school year and then behave differently toward different students.[3] Within months, this treatment affects student achievement. Students whose teachers don't expect a lot from them tend not to learn as much as students with similar socioeconomic backgrounds who are taught differently.

In some schools in underserved neighborhoods and communities, teacher expectations are so low that students who show even the minimal level of skills are given high grades that would be unwarranted if the students were attending a more affluent school with more rigorous coursework. This practice—a hybrid between grade inflation and social promotion—does an incredible disservice to students, because it misleads them into believing that they are far better prepared than they really are and that they possess the necessary skills to succeed at a university.

In addition to low teacher expectations, society's negative stereotypes can insidiously affect the performance of students from underrepresented groups. Claude Steele, internationally recognized social psychologist and Stanford University professor, studied the power of the "stereotype threat." Steele's basic premise is that a person's "social identity"—defined as group membership in categories such as age, gender, religion, and ethnicity—has significance when "rooted in concrete situations," such as a test environment.[4]

Steele has shown that when a person's social identity is attached to a negative stereotype, that person will tend to underperform in a manner consistent with the stereotype. For example, when African American students took a test after being told that white students typically outperform them on that test, the African Americans performed significantly worse than the average score for students from similar backgrounds. Steele attributes the underperformance to the students' anxiety that they would perform according to the negative stereotype. In other words, it's a self-fulfilling prophecy. The anxiety manifests itself in various ways, including distraction and increased body temperature, all of which diminish performance level. These are the types of unspoken, yet dangerously powerful, forces at work against people of color and women, which puts them at a disadvantage, even at so-called "fair" measures of performance.

At Kristen's high school, her teachers assumed that any students who didn't come from the town's professional families were destined to live and work in the agricultural economy outside the university town. Not Kristen. In addition to her part-time job at the bank, she volunteered ten hours per week with a health center, traveling in a county health department van with medical students, physicians' assistants, and doctors. They would stop in poor, rural towns that had no other source of medical care. Although the medical field per se didn't appeal to Kristen, listening to the patients' stories redoubled her commitment to her studies. Being poor was risky and depressing. Kristen wanted to make money—and plenty of it.

Kristen enrolled in all the advanced placement courses offered at her high school. She took the SAT at the suggestion of her bank manager, who also paid half of her test fee and gave her the test day off. Even though she passed on the option to have her test scored by hand for verification purposes (which can cost up to $100), her score was the highest in the state.

Kristen's grades and her stellar SAT scores brought her to the attention of college admissions officers. But when she went to her college interviews, Kristen repeatedly failed to impress the men she met. Her clothes were awkward. Her speech was simple and direct.

No one had taught her to use qualifiers, to be demure, or to use what researchers call "tentative speech" deemed appropriate for women, such as disclaimers (*I'm no expert, I suppose, I may be wrong but*), hedges (*kind of, you know, maybe*), and tag questions (*Isn't it? Don't you think? Right?*).

Social psychologists have documented that men, but not women, find direct female speakers to be less trustworthy and likable.[5] Similar research found that women with more confident communication styles involving such traits as rapid rates of speech, firm voice tone, few hesitations, upright posture, calm hand gestures, and frequent eye contact were perceived by male participants as threatening (Carli 1989).

These same communication patterns almost cost Kristen her full-ride academic scholarship to Harvard. A panel of male interviewers found her to be overly self-assured and entitled for a low-income farm girl. However, in the end, her high school transcripts, recommendations, and best-in-state SAT scores got her accepted to the university.

Another girl in Kristen's senior class also made it into the Ivy Leagues, though with considerably less effort. Her grades and test scores weren't as good as Kristen's, but her parents and her grandfather were alumni and generous donors, giving her an edge as both a legacy and development applicant. According to the *Economist,* legacy students are two to four times more likely to be admitted to the best American universities than their nonlegacy peers (Unnamed author 2004). These admissions are not based on any accomplishments but on accidents of birth. And in the United States, underrepresented students of color are generally less likely to have had parents who attended any college.

There are hidden barriers, indeed, for many people who are born into poor families, while those born into wealth and privilege enjoy many hidden advantages. From "Mozart in the Womb" to private, $75-an-hour reading tutors, children of privilege are better prepared for corporate success from the start. These advantages impact performance and perspective in the workplace and should be considered by managers when making hiring and performance-related decisions.

The Ivy League–bound girl in Kristen's senior class joined her parents at breakfast each morning with a copy of the *New York*

Times. Their houseguests included prominent professors and businesspeople. She joined her mother on work trips to stimulating conferences, she dined with her grandparents at white tablecloth restaurants, and she flew to Europe in the summer and skied at Lake Tahoe in the winter. She learned, almost by osmosis, how to hold a conversation about politics, what to pack for a journey abroad, and how to behave among important professionals. The graces and courtesies came naturally to her, bragged her parents. But these skills were learned traits.

Kristen, Eric, and Miguel had to compete for college admission with students who were born into families that knew about the importance of bolstering college applications *and* could afford to provide their children with advantages that would catch the eye of admissions officers. For example, a privileged girl in Kristen's senior class spent ten hours per week in the summer months working in the local university's oncology research laboratory with a friend of her parents. And other wealthy students enrolled in "college prep" summer programs, which can cost upward of $7,000, to travel to third-world countries, where they spent the bulk of their time traveling, but they also visited and volunteered at orphanages and clinics. Such tours are specifically designed to boost the "volunteer and service" component of college applications.

A report by the Pell Institute for the Study of Opportunity in Higher Education found large gaps in ranges of income among college students (O'Brien and Engle 2005). The news is both predictable and sad: most high-income teens go on to college, while most low-income teens don't. Those who do go to university tend to go to lower-ranked schools—frequently public, two-year community colleges. As any Ivy Leaguer can tell you, African American and Latino students are poorly represented at top universities.

Often what keeps such students out of the halls of the top schools is not academic performance but circumstance, life's matters-of-fact over which no one has control. The family into which you were born, your childhood neighborhood, and your parents' educational background are key determinants of your future: success or failure, open doors or dead ends, easy access or opportunities denied.

As a diversity trainer, I realized that these gaps in opportunity had a strong impact on the workplace as well. Thus, my work has vastly expanded to include training and support for diverse young adults facing unreasonable challenges. The idea is this: With the right support, they can reach beyond their difficult situations and become productive, contributing, and whole adults who bring their wealth of talents and skills to America's top businesses. These are astounding young people, who are determined to make it. Their resolve and courage are an inspiration. Consider the following story.

As a child, Leslie was shifted from one house to the next—from distant relatives, to friends, and then to a group home in Texas. At times, she was physically and sexually abused. Her mother, a stripper and occasional prostitute, ended up in prison.

When Leslie was fifteen years old, an aunt took guardianship; however, by then Leslie had serious behavior problems at school, had been admitted to a mental health facility for a brief stint, and had an array of tattoos that could not cover the scars of the physical and sexual abuse she had suffered as a child. Despite her tumultuous childhood, tough girl facade, and circumstances beyond most people's imagination, Leslie had one area with no deficiency: her resiliency and determination to succeed. This will never show up on a resume. But it will be evident when Leslie reaches the workplace, bringing a commitment, backbone, and certitude that can't be taught in any business school.

As a student in the Level Playing Field Institute's Summer Math and Science Honors (SMASH) Academy—a program designed to help high-achieving African American, Latino, and Native American students with an interest in science, technology, engineering, and mathematics—Leslie lives in a somewhat schizophrenic world. In one realm, she feels the pull of peer pressure, gang involvement, and the chaos of her family life and upbringing. But in the other, she has the support, encouragement, and high expectations of the SMASH environment.

Though full of promise, Leslie lacks direction, parental stability, a sufficient household income, and a well-financed school district—factors that really matter when it comes to the college admission process. Applications don't ask often enough about the life circumstances one has surmounted, which may actually be a more telling indicator of one's true character, personality, and ability to succeed in life. Rarely have admission essays asked students to write about how far they've come, what demons they've fought, and what twists of fate they've overcome to stay alive.

Indeed, when students take the gamble to disclose these factors, they risk further stereotyping or well-intentioned showcasing that borders on exploitation: "Oh, let's invite Leslie to our fund-raiser, put her story on our Web site, and have her recruit at all of the underresourced schools in the area." Her tragic experiences become her sole defining characteristic, ironically depriving her of opportunities to catch up—study halls, tutoring sessions, time in the library—while she's out on the road working as the poster child. I do expect Leslie to succeed, to make her way out of her difficult circumstances and enjoy an exciting and rewarding career. I do not expect her to reveal her traumas to anyone in the workplace, neither during job interviews nor to colleagues. Yet the signs will always be with her, in the challenges and strengths she's gained from her past.

DISMANTLING EDUCATIONAL BARRIERS

Considering the dramatic lives of many economically disadvantaged but highly gifted youth, it is little wonder (though a long time coming) that the actual role of race and class in the college admission process is drawing greater attention at the nation's top schools. As a result, the decades-old practice of early admission is under increased scrutiny and, in many cases, intense criticism. According to data collected by the National Association for College Admission Counseling (NACAC), 16 percent of U.S. four-year colleges and universities offer the option of "early decision" or "early action" to students (Hawkins and Lautz 2005).

This practice of students committing to a top college early in the admission game has been widely accepted, even to the point of incurring hefty penalty fees if a person reneges on the commitment. But lately, concern that these admission policies favor wealthier students is mounting, since financial aid packages are not available early in the admission season. Thus, cost wouldn't be a factor for a student who chooses to make a binding decision that may come with incentives such as early choice of housing. Nor would a cash penalty be of great concern, should that student receive an even better offer elsewhere. Meanwhile, equally qualified applicants from lower-income households would have to consider the financial aid packages first in their decisions, and these students aren't likely to be able to afford a withdrawal fee. Studies have shown that the odds of getting admitted to a top school via early decision or early action are better than getting into that same institution through the regular admission cycle.[6] Hidden bias begets hidden barriers.

This is another example of how bias masquerading as a perfectly acceptable admission policy can give those with privilege an unfair advantage. It's one of many factors that prove the playing field in higher education is not even close to being level, despite decades of attempts to make it so. No one intends to be malevolent; these are merely the unintended and unexamined consequences of policies that, at first glance, appear neutral. After all, how can a policy discriminate if it doesn't say anything about a demographic characteristic?

But some admission directors and university presidents are catching on. In a newspaper interview, Pete Caruso, chair of NACAC's Admission Practices Committee and associate director of undergraduate admission at Boston College, noted that the "super early decisions can also be unfair to students whose high school counselors don't or can't work in the summer to provide a student with the materials he or she would need to apply as early as their peers."[7]

In September 2006, Harvard ended its early admission policy, followed one week later by Princeton. No widespread "Harvard effect" resulted at other top U.S. schools, however. When contacted by *Inside Higher Ed,* officials at Columbia, Dartmouth, the University of Pennsylvania, and Yale all stated that they were "content with their current policies, which they say take into account the financial needs of lower-income students and enable them to create a diverse class" (Powers 2006).

With one unfair advantage under scrutiny, a host of other lingering admission practices that favor wealth over true merit, such as legacy admissions for children of alumni and rampant preferential treatment for children of big donors or celebrities, should be considered. These types of corrupt admission practices are documented in Daniel Golden's 2006 book, *The Price of Admission: How America's Ruling Class Buys Its Way into Elite Colleges—and Who Gets Left Outside the Gates.* In this exposé, the Pulitzer Prize–winning reporter for the *Wall Street Journal* lays bare with names and test scores how America's rich, famous, and politically powerful buy their children's acceptance into Ivy League schools, winning spots ahead of more deserving applicants.

In fact, the advantage for the rich often begins before an application is even submitted. Before the college applications hit the mailbox, parents with the financial means are pouring thousands of dollars into essay-writing coaches, entrance exam coaches, camps, expensive SAT prep courses, and tutors to prepare their children to compete for entry. With all the high-priced coaching for children of the rich, can their applications truly be viewed as equal to those of poorer students whose parents can't afford the costly prep work? Can the applications of two students be fairly evaluated when one received years of SAT prep and personalized coaching sessions and the other had no such luck?

One answer is for universities to require mandatory disclosure by students and parents of each and every form of purchased help. Parents could disclose and certify the level of college coaching their child received, including the amount of assistance provided by a high school; any private college counselors/coaches retained; the number of PSAT, SAT, and any other standardized test preparatory classes taken; the number of times the tests were actually taken; any assistance on essay writing; and activities pursued to bolster the student's record (for example, community service activities, trips, how unpaid internships were obtained, and so on).

Another solution, already at least partially in place at many universities, is to summarize characteristics of a student's high school to put an individual's achievements into context. For example, if two students from different schools have comparable high school transcripts and each took three advanced placement classes, it should matter that at one student's school this was the total number of AP courses offered, while in the other student's school, twenty-five AP classes were available. Similarly, if a student's SAT score was 610 in math, it's reasonable to consider whether that represents the 90th percentile or the 30th percentile among that student's classmates.

With a broader understanding of raw talent versus coached and coddled talent, admission committees can make better decisions. With a full understanding of how perks available to children of the well-to-do put children of lower socioeconomic groups at an unfair disadvantage, we can begin to bring an end to a system of reinforcing wealth and privilege and create a fairer admission process. In other words, we can support meaningful efforts to level the playing field and make our institutions of higher education more meritocratic.

And what does this mean for business? Recruiters touting a desire to hire a diverse staff frequently complain of a limited pool of people of color. The first step in fostering a diverse environment needs to come well before they are reviewing resumes. It is a role and responsibility of corporate leaders to press for hidden barriers to be removed early in their communities, in schools and elsewhere. Businesses will, in the end, reap the benefits for prompting changes in schools.

The link between educational success and career success is well documented and undisputed. In 2006, U.S. Secretary of Labor Elaine L. Chao stated that "Research over the past 10 years showed that the unemployment rate for high school dropouts is nearly twice as high as it is for those with high school degrees. And their unemployment is three times as high as those who graduate from college." Conversely, more education and training lead to higher earnings. Chao said, "In a 2002 study, the Census Bureau estimated that the average holder of a bachelor's degree earns twice the lifetime earnings of a high school dropout. Advanced degree holders earn more than three times as much."

This is particularly true for those with law degrees. But new research forces us to rethink what standardized tests like the LSAT really measure and whether they are, indeed, the best indicators of who will be successful. A multiyear study by two professors at the University of California at Berkeley (Hall 2005) showed that LSAT scores and GPAs do not predict actual success as a lawyer. In fact, their research shows that, at best, they predict law school performance—and the LSAT is only partly effective at that.

What's worse, a number of standardized tests are under fire due to the disparity in score results across racial lines. A 1999 report by the College Board studied the pervasiveness of score differences by racial/ethnic groups on high-stakes tests like the SAT, GMAT, and LSAT. In review after review and test after test, white students outperformed African American and Latino students, illustrating a gross inequity for minorities due to "inadequate academic preparation, poverty, and discrimination" (Camara and Schmidt 1999).

DIPLOMA JUSTICE: WHY JUDGING A CANDIDATE BY HIS OR HER SCHOOL CAN BE A MISTAKE

Harvard, Yale, Stanford, Princeton. Children of a certain income and education level grow up knowing about those schools, understanding the subtle rankings between a top-tier and a second-tier university. But this isn't obvious information, especially for disadvantaged students who rarely receive the important counseling to understand that the university they select when they're sixteen years old is going to affect their career opportunities and salary potential for the rest of their lives. It's more likely that other, stronger influences affect their decisions, such as family. I frequently encounter the following situations with students in the Level Playing Field Institute's education-related programs.

Jocelyn excels in calculus. A Mexican American and the oldest of five siblings aged four to twelve, she is quiet and diligent—a future STEM (science, technology, engineering, math) professional in a world that needs more scholars of color. But Jocelyn is also extremely loyal to her family and protective of her siblings. In fact, she feels a responsibility to them more akin to a mother than a sister. So while Jocelyn has the ability and potential to attend a top-tier, private university, she is considering a less prestigious college, because it is a bus ride away from her home and she will be able to look after her siblings.

The sense of family connectedness and responsibility to siblings is particularly strong in some cultures, especially when a first-generation college student encounters feelings of resentment in the family, emanating from a lack of understanding of the importance of higher education. Many families see the time spent studying as selfish when the family needs help putting food on the table or looking after the elderly or very young. When daily needs remain unmet, the promise of a more comfortable future seems remote. Companies looking only at top-tier university students may miss out on dauntless and resolute math whizzes, like Jocelyn, who are as full of character, loyalty, and promise as they are of quadratic equations.

I recently met with recruiters at an international management consulting firm. They were reconsidering their policy to look at resumes only from students in the top 10 percent of their class at the world's top business schools. In the past, they had assumed that any worthwhile student would seek out the best school to which he or she could be admitted. Students would, indeed, choose the most prestigious school, regardless of other factors; therefore, it was highly efficient to recruit only the top graduates of the top schools. In other words, the recruiters would let the college admission process do the initial candidate selection for them.

But one incident made them reevaluate this policy. These recruiters told me that on the recommendation of a vice president who knew the parents of one rejected African American applicant, they made an exception and decided to interview him, even though he graduated from a second-tier business school. During their interview, the recruiters learned that the applicant had been accepted into the top business school in the country but had opted to attend a less prestigious university to be closer to his father, who was dying of cancer. The firm hired him, impressed with his character. More important, as this rising star more than proved his worth, the firm began rewriting its recruiting policy.

A dean of one of the nation's top law schools, who is committed to boosting diversity on his campus, came to me with a slightly different dilemma. One of the school's applicants, a promising African American woman, had turned down her partial scholarship to accept a full scholarship at a far less prestigious, rural law school. "It happens all the time," the dean said. "These kids have no idea that a degree from our school all but guarantees better summer internships, which lead to better job offers, better starting salaries, and a hiring bonus that would probably pay back any loans they needed to cover their tuition here."

BARRIERS TO SUCCESS IN UNIVERSITY

Eric was lucky. His high school counselor saw his promise, walked him through college applications, and helped him get into Princeton University with a generous financial aid package. But after he started school, Eric began to wonder if he had made the right decision.

The hardest part about attending a high-status school for Eric was having people assume he would act a certain way because of his race. In class, every time something came up about African

Americans, professors would turn to him and ask, "What do you think, Eric?" Frequently he didn't know what to say. Heads would turn when he stepped into the business school library. His dorm mates pestered him to play basketball, a game he never learned to play well. Eric joined the gospel choir. He wasn't a particularly talented singer and he didn't care much for church, but the choir, made up of mostly African American students, made him comfortable.

One day the College Conservatives held an "Affirmative Action Bake Sale," offering cookies at $1 for white males, 50 cents for white females, and 25 cents for students of color. Eric, furious, stopped to watch and considered buying a few of the reduced-price cookies and tossing them at the smug salesmen. But then he saw the dean of his department walking by, a man he was hoping would write him a recommendation for business school. Eric greeted the dean, laughed at his joke about the bake sale, and slowly walked away with his hands in his pockets. Several years later, he received that recommendation and sent it along with his application to Stanford Graduate School of Business. His application included the subtly coded language used in both academic and corporate recruiting to indicate that a candidate is a minority: Association of African American Students, gospel choir, participation in the Minority Mentoring Program.

At Stanford, Eric explained that his goal was to work for a major, cutting-edge corporation, probably in marketing or business development. His advisers repeatedly tried to steer him into ethics, organizational development, and non-profit management courses. In class role plays, he was usually assigned the part of the union representative or office whistle-blower. Eric was the only black person among the one hundred students in his corporate entrepreneurship course. "At least I won't disappear in here," he thought to himself as he settled into his seat. But the professor rarely caught his eye and never called on him. Eric mused as to whether it was worse to be singled out for race-based questions or to be ignored on all topics. Was he ever going to be just another guy in class, an individual?

Starting his summer internship, Eric was assigned to shadow a managing director at a world-class consulting firm whose expertise was strategic marketing. Eric wore a suit—the same one his grandmother had bought him for his college graduation, but that wasn't good enough. Twice on his first day, office security asked him to show his company ID. Eric's pay on this internship was double his mother's annual income, a fact that evoked feelings of both pride and confusion. He had come far from his college summer internship years ago, which paid $10 an hour, decent enough for an intern. But Eric was barely getting by on $5 of that hourly pay, giving the rest to his younger brother, also a promising student, who needed to take a summer school course that was a prerequisite for attending an outstanding university. The course wasn't offered at their high school. If Eric's younger brother didn't take this course, he would be barred from applying to one of the best universities in the country.

Eric learned two important lessons during that internship: first, more than anything, this was the work he wanted to do. The work was stimulating, challenging, and exciting, and he was good at it. Second, it is absolutely necessary to find his community, his support group, a place where he didn't feel like an outsider and where he didn't have to check his identity at the door. Eric often went out for drinks with two fellow interns: a curly-headed man who was originally from the Philippines and an African American woman who was also the first in her family to graduate from college, let alone have aspirations of attending business school. They, too, had been asked to show their company IDs multiple times during their internships, and together they prepared polite comebacks and laughed over the snappy, sharp words they wished they could use instead.

Years later, when Eric was several years into a promising career, he lost his temper one afternoon on his way to a meeting when a client's security officer put him through a rigorous screening, requiring two IDs and his business card, before allowing him into the bank of elevators. Later, Eric's manager asked him why he lost his cool and suggested that he would have appeared more professional to laugh off the encounter. Perhaps a more tuned-in manager who was aware of Eric's background would have been more supportive or understanding. Eric shook his head. He couldn't explain that he still clung to the hope that someday he would be seen as an equal in the business world, not as an outsider.

BARRIERS TO GETTING THAT FIRST JOB: TRACKING AND PRIVILEGE

Eric had opted to mention his race, albeit subtly, when applying to college and business school. But he had never told his academic advisers, neither on paper nor verbally, that he was gay. When he was being recruited by some of the nation's top firms, he wondered if it wouldn't benefit him to mention his sexual orientation or at least scope out a firm's gay-friendly reputation (or lack thereof) before offering a resume. In the end, he decided that although his race might work against him, it was something he certainly couldn't hide. As for being gay, he stayed in the closet.

Around this time, Miguel was also applying for his first professional job. He had made it from the chaos of his aunt's apartment in inner-city New York, through a lousy public high school, into a community college, and then he was plucked to attend a private, prominent university as a junior transfer. Following his undergraduate degree, he taught public school in a neighborhood similar to one in which he had grown up, as part of a special program that didn't require him to earn teaching credentials. After a few years of this exhausting and rewarding work, he attended one of the nation's top business schools, hoping to give back to his community in a different way. Now he was golden, right? He had excellent grades, a prestigious MBA from Wharton, key recommendations, and an obvious drive to succeed.

Still, Miguel didn't get hired by his top-choice firm. The recruiter was impressed, flew him across the country for his interview, and suggested a hiring bonus might be available. But when the choice came down to Miguel and a young, white professional graduate from an equally prestigious school, Miguel lost out. Why? He just didn't seem to be the "right fit."

During a diversity training seminar at a bulge bracket investment bank, I gave two resumes to the participants (all were senior managing directors from around the world). With the exception of the firm's chief diversity officer, all were men—and all were members of the majority racial, ethnic, and cultural group in the country in which they lived and worked. The first resume that I distributed was from an orphan, whose biological mother was a Filipina and father was African American. At ten months, he had been adopted by a Japanese American woman who was then sixty-five. Sometimes he went hungry, and all of his clothes and the furnishings in his room were hand-me-downs. Yet he felt fortunate to have love, a roof over his head, and running water. He spent summers building outhouses in Mexico with his church group for those he considered less fortunate. He made it into a top public university and was on financial aid. He paid for business school with loans.

The second resume was from a white, privileged young man who attended a top independent high school, an Ivy League university, and the same business school attended by the African American/Filipino man. As the son of a CEO, the Caucasian student had summer jobs at companies where his father was an investor—but only for part of the summer so that he could spend several weeks traveling or at the family's island summer home. Despite the enormous chasm in their circumstances growing up, the two young men basically had the same business school education and similar grades. Their standardized test scores were quite different, however, as were their letters of recommendation. These reflected their divergent circumstances.

The managing directors at the investment bank prided themselves on being meritocratic, and they also knew that this exercise was part of a mandatory diversity training session. Nonetheless, they conceded that they would choose the wealthy, white young man for reasons of fit. He would be able to "hit the ground running." He would know how to dine with business tycoons, speak the language, and share stories of prep school and summers on Martha's Vineyard. It's not his race, they explained; it's just that they felt more comfortable with him, and he seemed more likely to succeed in the position.

This is a mirror meritocracy, not a real one. If we reward privileged experience, however unfairly or accidentally conferred, the gap can only widen. Any company aspiring to hire the best talent would hire for potential, not unearned opportunities. The usual choice may be a comfortable choice, an easy choice, if you don't mind the status quo. But it's no way to shape a company that values innovative approaches and can learn from diverse input. (For readers interested in how subjective our evaluations of resumes really are, Appendix A provides an interesting exercise.)

CONCLUSION

The young man whose resume was selected by the managing directors in my training session is in a river of success that will carry him along until he makes an effort to come ashore. In contrast, Eric, Miguel, and Kristen made repeated attempts at trying to get into the river and stay in, without being fished out or washed ashore. Their challenges began before they were born and continued as they pushed for successful careers. One might argue that this struggle made them better, more committed, harder workers—and this could be true. But more often than not, the struggle beats them down, adding to a growing, underutilized resource of untapped potential. At the very moment that the United States and global economies need all of the talent they can find, some companies are driving it out the door.

There is an alternative. Most corporations today say that they are committed to building a genuine, multicultural, and diverse workforce. Their customers demand it, global pressures require it, and as I've shown throughout the book, the costs of hidden barriers and bias are prohibitive. By understanding and working to address the early sources of hidden barriers and bias, by working with their communities and schools, and by understanding that many skills and challenges will never show up in a resume, today's business leaders can stimulate bona fide change.

CHAPTER TEN

TOWARD A NEW FRAMEWORK

Affirmative action programs in workplaces and universities have become synonymous with unfair advantage, yet no one blinks when top student athletes, legacy applicants, or the children of big donors receive an extra advantage. How did "affirmative action hire" become synonymous with "unqualified"? Why is "diversity" now a dirty word?

In the mid-1980s, while training senior managers of top-tier corporations, investment banks, and law firms, I used a case study to focus on gender issues. Jackie, the name given to the disguised character, was the only woman to join a joint venture team. Her first day on the job, she discovered the following greeting on a note stuck to her computer screen: "WELCOME TO THE AFFIRMA-TIVE ACTION HIRE." Jackie, in real life and in the case, was a Caucasian woman.

Across continents, I have asked global business leaders to inter-pret this note. Typically, the group would be about two dozen men of the predominant race and perhaps one white woman in the American groups. In the mid-1980s, the groups would say an unsigned message to an "affirmative action hire" was neutral. Noth-ing offensive here, just a simple greeting. A few would suggest that it carried a genuine welcome, perhaps from a secretary in the area who was lonely for female company; or it could be from a team member who welcomed a different point of view but didn't want to lose face by signing it. Almost no one was willing to proclaim it as an unadulterated negative view, unless it was accompanied by other evidence.

Today, a similar case study put to a group of banking, law firm, or consulting firm partners gets a very different response. The current case has a client stating that the deal or project is too important and complex to be staffed with any "affirmative action hires." When today's training participants are asked the same questions as their predecessors, the unanimous vote is that the expression "affirmative action hire" is negative and refers to people of color who aren't actually qualified to occupy their positions. And these are supposedly the younger, "hipper," new leaders of the post–civil rights era.

In the United States, a profound disconnect exists between aspirations of meritocracy and the mistaken notion that we have already achieved the goal. We declare our beliefs that everyone should be rewarded based on his or her abilities and achievements, not because of accidents of birth. But in our zeal to see and reward individual accomplishment, we are often oblivious to the systemic and unfair advantages enjoyed by many. Dozens of times, a venture capitalist, CEO, or director of a Fortune 1000 company has said to me, "I don't care if the person is green or purple, has three eyes and six legs. I'll hire the best and brightest candidate who can get the job done." This is often evidenced by a candidate possessing the best resume or the best business plan or having the best reputation. Yet the same high-level professionals conveniently forget that neither resumes, nor business plans, nor reputations randomly come to their attention; they're sent by someone they know, someone they trust, and someone who has access. Access and connections are critical to success in big business, and millions of potential stars, driven and intelligent workers, don't have them.

Numerous studies, some of which were detailed in Chapter Five, have been conducted confirming that we all have hidden biases. Whether the studies are conducted with hiring managers, academic journal reviewers, or any number of other populations, the results show us again and again that in our quest for objective criteria and in our self-confidence that we've transcended prejudice, we are merely deluding ourselves. In light of such findings, how can we claim that we hire only the best candidates? What do we actually mean when we say "best" or "most qualified"?

Appendix A contains a deconstruction of two resumes, challenging us to think about how to weigh experiences derived from accidents of birth. Do we continue to reward the child of privilege who builds a resume on family connections? Do we continue to punish the child of adversity who can't get to the study group because he or she spends three hours a day on public transportation to and from minimum-wage jobs? Or do we discount the privileged person for his or her ease of accessibility and augment the less fortunate person for his or her Herculean efforts and tenacity?

Unfortunately, self-delusion, in addition to some blatant racism, also plays a large role in recent efforts to kill affirmative action. Consider California's Proposition 209, which states, "The state shall not discriminate against, or grant preferential treatment to, any individual or group on the basis of race, sex, color, ethnicity, or national origin in the operation of public employment, public education, or public contracting" (California Secretary of State 1996). That and its more recent clone in Michigan play on both our hope for fairness and our deeply embedded, but increasingly subtle, racism.

Our genuine desire is that each person get a fair chance—based on his or her abilities and accomplishments—of succeeding or failing, whether that's scoring high on a standardized test, being admitted to a selective college, or being granted an entry-level position at a well-regarded, growing company. However, we continue to ignore the totality of life experiences that can put one person on the success path while leaving another unable to traverse the hostile terrain and secret passageways leading to this path. We all want a race-blind society, but refusing to collect the evidence of opportunities and treatment by race (or collecting and then hiding the data) simply isn't working.

DIVERSITY TRAINING: PART OF THE PROBLEM OR PART OF THE SOLUTION?

Diversity training with a committed management team, a trainer who goes well beyond the downloadable teaching kit, and the appropriate time and space to delve deeply into the issues can be effective. Sadly, one or more of these necessary components is usually missing from such training.

Tell your employees that they are required to attend diversity training and they'll think they're being punished. At its conclusion, "high praise" equates to "That wasn't as bad as I thought" or "I actually learned something."

On the way into the session (for those who couldn't come up with an excuse to avoid attending), one senior manager will invariably turn to a white woman or, more likely, to a person of color and say something like, "If you'd stop complaining, we wouldn't have to waste our time going to these sessions." It never occurs to him that if he stopped blurting out stereotypes and insensitive jokes, no one would complain.

And what corporate trainer hasn't heard an arriving attendee say, "Hey, is this where we learn to harass?" considering this to be a witty, original remark? It's difficult to imagine that this same person would walk into a compliance course loudly inquiring, "Hey, is this where we learn to embezzle?"

A sad example of the lack of progress on this front is California's new law that mandates training on sexual harassment to every workplace in the state with fifty or more employees. Folklore has it that the state legislator sponsoring the bill wanted to get back at Governor Arnold Schwarzenegger, for whom allegations of unwelcome sexual attention emerged late in his first bid for governor. But the legislation—be it well intentioned or mean spirited or both—has probably been most effective at polarizing groups and lining the coffers of those who come up with unrealistic, insultingly simple, do this/don't do that training programs. Harassment or diversity training in a vacuum, in an off-the-shelf, check-the-box context ("you can download a curriculum set from the Internet or buy the package at any major bookstore") is counterproductive. Such laws represent empty solutions.

One look at the demographics of California's workplaces would send a strong signal that focusing on sexual harassment alone, while ignoring all the complexities and nuances of working side by side with a burgeoning population from dozens of Latin American and Asian countries, is seriously misguided. According to the U.S. Census Bureau and Department of Commerce, more than 90 percent of the country's population growth between 1995 and 2050 will come from racial minorities. And California leads the pack in terms of overall population growth and the size of its Asian and Hispanic populations.[1]

Pricey Excuses: A Top Moneymaker Is a Top Harasser

The degree to which business is measured by its positive or negative social impact is currently in flux. Our renewed attention to global climate change illustrates the shift: Some businesses are now being measured based on their environmental impact, with a last resort of buying carbon offsets to balance their actions. Corporate fraud scandals have also prompted some to judge a company by its financial and investment ethics. But what would we see if companies were ranked as to fairness and ability to attract, retain, and motivate a diverse workforce?

If we develop rigorous metrics for evaluating a company's true commitment, mandating two-hour training sessions won't be necessary; every business will weave measuring and mitigating hidden bias and hidden barriers into the fabric of its operations. It's crucial to note that this will happen in conjunction with a company's bottom line—annual revenues and quarterly reports. If the equity analysts dinged a company's rating because its turnover costs were eating up too much of the bottom line, equality and fair workplaces for most would become a reality.

I have been invited on countless occasions to meet with members of the board of directors, the CEO, or the executive committee of a major corporation, investment bank, hedge fund, law firm, or other professional services firm about an allegation of bias, harassment, or discrimination against someone viewed as a star performer. Three responses are predictable: The accuser(s) is (are) doubted or discredited, the alleged behavior is minimized, and the accused's contribution to the bottom line is emphasized. What then ensues is a discussion about how to buy off the victim to avoid potential lawsuits. Indeed, I have encountered more than one situation in which a chronic bigot or sexual harasser is supported by senior management with this logic: "I can either fire a rainmaker who brings in millions every year, or I can settle this lawsuit for $250,000. What do you think I'm going to do?" Even if the ethics of the argument were reasonable, the arithmetic isn't. The repetitive costs of workplace bigotry and harassment are far higher than the price tag of a single lawsuit.

Beyond the math, can anyone imagine the same discussion about an embezzler or an inside trader? Why isn't being a harasser or a bigot considered just as tragic a character flaw and, therefore, a business liability? Why do otherwise brilliant businesspeople add up the ledger in such a simplistic way—without considering the cost of demoralizing the workforce or the reputational risk of deterring any top talent who has a choice of employer? The answers are not particularly complex. Fear of litigation, fear of upsetting a somewhat productive workforce, and fear of angering other managers are involved. Greed drives the large and immediate return from a moneymaker. And ignorance prevails with a general lack of understanding of the true costs of bias. Yet, as stressed throughout this book, the real costs are steep and obvious. If the word on the street, on the Web, or in the headlines is that a particular company tolerates inappropriate conduct from those who bring in enough revenue, a talented potential employee who wants to win in a fair system will likely choose to work elsewhere.

One of the most bizarre tales in my career started when I was contacted by the lawyer for a venture capital–backed startup. The founder, Brad, was a brilliant engineer who had a penchant for violent pornography. It seems that this man sent an e-mail to thirty-one people in the company, most of whom had been with him since the company's early days. The e-mail was a video link to "snuff" pornography with no explanation of the content; recipients opened it unaware and were shocked by what they saw. All agreed that it was "way over the top." It wasn't long before everyone in the company at least knew about this e-mail if they hadn't actually seen it. Several dozen people outside the firm had received a forwarded copy, mostly with commentary about how disgusting it was. For his part, Brad was unabashed and defensive.

The head of HR (a woman) and the chief operating officer (a man) decided to call the law firm that handled their company's intellectual property issues, term sheets, and contracts. Without any depth in employment law, the firm nonetheless considered itself a "full-service" firm for startups. The advice of the junior associate assigned to employment issues was to establish a sexual harassment policy immediately (the firm didn't have one, despite the fact that it was mandated by law in that state). In addition, he said Brad must be suspended, pending counseling, and the whole firm had to go through sexual harassment training. Unquestioningly, the COO and head of HR began implementing this strategy.

First, the pair authorized the law firm to draft a policy. The firm provided the state's boilerplate policy, which was available free of charge from the state regulatory agency's Web site, with no customization, and the law firm charged its usual fees.

Second, the following e-mail was sent to me:

> Dear Dr. Klein: You were referred to us by an attorney at [*startup support law firm*]. We are in need of your professional counseling services regarding sexual harrassment [sic] for an employee of ours. Please give me a call at your earliest convenience to make arrangements. The employee is currently suspended from work pending this counseling. Thanks.

After receiving this e-mail, my office responded by saying that we needed to understand the context and the steps being taken. We could, indeed, provide a counselor, but we recommended against the overall approach dictated by the lawyers. To us, this looked like an overreaction that might set Brad up as a martyr. The lawyers wanted the appearance of action—a rigid policy, mandatory reporting and investigation (that didn't fit the culture), a suspension with pay, and time out of the office for a very brief counseling session (that had no substance, since Brad maintained that he hadn't done anything wrong). My view was shaped by the COO's report that Brad did not believe his actions were inappropriate. In fact, Brad became hostile, saying that this was an indication of what was wrong with the company overall—it had lost its startup, freewheeling spirit and was becoming a corporate bureaucracy. He also said that because the thirty-one employees had not told him they did not want to be on his e-mail distribution list, they had, therefore, implicitly consented to receive whatever he might send. They were free to view it or ignore it, and they could delete it if they didn't like it.

Crises can become opportunities. I suggested that employees be interviewed regarding the impact on the work environment and their confidence in the company's leadership in the wake of the founder sending out violent pornography. This was the perfect time to determine overall what was working about the company culture and what wasn't. Was the company ruled by fear and threats that would eventually tear it apart? If the founder had no regard for others' boundaries, was this an early indicator of his ethical compass? "Snuff" pornography is illegal—so would his next action be financial boundary manipulation or other illegalities? What were the observations and concerns of employees? Did they think that they had any access to the board to discuss issues? In the end, the answers lay once again in fear, greed, and ignorance. This company was a swiftly climbing risk taker and moneymaker. Anything that could get in the way of that was considered counterproductive and to be avoided. The COO concluded that my advice, though it made sense, was too time-consuming to implement.

Instead, the COO decided to send Brad to my office for counseling that very afternoon. "Without Brad in the office tomorrow, the company would tank," he said. In addition, he said my fee was too high. It's clear he viewed my fee as an unfortunate, extra expense, while the fee charged by his lawyer for lifting a model policy, verbatim, from a state Web site was an accepted cost of doing business. This was a classic risk management approach: the COO was going through the motions with no regard for the deeper issues. Being proactive and working to prevent problems before they explode would have identified these dynamics, allowing the company to avoid persistent, costly, and time-consuming problems.

Despite the era of dotcom boom, substantial funding from prominent venture capital firms, and a product designed to solve real problems, this startup never achieved its potential. After a couple of years of lagging morale and confused product strategy, a new CEO and management team of industry veterans were brought in to turn the ship around.

Figure 10.1 depicts another example of a "reply all" e-mail wreaking havoc—although this e-mail content is merely offensive, not potentially criminal in nature. Two separate approaches to the situation lead to significantly different outcomes.

How did key issues impacting morale and productivity end up labeled as "diversity management" and get relegated to the legal department as a risk to contend with instead of a strategic advantage (as the platitudes on company Web sites proclaim)? Why do employees and clients/customers tolerate this dishonesty? There is a better way.

FIGURE 10.1 INAPPROPRIATE REPLY-ALL E-MAIL

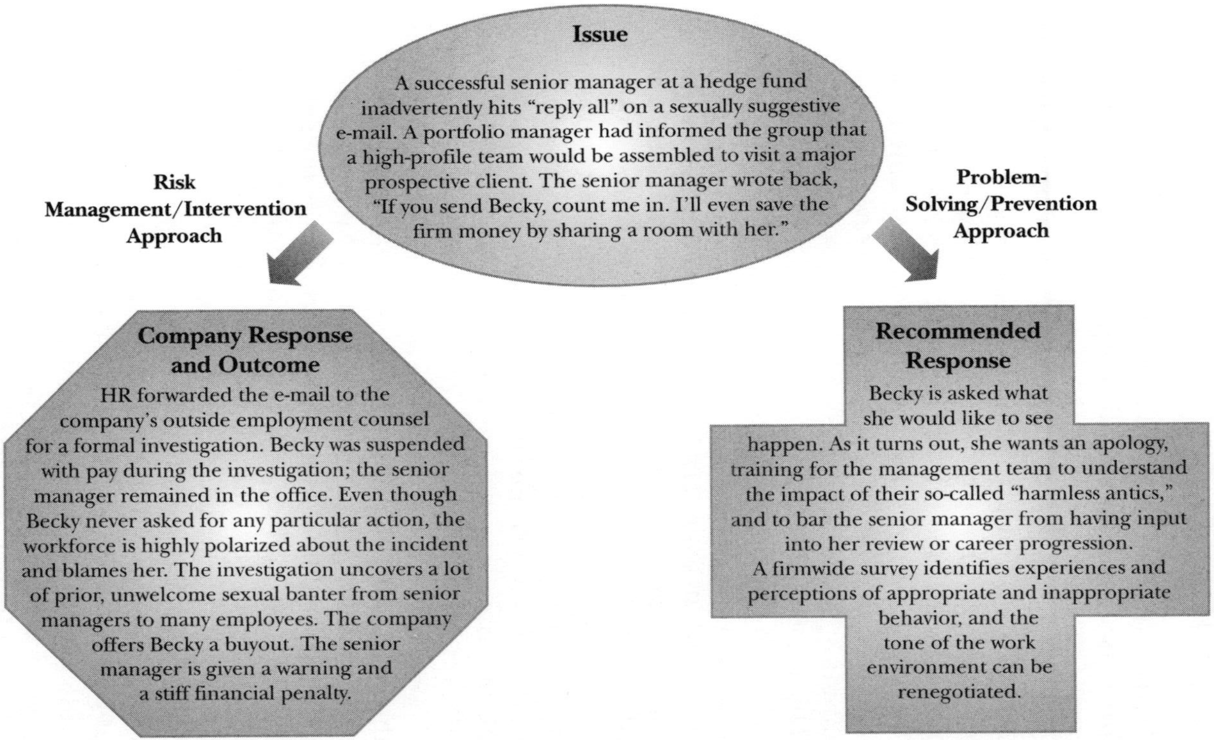

Issue

A successful senior manager at a hedge fund inadvertently hits "reply all" on a sexually suggestive e-mail. A portfolio manager had informed the group that a high-profile team would be assembled to visit a major prospective client. The senior manager wrote back, "If you send Becky, count me in. I'll even save the firm money by sharing a room with her."

Risk Management/Intervention Approach

Company Response and Outcome

HR forwarded the e-mail to the company's outside employment counsel for a formal investigation. Becky was suspended with pay during the investigation; the senior manager remained in the office. Even though Becky never asked for any particular action, the workforce is highly polarized about the incident and blames her. The investigation uncovers a lot of prior, unwelcome sexual banter from senior managers to many employees. The company offers Becky a buyout. The senior manager is given a warning and a stiff financial penalty.

Problem-Solving/Prevention Approach

Recommended Response

Becky is asked what she would like to see happen. As it turns out, she wants an apology, training for the management team to understand the impact of their so-called "harmless antics," and to bar the senior manager from having input into her review or career progression.

A firmwide survey identifies experiences and perceptions of appropriate and inappropriate behavior, and the tone of the work environment can be renegotiated.

Why Bias and Barriers Have Been Hidden

During the dotcom boom at the turn of this century, I asked the partners at a prominent Silicon Valley venture capital firm whether any of the startup companies in which they were major investors and board members had ever faced a discrimination lawsuit. One hundred percent of the Caucasian male hands shot up (the only demographic in the room). I then asked whether any of the situations giving rise to the charges had made their way to discussion at the weekly partners' meeting. All hands remained down, fiddling with their BlackBerries. Why was this the case? It's the cost of doing business. It's not a fixable situation. It descends like the weather. This is especially striking coming from a group of men who considered themselves to be powerful change makers and masters of their universe.

A strikingly similar conversation took place in the same time frame at a gathering of liberal environmental activists and funders. Although this group had gender parity in attendance, they were lacking in racial diversity. Their multiday strategy meeting was devoid of any discussion of the organizations they ran and/or funded. Their obliviousness to the quality of worklife in these workplaces, whose employees were expected to carry out their noble mission, rivaled that of the venture capitalists.

When the conversation at a break turned to my concern about the lack of diversity at the meeting at which agendas were being defined, I began to hear about their discrimination lawsuits. In an eerie echo of the venture capital partnership, the members of this group—responsible for dozens of non-profits—had all been sued for harassment or discrimination. No one considered the issue worthy of formal agenda time. Though the "tree huggers" and "vulture capitalists" (as they disparagingly refer to each other) could have responded in unison to these shared concerns, this was not the case. Instead, when the lawsuits emerged, each of them had called their outside employment lawyers—partners at big firms, whose jobs were to defend the charges. No one saw the opportunity (let alone a wake-up call) to examine and improve their respective work environments or how they were impacting employees' perceptions and experiences, thus undermining the activists' and funders' ability to achieve the goals of their different enterprises.

A few years earlier, I had been called to advise on the case of a CEO at an international firm who had what is commonly known as a "zipper problem." (Sadly, divulging this much information still affords ample anonymity, as this describes a soberingly large subgroup.) Talk in the room between the outside directors and the outside lawyers turned to other potential harassment and discrimination problems on the horizon. I asked them to imagine that they had just been notified of a lawsuit filed with the EEOC naming a senior manager in the company and then to write down the name of the person they most suspected of appearing in the agency's notice. Each person dutifully, and without hesitation, scribbled a name, folded up his or her paper, and handed it over. On each slip of paper, one of two names was written—one garnering more than three-fourths of the write-ins. I read the name and asked, "Why is he still here and charged with the responsibility for tens of thousands of employees and billions of dollars of revenue?" There was no response.

Companies need to add worklife to their business plans. This point is not lost on the most successful companies in this country. Flexible hours, telecommuting, workplace support, superb benefits, social responsibility to communities, and the less tangible day-to-day commitment to positive and respectful treatment are hallmarks of new approaches. Employee enthusiasm is soaring in response to simple steps that let all workers know they are valued.

THE NEW LEDGER

C-level executives have been known to spend millions of dollars to change a logo because they care so much about the reputation of their products and services. But these same executives fail to see the damage that occurs when their actions and inactions demotivate their employees.

The contrast between the approaches of two top-tier, global professional services firms is telling. One spends millions of dollars each year sponsoring diversity fairs, conferences, research, and in-house training. It seeks spots on panels at national and international meetings, touting its commitment to diversity. It aggressively buys advertising and includes, as part of a senior manager's targets for the year, the attainment of a top spot on one of the many magazines' lists of best companies for women, racial minorities, working mothers, and/or gays and lesbians. Standing before the new trainees, all graduates of top schools, senior managers and outside consultants extol the firm's values and commitment to diversity. Invariably, a brash trainee asks (after the senior managers leave the room), "Yeah, but if the firm cares so much, why is *Mr. X* still here?"

Mr. X was an infamous "screamer," capable of transforming the toughest, most arrogant young star to quivering jelly. *Mr. X*, of course, was also Prince Charming with clients and business leaders. He was a rainmaker. Every time his inappropriate behavior was tolerated, senior management danced around the answers to new associates' questions about their seeming hypocrisy and fueled cynicism and distrust within the ranks. On multiple occasions while conducting diversity/sensitivity training at the firm, I've heard some variant of this statement: "I wanted to believe they took this training seriously, but I know it's just BS. They're only covering their backside to try to avoid being sued."

The second firm differs in appearance and substance. It doesn't seek the limelight, nor is it mentioned on "Best of . . ." or diversity lists. The firm has a genuine commitment from management to model and enforce a bias- and barrier-free workplace. The approach has many prongs. New associates are asked whether they see a gap between what the firm espouses upon hiring and their experiences in their first year. One hundred percent of new employees believe that the firm is honest about its expectations that employees put work first in their lives, that they not accept a job if they want a balanced life, and that long hours and brutal demands are the norm. But employees can also count on opportunities for front-row seats at some of the most interesting deals and innovations unfolding in global business.

Maybe this is not our ideal world, but treating employees as grown-ups and letting them make their own informed choices is far healthier than subjecting them to an overdose of spin. The firm also has an informal complaint channel, whereby anyone can go for advice and a sanity-check about experiences they find uncomfortable. In other firms, a formal complaint system is the only option, and associates who use it get labeled as "weak" and are, thereby, written off. As discussed in Chapter Six, these formal complaint channels often do more harm than good.

"Employee engagement" is a popular altar at which millions of dollars, euros, and yen are being burned. Just as with branding, senior management may be missing the obvious: the larger the gap between what is stated and what is practiced, the shorter the path to employee cynicism and disengagement. Here are some other intriguing gaps:

- Stated: Our employees are our most valuable asset.
  Practiced: Our offer letters to new hires tell them that they can be fired at any time, for any reason or no reason.
- Stated: Our most important assets walk in the door every morning and out the door every night.
  Practiced: We outsource as many jobs as we can.
- Stated: We strive to be the employer of choice.
  Practiced: Our general counsel won't let us use the word "fairness" in any of our HR or diversity documents.
- Stated: Diversity is part of our strategic business advantage.
  Practiced: Each year the senior women draw straws, and the loser goes to the Catalyst awards dinner. Each year we buy a table at Jesse Jackson's Rainbow PUSH event and find some low-level minority employee to attend, giving the remaining seats to non-profit community groups.

DISCRIMINATION LAWS' DOUBLE-EDGED SWORD

The Civil Rights Act of 1964 was a landmark law. It was necessary to help curtail blatant racial discrimination in the United States. However, after more than forty years, it is not the right tool to address bias today.

The legal framework has had several unintended, counterproductive consequences: Companies now fear being sued for discrimination, so they are reluctant to do the analytics to detect and track bias and barriers that they routinely do for any other strategic business issue—employee surveys, assessments of bias in managers, and linking these data to measures of profitability and productivity. Companies do not value or work to improve what they don't measure.

Ironically, discrimination law might actually be the worst obstacle to true diversity:

- "Fear of discrimination lawsuits" is the reason cited most often by senior managers for not determining what they need to know about their employees' quality of worklife: "We can't survey our employees on their experiences and perceptions of inappropriate conduct—it will be Exhibit A in the lawsuit against us."

- Although scores of companies conduct diversity training (either in-house or through outside consultants) and truly want to know whether it is effective, collecting pre- and post-training data on managers' biases is "out of the question," again primarily out of concern for litigation.

- Many managers divide the world into "protected classes" and "nonprotected classes" (both an incorrect reading of the law and a self-destructive business practice) and then walk on eggshells with the former. A room full of white male managers is told that they can't fire a senior manager of color or a white woman without having ample documentation and many levels of review. However, they can fire a white male under forty for no reason at any time. So whom would you hire?

- In the United States, if men and women are harassed equally, it's not unlawful. Although this is not used often as a defense, it was the opinion of the courts in at least one case.[2] It points out the unintended consequences of trying to force-fit objectionable behavior (in this case, sexual harassment) into a preexisting mold (discrimination law).

- Nearly thirty years later, we have a new example of the limits of force-fitting an issue of workplace fairness into a discrimination mold: the Equal Employment Opportunity Commission reported an alarming 23 percent rise in pregnancy discrimination claims from 1996 to 2006. However, the *Wall Street Journal* points out that the new EEOC guidelines making it easier for parents to sue employers don't create a new protected class. "It could be permissible under federal law, for example, for a company to refuse to hire parents—as long as the rule is sex-blind, affecting fathers and mothers equally" (Shellenbarger 2007).

- Much egregious behavior carries no legal risk to the employer. For example, it's not illegal for a manager to be an equal opportunity jerk, as the company (mentioned earlier) attempting to be the diversity poster child learned with *Mr. X*. Indeed, as was detailed in the survey results presented in Chapter One, the incidence of behaviors such as bullying, public humiliation, and making someone the target of a joke is far more prevalent than behaviors we normally consider to be bias, harassment, or discrimination. When a CEO believes that his managers can throw a chair at an employee or hurl obscenities but can't tell a female subordinate that she looks nice today, something is seriously wrong.

Although business blames discrimination laws and/or the fear of lawsuits for the less-than-stellar progress in achieving diverse, bias-free workplaces, this argument is disingenuous. Sure, there's some fear of litigation. But more often the decisions are driven by greed or ignorance. And when it comes to other issues—that is, if a business believes that laws or regulations are in its way—it mobilizes decisively to change them.

Other victims of the legal framework and fear of lawsuits are the complaint-handling systems that companies implement. All research points to employees wanting to retain control of their complaints and have a completely confidential channel, such as an ombudsman—the impartial problem solver mentioned in Chapter Six. In the United States, it is sometimes ambiguous whether bringing an issue to an ombudsman constitutes making a complaint and putting the company on legal notice. Therefore, the standard for company policies is that all complaints *must* be investigated, which takes the control and confidentiality away from the person who already feels mistreated. As a result, employees don't come forward until they believe the situation has deteriorated so badly that they have nothing left to lose. At this point, most situations are difficult to repair well enough so that the people involved can continue to work together.

The U.S. framework is one of categorizing individual rights and mistreatment because of membership in a particular group ("protected class") rather than a framework of dignity and respect for everyone. Consequently, groups are pitted against one another for a share of the pie rather than everyone benefiting when the pie is fair for everyone.

The days of "No Blacks" signs at the drinking fountain have passed, but the days of racist jokes at the water cooler are definitely still here. Most bias-related behaviors these days are subtle, and no rigorous analysis of the cumulative effects of enduring subtle bias has been undertaken. A 2003 Level Playing Field Institute/ University of Connecticut Center for Survey Research & Analysis study (discussed in Chapter Two) revealed that "stereotyping is the [workplace] bad behavior reported most by people from every racial and ethnic group." Stereotyping occurred far more often than any form of discrimination or harassment, yet no one has studied how it unfolds in the workplace.

FOUR SIMPLE STEPS

When discrimination laws were written, most people in the work-place were white and male. This has changed. In the United States today, more women and minorities are represented in the work-place, both at the ground level and in management, than ever before. Discrimination law revision isn't typically on the agenda amidst the barrage of corporate lobbying at the state and federal levels. But the time has come, and is long overdue, for advocacy in this area. Sweeping changes are needed to facilitate corporations addressing hidden biases and barriers. These are simple to address, and their impact on the workplace and on corporate America's bottom line could be significant.

Here are the four basic legal changes I propose:

1. Reinvigorate self-critical analysis privilege to allow companies to collect data about their workforce in good faith, provided they take steps to act on the data.
2. Reinvigorate ombuds privilege to have the law be consistent with social science research.
3. In the longer term, redefine employer negligence as not look-ing at hidden bias and hidden barriers and taking active steps to mitigate them. It is more important that this concept be adopted by those who evaluate management quality and assess the value of a company than to create new laws that would fur-ther entrench the risk management stance. Simply put, com-panies that are well managed focus on how employees are treated and actively identify and remove hidden barriers.
4. Consider ending the prerogative of employers to fire any employee at any time for no reason. If the prevailing norm

were of "just cause" for termination, as it is in most of the developed world, trying to force-fit unfair treatment into a discrimination framework would no longer be necessary.

If you can't ask people specific, detailed questions about their perceptions and experiences, it will be impossible to establish a baseline measure of any company; therefore, it is impossible to determine whether the situation is getting better or worse (except with the grossest measures of number of certain types of people at certain levels) and how experiences across different groups vary.

WHO IS RESPONSIBLE?

All of our hands are a bit smudged; however, those in power (business managers, owners, and CEOs) hold the bulk of the responsibility for painting a glossy finish of "diversity" on their organizations while allowing barriers and bias to continue. But those with less power, the schoolteachers, medical providers, counselors, and landlords who place limits on people based on how they look or where they come from, are also to blame. And employees who face discrimination themselves, who don't speak up, who turn on each other and carry on the same practices when they clamber past others, are also at fault. Diversity trainers with their sixty-minute lessons, the HR departments focused on making problems go away, and the lawyers who want to keep corporate liability down rather than solve the deeper problems are also at fault.

The issues become a Rorschach test—depending on our lens and the angle from which we view the inkblot, we can assign blame in different directions. Unfortunately, if you scratch the surface of the hollow platitudes on both sides ("The most dedicated employees in the world work here" and "I can't think of any place I'd rather work"), you'll find a reservoir of deep distrust on both sides.

Those who have benefited from the current status quo point to their schools and companies as meritocracies and the elaborate mechanisms they have in place for "objective assessment." However, an ironic tautology is at work here: The current approach works for them, recognizes their talent, and rewards them; therefore, it must be fair. For them, the problem often lies with "the pipeline"—the inadequate supply of talent, in whatever form, that might be recognizable to them. These employees need to stop patting themselves on the back and start looking at how they can start easing the path for people with fewer opportunities.

Sometimes the finger of blame is also pointed at fellow employees—either the hypersensitive ones who can't take a joke or those who make false complaints. Everyone from managers who see this finger-pointing to those who engage in it should simply stop. Decades of research have shown that most employees put up with the barrage of unwelcome/inappropriate behaviors at work and are generally more reluctant to define these behaviors as "illegal" despite the prevailing laws. Nonetheless, the myth of the humorless employee who brings everyone's good-natured fun to an end persists. Similarly, senior managers cling to the notion that employees fabricate complaints to save their own jobs. Study after study points out how rare false complaints actually are. When you consider how difficult it is to prove an actual case of bias, harassment, or discrimination, it's not surprising that most employees would rather walk away than get branded a "whiner" or "troublemaker" at best, or even a "liar."

For those employees who do, indeed, have performance problems and raise countercharges, the process of proving the countercharge is usually complicated. Often, their files are full of nonspecific, generally laudatory performance appraisals, backed by average raises, no meaningful criticism, no meaningful assignments, and no promotions. If an employee has never been told he or she is doing a lousy job, the employee probably does believe that discrimination must explain the years of nonpromotion and the sudden flurry of documentation accompanying probationary status.

Employees will blame bigoted CEOs and management teams, but this is rarely constructive. Is it a conspiracy of the "Old Boys' Club" strategizing to drive out women, people of color, gays, and lesbians? No—the sad truth is that none of these groups matters enough to upper management to be the subject of any conspiracy. More often than not, people at the top are oblivious to the problems of their subordinates. But these same employees, through strategic and tactful communication, can change that.

Diversity consultants and trainers take their $1,000-plus per day and run, leaving behind simplistic nostrums such as, "We're not a melting pot, we're a salad bowl." It's a disingenuous and damaging practice. The consultants and trainers should take it upon themselves to dig deeper, require change, and demand that those who hire them truly commit to change. Without such a commitment, trainers and consultants should walk away from the prospective client.

The HR contingents (many of whom have never read the key publications of their industry) believe that they are saying "No, you can't do that" to managers while protecting the company from pesky employees. It's a misguided role. Instead, they need to learn about the challenges their employees and managers face, and they must learn to be the facilitators who smooth communications and who establish a culture of respect in the workplace.

The plaintiffs and defense lawyers believe that this is all a game of "gotcha" instead of a quest for fair, productive workplaces. In the end, they too must change if the interests of their employers are truly at heart. Their settlements should be solution oriented; the policies they provide should be aimed at resolving current problems and preventing future ones.

GUIDING PRINCIPLES

The best way to prevent all forms of bias is to create a workplace based on fairness and respect. Many organizations cite at least one of these three reasons for being willing to address bias:

1. **Litigation avoidance**   "We want to limit our exposure to lawsuits."
2. **Business case**   "Being inclusive of employees from a wide range of backgrounds helps us achieve our business goals and allows us to be sensitive to the cultural nuances of our customers and business partners."
3. **Human decency**   "It's the right thing to do."

The last reason—human decency—generally gets the least attention, especially in the United States. However, it has the strongest relationship to an organization's values, ethics, and overall culture. Being perceived as an "employer of choice" is heavily dependent on whether or not an institution is perceived as "fair." Fairness is a much broader concept than promoting diversity or not engaging in discriminatory practices. It often involves how senior management is perceived as performing on three dimensions:

- **Consistency**   Are the organization's mission, values, culture, and human resources systems in alignment? Does senior management "walk the talk"—that is, live the organization's values?
- **Transparency**   Are the organizational procedures and decision-making criteria evident, whether or not one agrees with them?
- **Accountability**   Are individuals at every level of the organization held accountable for their deeds and misdeeds?

Quality of worklife surveys conducted across thousands of organizations with millions of employees conclude that three dimensions of a workplace are of greatest importance to employees: equity, achievement, and camaraderie. These findings by Sirota, Mischkind, and Meltzer (2005) are consistent with those obtained by my for-profit consulting firm, Klein Associates, during nearly twenty years of work.

ORGANIZATIONAL COMMITMENTS AND A PRINCIPLE-BASED APPROACH

Like any other critical initiative, preventing bias requires a set of organizational commitments, the most important being a discernible commitment from top management. Senior management's view of the relative importance of any topic is conveyed both through action and inaction, and the consistency of words and deeds is of critical importance. For example, allowing abusive employees who are otherwise star performers to move through the ranks of the organization, while mediocre performers who barely cross the line in committing inappropriate behavior are dealt with harshly, sends a resounding message about company priorities.

Organizational commitment is also demonstrated through processes embodying honesty about the current state of the problem and the stages of improvement. Fears that the information might be used against the organization can lead senior manage-

Join today.
Start reading
tomorrow.

Join today and start receiving chapters
from popular books in your e-mail
tomorrow. Here are two ways to join
our free OnLine Book Clubs:

1. You can join by visiting our website
at:

www.jmcpl.ca

2. Use the computer in the library. Ask
library staff for instructions.

An apple a day is good for
your body.   A chapter a
day is good for your mind.

John M. Cuelenaere Public Library

125 12 Street East

Prince Albert, SK S6V 1B7

(306)763-8496

Join the Library's OnLine Book
Clubs and start receiving
chapters from popular books in
your daily email. Everyday,
Monday through Friday, we'll
send you a portion of a chapter
which will take about five
minutes to read.

After reading 2 or 3 chapters
from a book, you can decide if
you want to check the book out
of the library. Each week we
feature new books. You can
read fiction, nonfiction,
romance, business and young
adult books.

There's no charge for the book
clubs. You don't even need a
library card. Just give us your
email address and five minutes
a day, and we'll give you the
exciting world of reading. See
the back of this bookmark for
information about joining.

ment to be remarkably shortsighted and to neglect collection of rigorous data about the experiences and perceptions of employees.

Creating fairness and respect in the workplace takes intelligence, flexibility, and, most of all, dedication. The principles must be clear, but the practices must vary. We are humans and these are human issues, not spreadsheets with formulas. The goals are best accomplished through the comprehensive, consistent application of principles (rather than rigid rules) tied to the organization's mission, distinctive circumstances, and environment.

One example of the unsuitable use of a rigid rule is the zero-tolerance approach to sexual (and other types of) harassment. (Remember from Chapter Six that a *zero-tolerance stance* differs from a *zero-tolerance rule*.) Given that the definition of sexual harassment runs from unwelcome sexual comments or looks to sexual assault, adopting an approach of zero-tolerance toward all of these behaviors, regardless of severity, is simply not realistic—especially in multicultural and international organizations. Adding other types of harassment linked to group characteristics (race, ethnicity, sexual orientation, religion, disability, and so on) faces parallel challenges. All are on a continuum from subtle to severe, all have some degree of subjectivity inherent in their definitions, and all are interpreted through cultural norms. Failure to consider nuance, cultural differences, and context will likely have a chilling effect on the environment and/or result in inconsistent enforcement of the policy, which engenders cynicism among employees. Therefore, a rule-based, zero-tolerance approach is unlikely to be universally viewed as fair and, therefore, will not be uniformly followed, respected, or enforced.

Principles have a key, practical advantage over rules. Specifically, they are more flexible than rules, and they allow for the major message to remain consistent and be imparted, while the application can vary based on the specific aspects of the situation. Furthermore, various societal and cultural norms evolve over time to define behaviors once deemed acceptable to become unacceptable in a work environment. (Occasionally, the trend is in the other direction: behaviors once thought inappropriate in the workplace—such as men and women traveling together on business trips—are now acceptable.) A principle-based approach means that the larger picture can remain consistent, while the examples or specifics are permitted to change.

THE PRIZE

Whether responding to a crisis, delivering survey results, or conducting customized training, I often tell senior managers to focus on the message that they are sending to their employees through their action or inaction. By focusing on managing risk and attempting to hide from liability, management is issuing a resounding statement that employees aren't to be trusted, and at the end of the day it's "us" and "them."

So what are we trying to do? Here are three simple steps toward a solution. Implementing them will go much farther than you might imagine:

1. Each employee, from the CEO to the minimum-wage hourly worker, should think about his or her boundary between what's acceptable and unacceptable, what's welcome and unwelcome conduct in the workplace—from peers, bosses, customers/ clients, and other third parties. They should heighten their self-awareness, exploring biases and assumptions. They should recognize that a person's sense of humor, social norms, and appropriate conversation topics vary widely. No one person or culture is right or wrong—we're all just different.
2. Companies should make it clear that each employee has the right to draw a boundary between acceptable and unacceptable for herself or himself and that it is to be respected, without ridicule or ostracism.
3. If a person's boundaries are not respected, the person should have the right to speak up through an informal or formal channel, and the company should be expected to help enforce that boundary. The focus should be on a welcoming, respectful work environment for each person. That requires understanding, dialogue, and nuance.

The value of these three steps is high, both to a company's bottom line and to individuals who arrive at an organization ready to make a difference. When businesses start treating quality of work-life as a tangible benefit that can be measured, their progress is swift and their savings significant.

At the height of the 21st century bubble, a New York–based financial services firm brought me in to figure out how to solve their expensive and embarrassing turnover rate. The firm was hemorrhaging employees—everyone from the young hotshots recruited from top schools who had lots of promise and drive, to the seasoned moneymakers who were reliable, responsible mentors and who should have been committed to the firm.

I started with a series of interviews, focus groups, and surveys of current and former employees, as well as employees who had turned down job offers. I made many important, specific observations:

- Too few women at the top were also mothers.
- The company was a revolving door for people of color.
- The case-by-case basis on which they allowed flex-time or telecommuting amounted to favoritism with no discernible pattern of how one might earn it.
- Promotions went to those already anointed by the senior managers, and opportunities were never posted.
- Client entertainment was often conducted at strip clubs or at golf courses that had discriminatory membership rules.
- No clear guidelines were available for moving ahead, and only a few insiders actually knew whether they were on track for a senior position or on the verge of being asked to leave.

But the elephant in the room, the story I heard again and again, soon became overwhelmingly obvious: one of their biggest rainmakers was also a major harasser. Everyone said that his abusiveness was off the chart. He was crass, bigoted, and rude (especially toward women and people of color). The only group at the firm that was unscathed was gay and lesbian employees, since the harasser, himself, was gay.

I brought this sobering news to the executive committee and senior managers over dinner at a private club. Their response, as my report unfolded, was stunning. The several dozen senior Caucasian men and three Caucasian women barely heard me out before erupting in angry diatribes, grilling me and shouting at each other. Some were in denial. Others were furious that it had taken an outside consultant to bring them this incredibly obvious piece of information. The debate went on and on. But in the end, they did the right thing: they fired him.

The result was phenomenal, with countless benefits after the departure of a single, toxic individual—many that I hadn't even considered. For example, some of the employees who had left the company were now in a position to direct or withhold business from the firm. After firing the man and making several other structural changes related to performance feedback, complaint handling, and mentoring, the firm actually got more business from former employees than ever before. The firm continued to grow overall, and it also grew in the rankings of good places to work. And the favorable rankings were not from sources that they paid for—they were from objective trade journals that conducted real reviews of the workforce. Their numbers of senior women and people of color were noted for most improved.

I recently ran into the CEO of this firm. He said he was delighted to see me and that he had just reread my presentation, which was now several years old. "You were right," he said. Those simple but significant changes had made a lasting, positive effect on the corporate culture. The payoffs were many: employees thought that the firm was a great place to work. Turnover was down. Business was up. The bottom line was benefiting. Everyone learned an important business lesson.

Sometimes such lessons can be learned without incurring the initial damage. A startup tech company founder recently launched a new business with a model, certainly, to make plenty of money. But equally important, he said, was a firm set of clear values about the workplace and how people were to be treated. As a result, he has attracted top employees who want a positive work environment. These people want to telecommute. They want to be able to have cutting-edge work *and* a family or life outside the office. They want to participate in community events. The three most senior positions are now occupied by women engineers, all of whom left big companies because of being drowned out by the men, the pressure for face time, and the bullying, chair-throwing cultures. When fairness prevails, the people who rise to the top look different. The company is soaring financially, as much due to its product as to the environment it has created for its employees.

Many corporations won't take the first, important steps toward removing bias and barriers, due to liability concerns. They lack managerial commitment, as well as ideas, initiative, and the creative and aggressive energy it takes to address these issues.

In this book, I have shown you the human, societal, and financial costs of inaction and misguided efforts. I have detailed the price tags and have explained how to unearth and remove hidden bias and hidden barriers in organizations. My goal for three decades has been this: to create a more level playing field in corporate America. Now my tools are in your hands.

What's in a Resume?

Resumes are the most widely used measure of a person's qualifications in a job search, but what's really included in a resume? How accurately does a resume reflect the hard work, leadership, and innovation of a prospective employee? Resumes list accomplishments, not traits.

We asked a top recruiter from an internationally renowned recruitment agency to review the resumes that follow. Her overall assessment was that Michael had been "groomed for success." According to the expert, recruiters typically focus on the prestige of the schools a candidate has attended, as well as the prestige of any companies at which he or she was previously employed. She acknowledged that Fernando's attendance at a junior college, particularly in comparison with Michael's degree from Yale University, would be frowned upon. In addition, Michael's experiences as a student ambassador and a Senate page would trump Fernando's internships at the student bookstore and a local non-profit.

Our expert was of the personal belief that "resumes are just fact sheets," but she recognized that a typical recruiter does not factor in important traits such as initiative and creativity, especially when the recruiter has only about thirty seconds to evaluate a candidate. And although our expert herself favors "stories" over resumes, she often coaches candidates to place prestigious school and company names first in their resumes, even if decades have passed since they studied and worked there. She also acknowledged that a diversity search would place more weight on where a person started (that is, on the unlevel playing field) and the person's initiative and creativity to get to where they are. To her, Fernando displayed more initiative and creativity with less opportunity, while Michael's resume showed the prominence of his social networks and connections. She was concerned that a candidate like Michael showed no ability to "roll up his sleeves."

We strongly believe that resumes would be more accurate and meaningful predictors of a person's abilities if they were reviewed under a merit-based method as opposed to a privilege-based standard. For example, Fernando may not have attended an elite, Ivy League university like Michael, but Michael did not have to work a part-time job to help his family financially, nor did he have to be creative in seeking ways to pay for college. While it's true that Fernando did not learn to speak Spanish by studying abroad, as French-fluent Michael did in France, Fernando did manage to become fluent in Spanish by volunteering as an ESL teacher and interacting with native speakers.

Fernando's resume, although impressive, appears sparse in comparison to that of Michael. It shows no study-abroad programs in his high school—not that his parents would have been able to afford them anyway. He attended junior college to help manage costs and stay near his family and younger siblings, whom he helped to look after. He worked throughout the academic year at the student union bookstore to defray the cost of classes. His hard work and knack for numbers were recognized early on by the store manager, who promoted Fernando and asked him to be responsible for bookkeeping and budgeting—responsibilities for which the store had previously hired a seasoned accountant. As part of his responsibilities in managing the bookstore's finances, Fernando worked closely with the local credit union. His determination, ability to multitask, and intelligence so impressed the credit union manager that he informally mentored Fernando and encouraged him to apply for a transfer to a larger university.

Despite having a part-time job and taking care of his siblings, Fernando had strong academic credentials and was awarded a scholarship to attend the University of California. Although he immersed himself in his new surroundings and in courses at the business school, he found time to volunteer as a Big Brother. Based on the continued encouragement that Fernando received from his mentor at the credit union, Fernando interviewed with Goldman Sachs through three rounds and received an internship slot.

Many would still believe that Michael is the better-qualified candidate because his resume is filled with prestigious school names and even more prestigious employer names and volunteer experiences. Yet it is not obvious from his resume that Michael's attendance at a private boarding academy was a prominent factor in his success. Michael's school, Phillips Academy Andover, boasts 217 faculty members—29 in the mathematics department alone. The student-to-teacher ratio is five to one, and twelve academic departments offer 300 different courses, including eight foreign-language courses, each academic year. In 2006, the school's endowment was estimated at $670 million (see www.andover.edu). Unlike many other prep schools, Phillips Academy Andover does not require its students to perform community service. The boarding school has an elaborate college counseling program in which the staff is routinely in touch with the admissions directors at all of the top-tier colleges and universities.

What is even less obvious is that Michael's attendance at Phillips Academy Andover was secured by his parents' ability to pay nearly $36,000 per year in tuition. Michael's resume doesn't indicate that his father also attended Yale, where he remains an active donor, or that his mother "lunches" with corporate vice presidents and CEOs, whom she considers professional acquaintances and personal friends. His resume fails to acknowledge that his internships and foreign studies were secured by his parents' affiliations with prominent political figures and dignitaries. On many occasions, Michael's interviews were merely a formality.

Fernando and Michael managed to end up employed by the same prestigious bank, but the roads they traveled to get there are undeniably different. The road Fernando traveled was laden with obstacles, washed-out bridges, and no clear road signs. Michael's path was carved out by several previous generations of his family. A resume and a person's qualifications can be measured in many ways. Of course, it is easier and quicker to judge a person by the prestigious school he attended or by opportunities afforded to him because of social standing, and automatically assume a person is highly qualified. However, we may find that weighing a candidate's starting point, resourcefulness, and initiative may often be better indicators of his or her abilities and work ethic than an elite name alone. If we believe in a meritocracy, we should be measuring the distance traveled, not just whether or not a person has crossed the finish line.

If you were hiring a new employee and tasked with reviewing each of the following two resumes, whom would you hire? Why?

Michael J. Straton III
34506 Danover Avenue
Saddle River, NJ 07458
(201) 555–3304
michaeljstraton@gmail.com

EDUCATION
Yale University, BA, History, New Haven, CT – May 2006
- Captain of Men's Lightweight Crew Team
- President of Yale College Republicans
- Participated in Study Abroad Program in Cannes, France
Phillips Academy Andover, Andover, MA – June 2002
- Captain of Crew Team and Most Valuable Player
- Participated in Exchange Program at DaTong High School in Shanghai, China
- President of Phillips Academy Andover Student Body Association

WORK EXPERIENCE
Goldman Sachs, Summer Intern, New York, NY – May 2005
- Analyze financial data, extract and define relevant information for determining past financial performance and to project financial probability
- Review costs and perform cost-benefits analyses related to projects and programs
- Perform statistical, costs, and financial analyses of data reported in various systems
Rotary Club, International Student Ambassador, Paris, France – May 2004
- Compose report about globalization and the importance of cultural tolerance
- Take intensive language courses for three-month summer program
- Assist with cultural exchange program at the U.S. Embassy in Paris
United States Senate, Page, Washington, D.C. – June 2001
- Deliver correspondence and legislative materials within congressional complex
- Prepare chambers for Senate sessions and carry bills and amendments to the desks
- Attend morning classes at the United States Senate Page School

LANGUAGES & PERSONAL INTERESTS
Fluent French, avid sports fan, kayaking, and outdoors enthusiast

Fernando Cisneros
943 E. 1st Street, Apartment #3G
Los Angeles, CA 90043
(323) 555–4440
marcos_cisneros@yahoo.com

EDUCATION
University of California, BA, Economics, Berkeley, CA – May 2006
- Regents' and Chancellor's Scholarship Recipient
- Lipson Research Grant and Scholarship Recipient
- Social Justice Leadership Scholarship and Achievement Award

East Los Angeles Junior College, Los Angeles, CA – May 2004
- Big Brother & Sisters Program Participant

Crenshaw Senior High School, Los Angeles, CA – June 2002
- Junior Reserve Officers Training Corps (JrROTC)
- Student Council Member

WORK EXPERIENCE
Goldman Sachs, Summer Intern, San Francisco, CA – May 2005
- Analyze financial data, extract and define relevant information for determining past financial performance and to project financial probability
- Review costs and perform cost-benefits analyses related to projects and programs
- Perform statistical, costs, and financial analyses of data reported in various systems

Homeboy Industries, Summer Intern, Los Angeles, CA – May 2003
- Teach classes at non-profit that assists at-risk and former gang-involved youth
- Prepare business plan for job training program and verify document accuracy
- Develop financial reports for forecasting, trending, and results analysis

Student Union Bookstore, Sales Clerk, Los Angeles, CA – August 2002
- Stock supplies, conduct inventory of products, process orders with vendors
- Assist with preparing budget, process biweekly payroll and bank reconciliations
- Promoted to student manager, create weekly work schedules, open and close store

LANGUAGES & PERSONAL INTERESTS
Fluent Spanish, Volunteer ESL instructor at Cal America, Stiles Hall Big Brother

DETERMINING THE COST OF UNFAIRNESS

The financial cost of unfairness presented in this study is an estimate based upon the results of the 2007 Corporate Leavers Survey. The basic mathematical calculations used to determine the cost of voluntary turnover due solely to unfairness are as follows:

Population of employed civilians	×	Percentage of population who are professionals or managers	=	Number of professionals and managers in U.S. labor force

×	Percentage of managers and professionals who left solely due to unfairness	×	1.5 × total annual compensation of professional or manager	=	Cost of voluntary turnover due solely to unfairness

To determine the population of employed civilians, we consulted the 2000 U.S. Census. According to the census, the total employed civilian population within each demographic group and the number of professionals and managers within each group are as follows:

Race/ Ethnicity	Employed Civilian Population[1]	Percentage of Population Who Are Professionals or Managers[2]	Number of Managers and Professionals[3]
American Indian and Alaska Native	914,484	24.3%	222,220
Asian	4,786,782	44.6%	2,134,905
Black or African American	13,001,795	25.2%	3,276,452
Native Hawaiian and Other Pacific Islander	157,119	23.3%	36,609
Other Race	5,886,427	14.2%	835,873
Mixed Race	2,649,943	26.7%	707,535
White	102,324,962	35.6%	36,427,686
TOTALS	**129,721,512**	—	**43,641,280**

Unfortunately, the census did not report the number of Hispanics or Latinos in the employed civilian population. Instead, it reported the number of Hispanics or Latinos in the employed civilian population as a percentage within the other demographic groups: "Because Hispanics may be of any race, data in this report for Hispanics overlap with data for racial groups. Based on Census 2000 sample data, the proportion Hispanic was 8.0 percent for Whites, 1.9 percent for Blacks, 14.6 percent for American Indians and Alaska Natives, 1.0 percent for Asians, 9.5 percent for Pacific Islanders, 97.1 percent for those reporting Some Other Race, and 31.1 percent for those reporting Two or More Races."[4]

As such, we recalculated the employed civilian population for each demographic group by calculating the number of Hispanics or Latinos in each reported demographic group and subtracting that number from the number of employed civilians in each group.

Race/ Ethnicity	Employed Civilian Population	Percentage of Population Who Are Hispanics or Latinos	Hispanics or Latinos in Employed Civilian Population[5]	Employed Civilian Population[6]
American Indian and Alaska Native	914,484	14.6%	133,515	780,969
Asian	4,786,782	1.0%	47,868	4,738,914
Black or African American	13,001,795	1.9%	247,034	12,754,761
Native Hawaiian and Other Pacific Islander	157,119	9.5%	14,926	142,193
Other Race	5,886,427	97.1%	5,715,721	170,706
Mixed Race	2,649,943	31.1%	824,132	1,825,811
White	102,324,962	8.0%	8,185,997	94,138,965
TOTAL			**15,169,193**	

Next, we recalculated the percentage of professionals and managers within each demographic group. We knew the percentage of the employed civilian Hispanic or Latino population who were managers and professionals was 18.1 percent.[7] We calculated the percentage of professionals and managers in the other demographic groups by dividing the "new" number of professionals and managers in each group (minus Hispanics and Latinos) by the "new" employed civilian population in that group (minus Hispanics and Latinos).

Race/ Ethnicity	Employed Civilian Population	Percentage of Population Who Are Professionals or Managers	Number of Managers and Professionals
American Indian and Alaska Native	780,969	25.36%	198,054
Asian	4,738,914	44.87%	2,126,351
Black or African American	12,754,761	25.34%	3,232,056
Hispanic or Latino	15,169,193	18.1%	2,745,624
Native Hawaiian and Other Pacific Islander	142,193	23.85%	33,913
Other Race	170,706	14.2%	24,240
Mixed Race	1,825,811	30.58%	558,333
White	94,138,965	37.12%	34,944,384
TOTALS	**129,721,512**	—	**43,862,955**

The number of professionals and managers in each group was then multiplied by the percentage of Corporate Leavers Survey respondents who indicated that unfairness was the sole reason they left their employer.

Race/ Ethnicity	Number of Managers and Professionals	Percentage That Left Solely Due to Unfairness[8]	Number of Managers and Professionals Who Left Solely Due to Unfairness
American Indian and Alaska Native	198,054	9.5%	18,815
Asian	2,126,351	9.5%	202,003
Black or African American	3,232,056	9.5%	307,045
Hispanic or Latino	2,745,624	9.5%	260,834
Native Hawaiian and Other Pacific Islander	33,913	9.5%	3,222
Other Race	24,240	9.5%	2,303

Mixed Race	558,333	9.5%	53,042
White	34,944,384	3.8%	1,327,887
TOTALS	**43,862,955**	—	**2,175,151**

Based on the preceding calculation, an estimated 2,175,151 people left their jobs due solely to unfairness.

Many studies have estimated the cost of employee turnover as a multiple of total annual compensation.[9] The most conservative of these estimates is that turnover costs employers 1.5 times the total annual compensation of the employee lost. Using the average total compensation of professionals and managers, as indicated by the U.S. Department of Labor, Bureau of Labor Statistics,[10] we calculated the average cost of replacing one professional or manager as follows:

$$\begin{array}{ccc} \$97,677 & \times \quad 1.5 \quad = & \$146,516 \\ \text{Average total} & & \text{Cost of turnover} \\ \text{compensation of} & & \text{for one professional} \\ \text{professional or manager} & & \text{or manager} \end{array}$$

We then multiplied the cost of turnover for one professional or manager by the estimated number of people who left their job in the past five years solely due to unfairness.

$$\begin{array}{cccc} \$146,516 & \times & 2,175,151 & = & \$318,694,423,916 \\ \text{Cost of} & & \text{Estimated} & & \text{Cost of turnover} \\ \text{turnover for} & & \text{number of} & & \text{due solely to} \\ \text{one professional} & & \text{people who} & & \text{unfairness during} \\ \text{or manager} & & \text{left solely} & & \text{the past five years} \\ & & \text{due to unfairness} & & \end{array}$$

Lastly, we divided the cost of turnover due solely to unfairness during the past five years by 5 to arrive at the annual estimated cost of unfairness.

$$\frac{\$318,694,423,916}{5} = \$63,738,884,783$$

Thus, voluntary employee turnover costs U.S. businesses an estimated $63,738,884,783 a year.

The Corporate Leavers Survey:
The Cost of Employee Turnover
Due Solely to Unfairness in the workplace
Executive Summary

What happens when an Arab telecommunications professional, returning from a family visit to Iraq, is jokingly asked by a manager if he participated in any terrorism? Or when an African American lawyer is mistaken, three times, for another black lawyer by a partner at the firm? What is the effect when a lesbian professional is told that her employer covers pet insurance for rats, pigs, and snakes but does not offer domestic partner benefits? What about when a Latina information technology professional is told by her manager that she is too "ethnic" to be taken seriously?

They leave.

They leave without any of the attention given to the multi-million–dollar gender- or race-based discrimination lawsuits, but they and millions like them leave at an annual cost that exceeds the cumulative settlements for all sex- and race-based lawsuits reported by the Equal Employment Opportunity Commission from 1997 until 2006.[11] They leave at a time when people of color and women will soon constitute a majority of the global workforce, and they leave committed not to use their former employer's products or services and resolved not to recommend their employer to any of the professionals in their network.

The Corporate Leavers[12] Survey, a groundbreaking study conducted by the Level Playing Field Institute in January 2007, shows that each year in this country, more than two million professionals and managers in an increasingly diverse workforce leave their jobs, pushed out by cumulative small comments, whispered jokes, and not-so-funny e-mails. This rigorous study, the first large-scale review of this issue, shows that unfairness costs U.S. employers $64 billion on an *annual basis*—a price tag nearly equivalent to the 2006 combined revenues of Google, Goldman Sachs, Starbucks, and Amazon.com[13] or the gross domestic product of the 55th wealthiest country in the world.[14] This estimate represents the cost of losing and replacing professionals and managers who leave their employers *solely* due to workplace unfairness. By adding in those for whom unfairness was a major contributor to their decision to leave, the figure is substantially greater. This study also shows how often employees who left jobs due to unfairness later discouraged potential customers and job applicants from working with their former employer.

This extensive study of U.S. employees takes an in-depth look at (1) the effect of unfairness upon an employee's decision to leave an employer, (2) the financial cost to employers due to voluntary turnover based on unfairness, and (3) what, if anything, employers could have done to keep employees who left due to unfairness. We focused our study on professionals and managers in the corporate workforce who voluntarily left their employers or volunteered for a layoff within the past five years.[15] We began with a sample of 19,000 potential survey subjects to yield 1,700 professionals and managers who met our criteria and completed the survey.

Beyond the financial costs of unfairness, the Corporate Leavers Survey findings include the following:

- People of color are three times more likely to cite workplace unfairness as the only reason for leaving their employer than heterosexual Caucasian men and twice as likely as heterosexual Caucasian women.
- Gay and lesbian professionals and managers said workplace unfairness was the only reason they left their employer almost twice as often as heterosexual Caucasian men.
- Among the specific types of unfairness we inquired about, the behaviors that were most likely to prompt someone to quit were (1) being asked to attend extra recruiting or community-related events because of the employee's race, gender, religion, or sexual orientation; (2) being passed over for a promotion due to the employee's personal characteristics; (3) being publicly humiliated; and (4) being compared to a terrorist in a joking or serious manner.[16]
- More than one-fourth (27 percent) of respondents who experienced unfairness at work within the past year said their experience strongly discouraged them from recommending their employer to other potential employees. Similarly, 13 percent of these same respondents said their experience strongly discouraged them from recommending their employer's products or services to others.

- Responses concerning what employers could have done to keep them varied across demographic groups. Almost half of gay and lesbian professionals and managers said that if their employer offered more or better benefits, they would have very likely stayed. In comparison, 34 percent of people of color said they would have very likely stayed if their employer had offered better managers who recognized their abilities.

The most fundamental conclusion to be drawn from this study is this: overt and illegal discrimination is no longer the largest threat to recruiting and retaining the "best and the brightest." Unfairness in the form of everyday inappropriate behaviors such as stereotyping, public humiliation, and promoting based upon personal characteristics is a very real, prevalent, and damaging part of the work environment. We found that experiences of unfairness vary by demographics, and thus generic training and laws alone cannot adequately remedy this complex problem. By identifying, studying, and quantifying the problem of unfairness in the workplace, across demographics, we can work to remove the barriers and biases that create unfair workplaces.

To receive more information about the Corporate Leavers Survey and its findings, please contact Level Playing Field Institute at (415) 946-3030 or info@lpfi.org.

SOURCES OF CORPORATE LEAVER STORIES

Abbott Laboratories	Accel Partners	Agilent	Apple Computer, Inc.
Banque BNP Paribas	The Boeing Company	The Boston Consulting Group	Channel Point, Inc.
Charles Schwab	CIGNA	Cisco Systems, Inc.	Computer Associates
Computer Sciences Corporation (CSC)	Cravath, Swaine & Moore LLP	Deloitte Touche Tohmatsu	Donaldson, Lufkin & Jenrette
East Bay Municipal Utility District (EBMUD)	U.S. Environmental Protection Agency (EPA)	Ernst & Young	Escalate
Esprit	GAP	Genentech	Gibson, Dunn & Crutcher LLP
Goldman Sachs	Hannah Strategies	Hewlett-Packard	Hughes, Hubbard & Reed
IBM	InsurQuote, Inc.	Internal Revenue Service (IRS)+A41	Johnson & Johnson
Kleiner Perkins Caufield & Byers	Kraft Foods, Inc.	Levi Strauss & Co.	Lockheed Martin
Lotus Software	McKinsey & Company	Mercer Human Resource Consulting	Mervyns

Microsoft Corporation	Morgan Stanley	Morrison & Foerster	Music Television (MTV)
Netscape	New Enterprise Associates (NEA)	Paine Webber (now part of Union Bank of Switzerland)	PatientKeeper
Patton Boggs LLP	Paul, Weiss, Rifkind, Wharton & Garrison LLP	Pfizer Pharmaceutical Company	Pricewaterhouse Coopers (PwC)
Proctor & Gamble	Safeway Stores	Sanwa Bank	Simpson, Thacher & Bartlett LLP
Skadden, Arps, Slate, Meagher & Flom LLP	Stanford University	Studley, Inc.	Sullivan & Cromwell LLP
Televoke	Time Warner	Toyota	University of California, Berkeley
Weil, Gotshal & Manges LLP	Wells Fargo	WPP	Yahoo!

Non-profits

100 Black Men of the Bay Area, Inc.

Alpha Phi Alpha Fraternity, Inc.

American Arab Anti-Discrimination Committee San Francisco

American Indian Science and Engineering Society

ASCENT

Asian American Bar Association of the Greater Bay Area

Association of Women's Business Centers

Astia (formerly the Women's Technology Cluster)

Billy DeFrank LGBT Community Center

Black Ivy Alumni League

Black Recruiters Network Association

Business for Social Responsibility

Charles Houston Bar Association

Chinese for Affirmative Action

The Consortium for Graduate Study in Management

Filipina Women's Network

Forum for Women Entrepreneurs & Executives

Gay & Lesbian Alliance Against Defamation

Hispanic Net

Human Rights Campaign

Latino Ivy League

Lawyers' Committee for Civil Rights Under Law

Lawyers for One America

Leadership Education for Asian Pacifics, Inc.

MentorNet

National Association of Asian American Professionals

National Bar Association

National Black Law Students Association

National Black MBA Association

National Coalition of 100 Black Women, Inc. (Oakland–Bay Area Chapter)

National Gay and Lesbian Chamber of Commerce

National Native American Bar Association

National Society of Black Engineers

National Society of Hispanic MBAs

Network of Arab-American Professionals

Out & Equal Workplace Advocates

Public Advocates, Inc.

Robert Toigo Foundation

San Francisco La Raza Lawyers Association

San Francisco LGBT Community Center

Society of Hispanic Professional Engineers, Inc.

Stonewall Democrats

Upwardly Global

Women Lawyers' Division of the National Bar Association (Greater Washington Area Chapter)

Women of Color Action Network

Women's Bar Association of the District of Columbia

NOTES

Chapter 1

1. According to the Web site of the Executive Office of the President, Office of Management and Budget (see http://www.whitehouse .gov/OMB/pubpress/2006/2006-6.pdf).
2. See http://investor.google.com/fin_data.html; http://www2 .goldmansachs.com/our_firm/investor_relations/financial_reports/ annual_reports/2006/; http://library.corporate-ir.net/library/99/ 995/99518/items/230297/10K_A_10K.pdf; and http://media .corporate-ir.net/media_files/irol/97/97664/2006AnnualReport.pdf.
3. According to the United Nations Office of the Iraq Programme: Oil-for-Food (see http://www.un.org/Depts/oip/background/latest/ wu030304.html).
4. See, for example, Krebsbach, 2007.
5. China.org.cn (see http://www.china.org.cn/english/2006/Sep/ 180438.htm).
6. See, for example, Bounds, 2007.
7. According to the World Development Indicators Database, World Bank, April 23, 2007 (see http://siteresources.worldbank.org/ DATASTATISTICS/Resources/GDP.pdf).

Chapter 3

1. Quoted in "The New Post-Heroic Leadership," *Fortune*, February 21, 1994.

Chapter 4

1. Cited by American Institute of Stress, 2004.
2. Cited by Rosch, 2001.
3. Cited by National Institute for Occupational Safety and Health, 1999.
4. Cited by Broughton, 2004.
5. Bliss, 1998.

6. This figure is based on the hourly rate for "management, profes-
    sional, and related" employees working full-time in "private indus-
    try" (see http://www.bls.gov/news.release/ecec.t11.htm.)
7. The Wharton School of the University of Pennsylvania, 2004.
8. As quoted in Smith, 2004.

Chapter 5
1. As quoted in Vedantam, 2007.

Chapter 6
1. A comment attributed to Douglass, spoken to a friend after Doug-
    lass met with Lincoln at the White House; date unavailable.
2. Key findings: http://www.bayerus.com/msms/news/facts.cfm?mode
    =detail&id=summary06a. Press release: http://www.bayerus.com/
    msms/news/facts.cfm?mode=detail&id=survey06.
3. See http://web.mit.edu/negotiation/toa/TOAintro.html.

Chapter 7
1. Cited in Brunner, 2001.
2. Note, however, that the Ninth Circuit Court of Appeals ruled in
    E.E.O.C. v. National Education Association (September 2, 2005) that
    bullying behavior—even without sexual conduct—could be dis-
    criminatory if it had a substantially different impact on women than
    on men.

Chapter 9
1. As quoted in Hechinger, 2006, B1.
2. See, for example, Lee and Burkam, 2002; Dearing et al., 2001.
3. See, for example, Ferguson, 2003.
4. See, for example, Perry et al., 2003, 109–130.
5. See, for example, Carli et al., 1995.
6. See, for example, Avery et al., 2003.
7. As quoted in Capriccioso, 2006.

Chapter 10
1. Statistics from U.S. Census Bureau and U.S. Department of Com-
    merce, 1999, 1, 22, 48.
2. *Miller v. Bank of America,* 600 F.2d 211 (9th Cir. 1979).

Appendix B
1. U.S. Census Bureau, Census 2000 (see http://www.census.gov/
    prod/2003pubs/c2kbr-25.pdf).

2. U.S. Census Bureau, Census 2000 (see http://www.census.gov/prod/2003pubs/c2kbr-25.pdf).

3. The number of managers and professionals within each group is the product of the employed civilian population multiplied by the percentage of that population who are professionals and managers.

4. U.S. Census Bureau, Census 2000 (see http://www.census.gov/prod/2003pubs/c2kbr-25.pdf).

5. The number of Hispanics or Latinos in the employed civilian population is the product of the number of employed civilian population with Hispanics or Latinos included multiplied by the percentage of that population who are Hispanics or Latinos.

6. The employed civilian population is calculated by subtracting the number of Hispanics or Latinos in the employed civilian population from the employed civilian population with Hispanics or Latinos included.

7. U.S. Census Bureau, Census 2000 (see http://www.census.gov/prod/2003pubs/c2kbr-25.pdf).

8. As found in the Corporate Leavers Survey.

9. See, for reference, http://www.talentkeepers-services.com/talentkeepers/costcalc.asp; http://www.caliperonline.com/solutions/turnover.shtml; and http://www.dol.gov/cfbci/turnover.htm.

10. The average employer costs per hour worked for a professional or manager was $46.96 per hour. We multiplied this hourly figure based upon a forty-hour workweek and a fifty-two-week year to come up with an annual salary of $97,677 (see http://www.bls.gov/news.release/ecec.t11.htm.)

11. See http://www.eeoc.gov/stats/race.html; http://www.eeoc.gov/stats/sex.html.

12. The term "corporate leavers," as used in this report, is defined as those professionals and/or managers who voluntarily left or volunteered for a layoff from their corporate employers (as opposed to public, government, or non-profit employers).

13. See http://www2.goldmansachs.com/our_firm/investor_relations/financial_reports/annual_reports/2006/; http://investor.google.com/fin_data.html; http://library.corporate-ir.net/library/99/995/99518/items/230297/10K_A_10K.pdf; and http://media.corporate-ir.net/media_files/irol/97/97664/2006AnnualReport.pdf.

14. See http://siteresources.worldbank.org/DATASTATISTICS/Resources/GDP.pdf.

15. We focused on professionals and managers as opposed to entry-level, administrative, or similar employees, because professionals and managers are a source of invaluable expertise to employers and are thus the focus of recruitment, development, and retention

efforts. This is also the population in which the United States faces the greatest talent shortages in coming years.

16.   The actual incidence rate of being compared to a terrorist among the corporate leavers surveyed was small, 2 percent. However, when it did occur, it had a profound effect and was one of the behaviors most frequently associated with an employee's decision to leave solely due to unfairness.

References

Allegretto, S.A. "Social Expenditures and Child Poverty—The U.S. Is a Noticeable Outlier." June 23, 2004. Accessed February 15, 2007 <http://www.epinet.org/content.cfm/webfeatures_snapshots _06232004>.

American Institute of Stress. "Job Stress." 2004. Accessed February 15, 2007 <http://www.stress.org/job.htm>.

Avery, C., A. Fairbanks, and R. Zeckhauser. *The Early Admissions Game: Joining the Elite.* Cambridge, MA: Harvard University Press, 2003.

Bayer Corporation. "Disconnect over Women, African-Americans, Native Americans and Hispanic Americans as Untapped Talent Pool." May 9, 2006. Accessed February 15, 2007 <http://www.bayerus.com/msms/ news/facts.cfm?mode=detail&id=survey06>.

———. "Key findings," in *The Bayer Facts of Science Education XII: CEOs on STEM Diversity: The Need, the Seed, the Feed.* 2006. Accessed February 15, 2007 <http://www.bayerus.com/msms/news/facts.cfm?mode=detail &id=summary06a>.

Beagrie, S. "If You Only Do Five Things...." *Personnel Today,* September 23, 2003: 29.

Berger, P.L., and S.P. Huntington, eds. *Many Globalizations: Cultural Diversity in the Contemporary World.* New York: Oxford University Press, 2002.

Bertrand, M., and S. Mullainathan. "Are Emily and Greg More Employable Than Lakisha and Jamal? A Field Experiment on Labor Market Discrimination." *The American Economic Review,* 94(4) (2004): 1–31.

Binette, C. "NFL Achieves Highest Grade Ever for Racial Diversity from UCF Institute." August 24, 2006. Accessed February 15, 2007 <http:// news.ucf.edu/UCFnews/index?page=article&id=0024004105bd6043 9010c0c76ce2f006c6f>.

Bliss, W.G. "Cost of Employee Turnover." 1998. Accessed February 15, 2007 <http://www.isquare.com/turnover.cfm>.

Bounds, A. "EU Must Increase Giving to Meet Development Aid Pledges." April 2, 2007. Accessed June 4, 2007 <http://www.ft.com/cms/s/ 17b6ceb2-e0b6-11db-8b48-000b5df10621.html>.

Broughton, A.C. *Beyond Paycheck-to-Paycheck: Wealth-Building Strategies for Venture Capital Funds to Use with Portfolio Companies and Their Employees*. New York and Durham: SJF Advisory Services, 2004.

Brunner, N.R. "Does Your Potential Employer Measure Up?" July 1, 2001. Accessed February 15, 2007 <http://www.jobjournal.com/article _full_text.asp?artid=253>.

California Secretary of State. "Proposition 209: Text of Proposed Law." 1996. Accessed February 15, 2007 <http://vote96.ss.ca.gov/BP/ 209text.htm>.

Camara, W.J., and A.E. Schmidt. *Group Differences in Standardized Testing and Social Stratification*. College Board Report 99–5. New York: College Entrance Examination Board, 1999.

Candland, C.C. "Blended Staffing Strategies Prepare Companies for Talent Shortage." July 1, 2003. Accessed April 19, 2007 <http://www .suite101.com/article.cfm/human_resources/97449>.

Capriccioso, R. "The Earliest Early Admissions." August 8, 2006. Accessed February 15, 2007 <http://www.insidehighered.com/news/2006/ 08/08/admissions>.

Carli, L.L. "Gender Differences in Interaction Style and Influence." *Journal of Personality and Social Psychology*, 56(4) (1989): 565–576.

Carli, L.L., S.J. LaFleur, and C.C. Loeber. "Nonverbal Behavior, Gender, and Influence." *Journal of Personality and Social Psychology*, 68(6) (1995): 1030–1041.

Chao, E.L. Remarks delivered by U.S. Secretary of Labor Elaine L. Chao at the Southern Women in Public Service Conference, Nashville, May 8, 2006.

Dearing, E., K. McCartney, and B.A. Taylor. "Change in Family Income-to-Needs Matters More for Children with Less." *Child Development*, 72(6) (2001): 1779–1793.

DeNavas-Walt, C., B.D. Proctor, and C.H. Lee. *Income, Poverty, and Health Insurance Coverage in the United States: 2005*. U.S. Census Bureau Current Population Reports, P60–231. Washington, D.C.: U.S. Government Printing Office, 2006.

Edelman, R., et al. *2006 Annual Edelman Trust Barometer*. New York: Haymarket Media, 2006.

Esposito, F., et al. "America's 50 Best Companies for Minorities." *Fortune*, July 9, 2001: 122–128.

Ferguson, R.F. "Teachers' Perceptions and Expectations and the Black-White Test Score Gap." *Urban Education*, 38(4) (2003): 460–507.

Frankel, B. "Top 50 2006: Methodology." *Diversity Inc.*, June 2006: 38.

Geletkanycz, M.A. "The Salience of 'Culture's Consequences': The Effects of Cultural Values on Top Executive Commitment to the Status Quo." *Strategic Management Journal*, 18(8) (1997): 615–634.

Gladwell, M. "The Talent Myth: Are Smart People Overrated?" *The New Yorker,* July 22, 2002: 28–33.

Golden, D. *The Price of Admission: How America's Ruling Class Buys Its Way into Elite Colleges—and Who Gets Left Outside the Gates.* New York: Crown, 2006.

Goldin, C., and C. Rouse. "Orchestrating Impartiality: The Impact of 'Blind' Auditions on Female Musicians." *The American Economic Review,* 90(4) (2000): 715–741.

Hall, L.E. "What Makes for Good Lawyering? A Multi-Year Study Looks Beyond the LSAT." *Boalt Hall Transcript,* Summer 2005: 22–27.

Hansen, F. "Diversity's Business Case Doesn't Add Up." *Workforce,* April 2003: 28–32.

Hawkins, D.A., and J. Lautz. *State of College Admission.* Alexandria, Va.: National Association for College Admission Counseling, 2005.

Heathfield, S.M. "Why You Really Ought to Want to Love Your Work." 2000. Accessed February 15, 2007 <http://humanresources.about.com/od/careerplanningandadvice1/a/loveyourwork.htm>.

Hechinger, J. "The Tiger Roars: Under Tilghman, Princeton Adds Students, Battles Suit, Takes on the Eating Clubs." *Wall Street Journal,* July 17, 2006: B1.

Heymann, J., A. Earle, and J. Hayes. *The Work, Family, and Equity Index: How Does the United States Measure Up?* Boston: Project on Global Working Families and Montreal: Project on Global Working Families/Institute for Health and Social Policy, 2007.

Horvath, M., and A.M. Ryan. "Antecedents and Potential Moderators of the Relationship Between Attitudes and Hiring Discrimination on the Basis of Sexual Orientation." *Sex Roles,* 48 (3/4) (2003): 115–130.

Joyce, A. "Verizon Bias Suit Deal Sets Record: Pregnancy Case Yields Payout of $48.9 Million." *Washington Post,* June 6, 2006: D01.

Kalev, A., F. Dobbin, and E. Kelly. "Best Practices or Best Guesses? Assessing the Efficacy of Corporate Affirmative Action and Diversity Policies." *American Sociological Review,* 71 (2006): 589–617.

Kazmierczak, M.F., J. James, and W.T. Archey. *Losing the Competitive Advantage? The Challenge for Science and Technology in the United States.* Washington, D.C.: American Electronics Association, 2005.

Keys, P.Y., K.M. Ellis, P.T. Newsome, and S.S. Friday. "Shareholder Benefits of Diversity." Paper presented at the Stephen A. Buser Colloquium Series in Financial Economics, Fisher College of Business, Ohio State University, April 2003.

Krebsbach, K. "Inside the Outsourcing World of India." January 2007. Accessed June 4, 2007 <http://www.banktechnews.com/article.html?id=20070102SM9O2E2D>.

Lee, V.E., and D.T. Burkam. *Inequality at the Starting Gate: Social Background Differences in Achievement as Children Begin School.* Washington, D.C.: Economic Policy Institute, 2002.

Level Playing Field Institute. *The Corporate Leavers Survey: The Cost of Employee Turnover Due Solely to Unfairness in the Workplace.* San Francisco: Level Playing Field Institute, 2007.

Level Playing Field Institute and University of Connecticut Center for Survey Research & Analysis. *The HOW-FAIR Study 2003: How Opportunities in the Workplace and Fairness Affect Intergroup Relations.* San Francisco: Level Playing Field Institute and Storrs, Conn.: University of Connecticut Center for Survey Research & Analysis, 2003.

Lewis, T.T., et al. "Chronic Exposure to Everyday Discrimination and Coronary Artery Calcification in African-American Women: The SWAN Heart Study." *Psychosomatic Medicine,* 68 (2006): 362–368.

National Institute for Occupational Safety and Health. "STRESS . . . at Work." 1999. NIOSH Publication No. 99–101. Accessed April 19, 2007 <http://www.cdc.gov/niosh/stresswk.html>.

O'Brien, C., and J. Engle. *Indicators of Opportunity in Higher Education: 2005 Status Report.* Washington, D.C.: Pell Institute for the Study of Opportunity in Higher Education, 2005.

Payne, A. *Handbook of CRM: Achieving Excellence Through Customer Management.* Oxford, U.K., and Burlington, Mass.: Butterworth-Heinemann/ Elsevier, 2006.

Peoples, J.C. *Diversity Practices That Work: The American Worker Speaks.* New York: National Urban League, 2004.

Peppers, D., and M. Rogers. *Return on Customer: Creating Maximum Value from Your Scarcest Resource.* New York: Currency, 2005.

Perry, T., C. Steele, and A. Hilliard. *Young, Gifted and Black: Promoting High Achievement Among African-American Students.* Boston: Beacon Press, 2003.

Powers, E. "The Harvard Effect." September 13, 2006. Accessed February 15, 2007 <http://www.insidehighered.com/news/2006/09/13/harvard>.

Prickett, T.N., N. Gada-Jain, and F. Bernieri. "The Importance of First Impressions in a Job Interview." Paper presented at the annual meeting of the Midwestern Psychological Association, Chicago, May 2000.

Reichheld, F.F., and T. Teal. *The Loyalty Effect: The Hidden Force Behind Growth, Profits, and Lasting Value.* Boston: Harvard Business School Press, 1996.

Reichheld, F.F., and W.E. Sasser. "Zero Defections: Quality Comes to Services." *Harvard Business Review,* September–October 1990: 2–8.

Roberts, N.A., and R.W. Levenson. "The Remains of the Workday: Impact of Job Stress and Exhaustion on Marital Interaction in Police Couples." *Journal of Marriage and Family*, 63(4) (2001): 1052–1067.

Rogers, S.J., and D.C. May. "Spillover Between Marital Quality and Job Satisfaction: Long-Term Patterns and Gender Differences." *Journal of Marriage and Family*, 65(2) (2003): 482–495.

Rosch, P.J. "The Job Stress Epidemic." 2001. Accessed February 15, 2007 <http://www.isma-usa.org/newsletters/0401newsletter.pdf>.

Rosenthal, R., and L. Jacobson. "Pygmalion in the Classroom." *The Urban Review*, 3(1) (1968): 16–20.

Shellenbarger, S. "Government Eases Path for Parents to Sue Employers." *Wall Street Journal*, May 24, 2007: D1.

Sinclair, S., B.S. Lowery, C.D. Hardin, and A. Colangelo. "Social Tuning of Automatic Racial Attitudes: The Role of Affiliative Motivation." *Journal of Personality and Social Psychology*, 89(4) (2005): 583–592.

Sirota, D., L.A. Mischkind, and M.I. Meltzer. *The Enthusiastic Employee: How Companies Profit by Giving Workers What They Want.* Upper Saddle River, NJ: Wharton School Publishing, 2005.

Smith, T. "Terence Smith Talks with *New York Times* Columnist Tom Friedman About His Latest Trip to Bangalore, India, Where He Examined the Politics of Outsourcing American Jobs Overseas." March 9, 2004. Accessed February 15, 2007 <http://www.pbs.org/newshour/bb/asia/jan-june04/friedman_03–09.html>.

Steinpreis, R.E., K.A. Anders, and D. Ritzke. "The Impact of Gender on the Review of the Curricula Vitae of Job Applicants and Tenure Candidates: A National Empirical Study." *Sex Roles*, 41(7/8) (1999): 509–528.

Stuart, A.N. "Gap Analysis: Why Diversity Programs Work Better for Women Than for Minorities." June 1, 2007. Accessed June 4, 2007 <http://www.cfo.com/article.cfm/9216073/c_9277557?f=home_magazine>.

Trix, F., and C. Psenka. "Exploring the Color of Glass: Letters of Recommendation for Female and Male Medical Faculty." *Discourse & Society*, 14(2) (2003): 191–220.

Trompenaars, F., and C. Hampden-Turner. *Riding the Waves of Culture: Understanding Diversity in Global Business.* 2d ed. New York: McGraw-Hill, 1997.

Unnamed author. "The Curse of Nepotism: A Helping Hand for Those Who Least Need It." *The Economist*, January 8, 2004: 27.

U.S. Census Bureau and U.S. Department of Commerce (Minority Business Development Agency). *Dynamic Diversity: Projected Changes in U.S. Race and Ethnic Composition 1995 to 2050.* Washington, D.C.: U.S.

Department of Commerce (Minority Business Development Agency), 1999.

Vedantam, S. "In Boardrooms and in Courtrooms, Diversity Makes a Difference." *Washington Post,* January 15, 2007: A02.

Weiss, T. "M.B.A. Reality Check." August 1, 2006. Accessed June 4, 2007 <http://www.forbes.com/home/leadership/2006/08/01/leadership-mba-salary-cx_tw_0801mbacomp.html>.

Wentling, R.M., and N. Palma-Rivas. "Current Status of Diversity Initiatives in Selected Multinational Corporations." *Human Resource Development Quarterly,* 11(1) (2000): 35–60.

The Wharton School of the University of Pennsylvania. "Linking Marketing Metrics to Financial Consequences." December 2004. Accessed May 11, 2007 <http://executiveeducation.wharton.upenn.edu/ebuzz/0412/classroom.html>.

ACKNOWLEDGMENTS

A central premise of this book is that successful people rarely become so as a solo endeavor; they are usually presented with opportunities that open doors, plus a bit of luck, or at least fortunate timing along the way. I am no different. Any successes I have experienced were influenced by people who inspired me, believed in me, took a chance on me, or just happened across my path at the perfect moment.

My colleagues at the Level Playing Field Institute (www.lpfi.org) have been steadfast supporters of this work, and they remind me why revealing and removing barriers is so important. Our IDEAL and SMASH Scholars (www.lpfi.org/education) are constant sources of inspiration; they renew my hope in the future of this country. A great debt is owed to those who have run these programs: Cedric Brown, Irene St. Roseman, and Angela Lintz.

The *Giving Notice* team was phenomenal! My two co-authors, Kimberly Allers and Martha Mendoza, both distinguished journalists with previous books to their credit, showed me the ropes. Their writing talents are impressive and well known. The added joy was that they each brought their experiences and whole selves to the project.

As a first-time book author, I relied heavily on the guidance of Wendy Strothman and Dan O'Connell, my literary agents, and was never disappointed. I would never have found them if it weren't for a wonderful, enthusiastic, visionary, client-turned-friend: Robin Neustein. Rebecca Browning, my editor at Jossey-Bass, has been an enthusiastic advocate of this project since she first learned of it. At each stage of the process, I continue to be impressed by the caliber of people on the Jossey-Bass/Wiley team.

Everyone at the Level Playing Field Institute has been a champion of this project. The Workplace Programs team fanned out to collect stories through interviews, focus groups, and collaborations with a growing list of prominent, non-profit advocacy organizations. Led by the always optimistic and committed Caroline Barlerin, the team included Sean Aquino, Kiko Asmerom, Dawn Dow, Dr. Mini Kahlon, Martha Kim, Rhonda Ngom, Lakiba Pittman, Dr. Jim Spencer, Mary Kate Stimmler, and Michelle Thomas.

Through all the decades of my career, Kevin Smith has been my methodologist, pushing for precision and rigor in how we ask questions and analyze data.

Special heartfelt thanks go to Dr. Greg Humpa, my long-term colleague and the book project manager, whose unflagging commitment and incredible competence made this effort much more enjoyable than it otherwise might have been. In ways large and small I am often reminded that Greg's commitment to our work greatly improves the quality of my life.

The steady pillars in my life are my women friends. They are my contemporaries who helped chart social movements, shaped my thinking, and have been the best buddies to laugh and cry with over the decades: Dr. Laurien Alexandre (a.k.a. "my oldest friend in the whole world"), Chris Crandall, Dr. Nan Stein, and K. C. Wagner. Marsha Simms, a client-turned-friend, deserves special thanks for her remarkable ability to juggle being well respected in the business world and being a champion for social justice.

For levity, loyalty, and distraction, my two labradoodles, Cosmo and Chandler, can't be surpassed. They snoozed through many a planning meeting and discussions about the project and enthusiastically greeted Corporate Leavers coming to our office for interviews and focus groups.

But, ironically, two men made this work possible in different ways: my father, Dr. Phil Klein, from whom I learned about ethics and leading a life of integrity, and my husband, Mitchell Kapor, who has been a soul mate on every level, offering more insight, encouragement, and love than anyone could hope for.

The Author

Freada Kapor Klein, Ph.D. is a pioneer in the field of workplace bias and diversity, having designed and analyzed surveys, conducted training, and consulted for workplaces around the world. At age twenty-four, she co-founded the first organization in the United States focused on sexual harassment. In 1984, she obtained her Ph.D. in social policy and research from the Heller School at Brandeis University and served as the first Director of Employee Relations at Lotus Development Corporation.

For two decades, Klein has had a wide-ranging consulting clientele—including top-tier international law firms, Wall Street investment banks, and high-flying Silicon Valley startups—with a focus on issues of bias, harassment, and discrimination. She has served as an expert witness in dozens of lawsuits and has been an often-quoted voice in the business press and national broadcast media during the past fifteen years.

Klein is the founder of the Level Playing Field Institute, a non-profit organization promoting innovative approaches to fairness in higher education and the workplace. The Institute is dedicated to revealing and removing barriers from the classroom to the boardroom. She is also co-founder of the IDEAL Scholars Fund, which invests in high-caliber, underrepresented students of color at the University of California at Berkeley, Klein's undergraduate alma mater.

Klein, her husband Mitchell Kapor, and their two labradoodles live in San Francisco.

INDEX